# 100 Hikes in™
# COLORADO

# 100 Hikes in™
# COLORADO

## Scott S. Warren

THE
MOUNTAINEERS

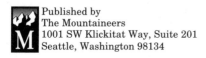

Published by
The Mountaineers
1001 SW Klickitat Way, Suite 201
Seattle, Washington 98134

Founded in 1906, The Mountaineers is a Seattle-based non-profit outdoor activity
and conservation club with 15,000 members, whose mission is "to explore, study,
preserve, and enjoy the natural beauty of the outdoors . . . . " The club sponsors
many classes and year-round outdoor activities in the Pacific Northwest, and supports environmental causes by sponsoring legislation and presenting educational
programs. The Mountaineers Books supports the club's mission by publishing travel
and natural history guides, instructional texts, and works on conservation and history. For information, call or write The Mountaineers, Club Headquarters, 300 Third
Avenue West, Seattle, Washington, 98119; (206) 284-6310.

First edition: first printing 1995, second printing 1996, third printing 1997

Published simultaneously in Great Britain by Cordee, 3a DeMontfort Street,
Leicester, England, LE1 7HD

Manufactured in the United States of America

Edited by Miriam Bulmer
Maps by Scott S. Warren
All photographs by Scott S. Warren
Book design and typesetting by The Mountaineers Books
Book layout by Virginia Hand

Cover photograph: Autumn aspen colors, Mount Wilson, San Juan National Forest
© F. Stuart Westmorland/Allstock
Frontispiece: Geyser Spring is one of Colorado's more unusual geologic features.

Library of Congress Cataloging-in-Publication Data

Warren, Scott S.
    100 hikes in Colorado / Scott S. Warren.
        p.      cm.
    Includes index.
    ISBN 0-89886-429-1
    1. Hiking—Colorado—Guidebooks.   2. Backpacking—Colorado
Guidebooks.   3. Trails—Colorado—Guidebooks.   4. Colorado—
Guidebooks.   I. Title.
GV199.42.C6W37   1995
796.51'09788—dc20                                         95-2481
                                                              CIP

# Contents

## Southern Mountains

# Map Legend

- - - - - - Primary trail      (S)   Start of hike

- - - - - Secondary trail      ) (   Mountain pass

- - - - - Land management      ∿   *Spring*
boundary

- - - - - Continental Divide      ■   Building or
structure

Canyon rim      ▲   Mountain summit

Perennial stream      ⋀   Campground
or river

Intermittent stream      ⋔   Picnic area
or drainage

4WD or high-clearance      ⬭   *Pond or lake*
2WD road

= = = = = = All weather 2WD      ⬟   Visitor center
road

Paved road      ⟨   Cliff dwelling

# INTRODUCTION

When most people think of Colorado, they think of mountains. And why not? With its array of mountain ranges, fifty-three 14,000-foot peaks, and thousands of slightly lesser summits, Colorado is the most mountainous of the Lower Forty-eight states. In fact, Colorado's average elevation of 6,800 feet makes it the highest state in the union. Surprisingly, despite these lofty statistics, only a third of Colorado's area is covered with mountains. Spanning much of the eastern half of this rectangular state are the Great Plains—expansive prairies broken up by the occasional shallow canyon and a lone butte or two—while the western quarter of Colorado is encompassed by the slickrock canyons and mesas of the Colorado Plateau. It is from these three provinces—the Rocky Mountains, the Great Plains, and the Colorado Plateau—that Colorado draws its geographic diversity, allowing it to provide some of the best opportunities for hiking and backpacking in the nation.

## Topography

Few places can match Colorado's widely varying topography. Moving from east to west, you first encounter the flat and seemingly featureless grasslands of the state's eastern plains. As part of the Great Plains, this land is naturally treeless, save for a few cottonwoods that sidle up to rivers and creeks. What grows here instead are a variety of grasses and some beautiful species of wildflowers. Looking out across this land, you might think at first glance that there are no places worth exploring. Longer contemplation would reveal the shallow canyons that dissect portions of this terrain, and a few buttes and mesas that interrupt the horizon on occasion.

As the plains roll westward, they suddenly run up against the dramatic rise of the Rocky Mountains. Defined in the northern half of the state by a chain of summits known as the Front Range, and by the Pikes Peak massif, the Wet Mountains, and the Sangre de Cristo Range to the south, Colorado's first battalion of mountains stands in sharp contrast to the horizontal stretch of the plains to the east. Within the space of only a few miles, these peaks rise to elevations of 13,000 and even 14,000 feet. Beyond them the mountains continue in such ranges as the Sawatch, Gore, Park, Elk, West Elk, and San Juan mountains. In all, Colorado encompasses some fifty different mountain ranges. In contrast to the singular grasslands environment that characterizes the eastern plains, the sudden changes in elevation that Colorado's mountains provide are responsible for a variety of different ecosystems, courtesy of the widely varying climates. Forming a natural boundary that separates the eastern slope and the western slope of the mountains, the Continental Divide also plays an important role in determining local weather patterns. Because the Divide winds for over 600 miles through the state, Colorado gives rise to a number of important rivers, including the North Platte, Arkansas, Rio Grande, San Juan, and Colorado, to name five.

*One of the many natural arches in Rattlesnake Canyon*

In the western portion of the state, the high mountains give way to the deeply dissected canyon country of the Colorado Plateau. Although this transition is not as abrupt as the one between mountains and plains, the contrasts are definitive. A land of relatively little rain, much of the Colorado Plateau can be considered upland desert, especially when compared to the snowy mountains to the east. Deep redrock canyons, high mesa tops, and an assortment of other features add considerable variety to the topography. Extending well into Utah, Arizona, and New Mexico, the Colorado Plateau encompasses about a fifth of Colorado.

## Climate

Colorado is a land of many climates. Among its high mountains, deep snows and below-zero nighttime temperatures grip the land for much of the year. With the arrival of spring, however, the snow begins to melt, and by June or July these mountain lands are experiencing more comfortable conditions. During July and August the mountains are racked on most afternoons by severe local thunderstorms. These storms typically feature brief but heavy periods of rainfall or hail, and plenty of lightning. Come September, these storms become less frequent and by the end of the month or in early October the first snows begin to fall. Although these initial wisps of winter typically melt off, heavier snowfalls soon follow to again close off the high country for the year.

While the mountains are gripped by heavy snows and cold temperatures in the winter, Colorado's western canyons may feature relatively mild conditions—plenty of sunshine and afternoon temperatures that hover near the 50-degree mark. During the summer months, the canyons can experience temperatures around the century mark. As for the plains region, winds and cold temperatures regularly buffet its open expanses in the winter, but the land remains mostly snow-free. In contrast, sweltering temperatures are commonplace in the summer across the plains.

## Flora and Fauna

**Eastern Plains.** In the areas where croplands have not replaced the natural prairie, the eastern plains of Colorado feature a comparatively homogeneous mix of grasses and forbs. Grasses include such species as blue grama, buffalo grass, Kentucky bluegrass, big bluestem, Indian grass, and cheatgrass; forbs include evening primrose, goldenrod, milk vetch, Russian thistle, prickly pear cactus, and yucca among others.

**Mountains.** The ever-changing elevations within Colorado's mountain lands translate into very different plant communities. Dependent mostly on elevation and, to some extent, on local topography, these ecosystems can be conveniently broken up into five distinct zones.

The *Upper Sonoran Zone*, which features stunted forests of pinyon pines and junipers, is typical of the lower foothills. It ranges from less than 5,000 feet to 6,000 feet.

Above that is the *Transition Zone*, which is characterized by taller ponderosa pines, as well as some Douglas firs and Gambel oaks. The Transition Zone begins around the 6,000-foot level and extends up to about 8,000 feet.

A bit cooler in overall temperature and blessed with more precipitation is the *Canadian Zone*. This zone still harbors some Douglas firs throughout, but also subalpine firs and Engelmann spruce. This Engelmann spruce–subalpine fir mix is widespread throughout Colorado's mountains above the 9,000-foot level. Aspen groves are also common in the Canadian Zone; typically, aspens pioneer disturbed ecosystems such as burn areas.

Creating a buffer between the Canadian Zone and the Arctic-Alpine Zone above, the *Hudsonian Zone* is home to hardy tree species such as the bristlecone and limber pines, as well as Engelmann spruce and subalpine fir. Because of the harsh climate that prevails at these elevations, spruce trees often grow in stunted and twisted thickets known as krummholz forests. Blasted by near-constant cold and wind, such trees have little chance of growing tall and straight.

Finally, above timberline is the *Arctic-Alpine Zone,* a treeless terrain dominated by flowering annuals and perennials, grasses, and occasional thickets of willow. Timberline in Colorado ranges from about 11,000 feet in the north to 11,500 feet across the southern portion. The Arctic-Alpine Zone features many of the same species of plants that are found above the Arctic Circle, such as phlox.

**Plateau.** West of the mountains, across the canyons and mesas of the plateau region, elevations are low enough to ensure that the Upper Sonoran Zone is most prevalent. Here, pinyon pines and junipers are the most common species of trees. Mountain mahogany, Utah serviceberry, Mormon tea, yucca, and a variety of small cacti are also plentiful.

**Riparian.** An additional Colorado community that is of great importance is the riparian ecosystem, which provides an important reservoir of plant and animal diversity, especially in the arid plateau region and the eastern plains. Blessed with a reliable source of water, such as a perennial or frequently flowing stream, riparian areas often support cottonwood, box elder, ash, and willow trees, as well as a variety of undergrowth such as wax currant, hawthorn, bulrush, cattail, and poison ivy.

Colorado's different provinces are home to an incredible variety of wildlife. Among the species that favor the mountains are mule deer, elk, bighorn sheep, mountain goats, black bears, perhaps a grizzly or two in the South San Juan Mountains, mountain lions, coyotes, bobcats, a few Canadian lynxes, pine martens, perhaps some wolverines, snowshoe hares, cottontail rabbits, a variety of squirrels, chipmunks, and various other rodents. Pronghorn antelope, white-tailed deer, badgers, and prairie dogs inhabit the eastern plains, while desert bighorn sheep are found in many parts of the plateau.

Among the hundreds of species of birds that call Colorado home are both golden and bald eagles, peregrine falcons, prairie falcons, American kestrels, prairie chickens, western meadowlarks, Steller's jays, Clark's nutcrackers, and magpies.

*From Beckwith Pass it is possible to spot the Castles in the distance.*

# Using This Book

This book serves to introduce hikers and backpackers to 100 of Colorado's best hikes. To lessen the impact on the environment, all of these hikes follow established trails. If you should happen to leave these routes to hike cross-country, do so at your own risk. While most of the hikes listed below access a particular destination, such as a lake or mountain pass, some follow loop routes to take in a variety of locations. Hikes from all regions of the state have been included, but, unsurprisingly, most hikes fall within the mountainous areas. Because no special effort was made to include only lesser-known hikes (that would have led to the omission of some truly incredible routes), some of the trails covered here are very popular. If crowds are not your cup of tea, be sure to plan your trip for the off-season if possible, or at least during a weekday.

## INFORMATION BLOCKS

Each hike begins with an information block that presents essential facts at a glance. These facts will help you decide whether or not a hike is right for you.

The *Distance* listing tells you the total mileage the hike requires. Wherever possible, this figure reflects the round-trip distance. In other words, for a hike along a trail that is 6.4 miles long, the distance figure would be 12.8 miles. In the few cases where a point-to-point hike is discussed, this line will state that the distance involved is "one way." You will need to arrange a shuttle for these hikes.

While determining the *Difficulty* of a hike is subjective at best, the ratings presented here reflect the hike's total elevation change, its overall grade, and, to some extent, its distance. (Condition of the trail is not a factor; all of the trails in this book are in pretty good shape.) The three ratings used are easy, moderate, and strenuous. Most short hikes would be rated as easy, but a short hike that climbs steeply might be rated as moderate or even strenuous. Similarly, some longer hikes may be rated as moderate or strenuous simply because they are longer.

As with the Difficulty rating, trying to determine the *Hiking time* of a route is an uncertain science. Not only do hikers walk at different speeds, but some make take more breaks than others. This book tries to balance each route's length with its overall elevation change to come up with a consistent determination of the total time that each hike should take. These times tend to be conservative to better prepare hikers of beginning abilities. Remember, they are only estimates.

The *Elevation* listing indicates the range in elevation covered by the hike. The first figure is the trailhead elevation, the second figure is the hike's high or low point, depending on whether the route gains or loses elevation.

The *Management* listing indicates which government agency actually manages a trail. Entries include the Bureau of Land Management (BLM), national forest (NF), national park (NP), national monument (NM), national grassland (NG), state park (SP), state forest (SF), and open space. In addition to identifying which agency you may obtain more information from, this listing also indicates a source for maps. Where the Routt NF is listed, for example, you might want to purchase a Routt National Forest map from the Forest Service before setting out.

*Wilderness status* indicates whether or not the hike crosses an established wilderness area (WA) or wilderness study area (WSA). These areas are covered by specific regulations (see the Wilderness Etiquette section of this chapter). In this day and age, this listing is most relevant where mountain bikes are concerned.

The *Season* entry reveals when a particular route will probably be free of snow. These listings are conservative; some routes may open up to a month earlier or close a month later, depending on how severe the winter has been or will be. Check with the managing agency if you have any questions concerning the condition of a trail or access to a trailhead.

The *USGS Map* listing indicates which 7.5-minute topographic maps apply to the hike. Because some of these maps are quite old, they may not indicate recent changes in a route or they may omit a new trail completely. The topo maps should be used in conjunction with other maps, such as those published by the U.S. Forest Service or the Bureau of Land Management.

## MAPS

Each hike in this book is accompanied by a map. While efforts have been made to include as much information as possible, these maps are meant to introduce a route and should not serve as your sole guide in the field. It is advisable to bring more detailed maps, such as topographic maps, national forest maps, and privately published trail maps.

## HIKE DESCRIPTIONS

Each hike description begins with an introductory paragraph, followed by detailed information on how to reach the start of the hike.

*Twin Lakes at dusk*

(Although these directions and the driving distances are as accurate as possible, it is helpful to have a good map on hand.) The text then presents a mile-by-mile guide to the hiking route, with descriptions of distances, grade changes, trail difficulty, trail condition, intersecting trails, and natural features such as forest types or geological formations. Historical anecdotes are occasionally included and some information on side routes is also provided, mostly to give the reader an idea about other hiking possibilities in the area. The final paragraph lists such technicalities as the availability of water, possible hazards, and specific regulations.

## Wilderness Etiquette

Many of the hikes listed below enter established wilderness areas where specific regulations apply. Some hikes explore the backcountry reaches of national and state parks, which have their own rules. Other hikes cross parcels of public domain that are open to multiple use. No matter which hike you choose, you should follow a set of commonsense rules that are environmentally friendly. Many of these edicts of wilderness etiquette are stipulated in the Wilderness Act of 1964.

As dictated by the Wilderness Act, all forms of mechanized travel are prohibited in wilderness areas. This includes hang gliders, motorcycles, and mountain bicycles. Because some off-road bicyclists feel that this regulation does not or should not apply to them, mountain bikes present a particularly pressing problem to land managers. Keep in mind that *all trails within wilderness areas, national parks, and national monuments are off-limits to bicycles.* Where mountain bikes are allowed, be sure to watch for the occasional out-of-control rider. While most bicyclists are learning that irresponsible riding will lead to additional trail closures, a few still feel their fun takes precedence over all other trail users.

The Wilderness Act also prohibits the use of chainsaws, generators, and other mechanized equipment in wilderness areas. Commercial enterprises such as livestock grazing, pack outfitting, and guide services are allowed by permit only. Because dogs can disturb both wildlife and other hikers, they are prohibited in the backcountry of national parks and monuments, as well as in most state parks, and in specific areas within national forest and BLM lands. The best plan is to leave your dog at home, but if you should happen to take your pet along, it is important to keep it under control at all times. Fish and wildlife regulations are enforced by Colorado's Division of Wildlife.

In order to lessen their impact on Colorado's wild areas, hikers should follow the regulations listed in the Wilderness Act of 1964 as well as additional "no trace" guidelines, both in the backcountry and when camping at the trailhead.
- Do not build campfires—use a stove instead.
- Avoid camping in sensitive areas such as mountain meadows and fragile desert soils.
- Camp at least 100 feet from all trails, streams, and lakes, and use existing sites whenever possible. Some heavily used areas may

have additional regulations concerning where you may camp.
- Never cut down standing trees—dead or alive.
- Do not leave behind any structures or nails.
- Do not dig holes and trenches, and do not level tent areas.
- Use biodegradable soap and bury all human waste at least 200 feet from water.
- Travel in small groups.
- Never cut across switchbacks or walk over sensitive areas such as cryptogamic soils.
- Pack out all litter.

Of course, it should go without saying that all plants, animals, rocks, and historical relics should be enjoyed only within their natural setting. These rules are the law within national parks and monuments, and in state parks. Although they do not always apply to areas administered by the U.S. Forest Service and Bureau of Land Management, they should be followed just the same. Where historical and archaeological artifacts are concerned, all antiquities of historic and prehistoric origin are fully protected on all federal lands. In recent years the looting of Indian artifacts has grown to become an alarming problem, especially in the southwest corner of Colorado. The best rule where ancient artifacts, cliff dwellings, and rock art are concerned is look but do not touch.

## Backcountry Safety

While hiking Colorado's backcountry can be a pleasurable experience, it can also be filled with hazards, especially for those who are unprepared. Before setting out into the plains, mountains, and canyons of the state, you should be aware of these hazards and how best to avoid them. The most common potential problems are described briefly below. The following books offer more detailed information concerning safety in the backcountry.

*Wilderness Basics: The Complete Handbook For Hikers & Backpackers,* 2nd ed., by the San Diego Chapter of the Sierra Club. Seattle: The Mountaineers, 1993.

*Mountaineering: The Freedom of the Hills,* 5th ed., Don Graydon, editor. Seattle: The Mountaineers, 1992.

### HYPOTHERMIA

Because the weather in Colorado's high country can change quite suddenly and without much notice, hikers need to be prepared for all possibilities. Even during the summer, the sun can be shining one moment and a storm might be brewing the next. Because winds, cold rain, hail, and even snow may accompany such changes in weather, hikers should be aware that hypothermia can become a life-threatening situation. Hypothermia occurs when the body's core temperature drops to dangerous levels. Symptoms include uncontrollable shivering, deteriorating speech, impaired judgment, drowsiness, and weakness. Often, the victim is unaware that he or she is sick.

While hypothermia can kill in only a few hours, it is readily treatable, even in the field. As soon as possible, replace wet clothing with dry and place the victim in a warm sleeping bag. It may also be necessary to huddle with the victim so as to share body warmth. Give warm liquids and high-energy food, and then seek medical help at once. Of course, the best plan of action is to avoid hypothermia altogether by staying dry in the first place, carrying spare clothing and rain gear, and eating plenty of high-energy foods.

## LIGHTNING

Certainly the most omnipresent threat to visitors in Colorado's backcountry is lightning. Indeed, lightning can strike anywhere and anytime there are clouds in the area. Thunderstorms build in Colorado's

*A small Aspen grove along the Rainbow Trail*

high country nearly every afternoon during the months of July and August. Often quite violent in nature, such storms hit the upper elevations with incredible ferocity. In short, you don't want to be in any high location—i.e., above timberline, on a mountain or ridge top, around canyon rims, or in other exposed places—where lightning would naturally strike. As with hypothermia, an ounce of prevention can go a long way. Plan your trip so that you are off the mountain by noon or shortly after. If you do happen to get caught in a storm, experts suggest that you huddle in a flat area or depression, get rid of any metal objects, and stay away from trees. Deeper caves can provide a safe hideout, but avoid tents, shallow alcoves, the base of rocks, and gully bottoms. The safest place to be, by far, is in your vehicle.

## FLASH FLOODS

Although flash floods are not particularly common in Colorado's high country, they occasionally occur in the canyons of the plateau region and even in some drainages in the eastern plains. The tricky thing about flash floods is that you may experience sunny weather while it is raining torrents upstream somewhere else. In these cases, a wall of water can crash down upon an unsuspecting hiker with little or no warning. If you are caught off-guard, get to higher ground immediately. Do not try to cross flooded areas until the water has subsided.

## WILDLIFE

Although most hikers don't perceive Colorado's wildlife as a threat, there is always the possibility that injury can result from contact with some species. In recent years, attacks on humans by both mountain lions and black bears have been on the rise across the country., largely due to an increase in the number of people living near wild areas. Where hikers are concerned, a little common sense and sensible precautions should prevent most conflicts. Hang your food bag at least 10 feet up in a tree and away from your tent. The smell of food is the surest way to invite a bear into your camp. As for mountain lions, because they still have a healthy fear of man in Colorado's unpopulated areas, they are not usually considered a menace. Rattlesnakes are common in the lower elevations, but they too shy away from people when they can. Running into a rattler is most likely if you leave the trail to explore rocky areas.

## GIARDIA

Within the last two decades, *Giardia* has become so widespread that you should always assume that no surface water—streams, creeks, lakes, and so on—is safe to drink without being treated or purified first. A microscopic organism, *Giardia* causes severe diarrhea one to two weeks after it gets into your digestive system. Fortunately, *Giardia* is easy to avoid. While most chemical treatments do not safeguard against *Giardia*, boiling water for 10 minutes or longer does. There are also some effective filter systems available on the market today; read the label to make sure your system can screen out *Giardia*. If

*A prehistoric cliff dwelling in Sand Canyon*

you are out just for the day, the simplest means of prevention is to pack along enough water for the entire hike.

GETTING LOST AND FOUND

Like many outdoor skills, the ability to find your way through the backcountry is enhanced with experience. While most of the hikes in this book are straightforward enough to introduce novice hikers to Colorado's backcountry, the possibility of getting lost nevertheless exists. To deal with this, first-time hikers should not travel alone and veteran hikers should think twice about soloing on harder routes. In any case, you should always let someone know where you are going and when you will return. If you plan to leave established trails, be prepared with a compass, topographic maps, and the orienteering skills to use both. If you do get lost, remain calm. With luck, another hiker will happen along shortly. If not, a search party will eventually be sent once whoever you told realizes you are overdue.

## Before You Go

When planning a hike, a little preparation can make all the difference in the world between having a fun and successful excursion or enduring a miserable and even unsafe experience. The best place to begin is in selecting your equipment. You will certainly need sturdy yet comfortable hiking shoes. Good soles and plenty of ankle support are especially important when tackling steep and rocky terrain. While shorts and a T-shirt might seem like enough clothing when you set out, be sure to pack long pants and long-sleeved shirts as well. A warm jacket is a must, as is proper rain gear—a poncho or rain parka and pants. Because exposure to the sun is intense in alpine areas and in the canyons and plains, you may also want to bring a wide-brimmed hat.

Whether you are setting out for the morning or overnight, you will need a comfortable pack. The market is filled with high-tech packs that make carrying weight as painless as possible. A lightweight tent, a warm sleeping bag, and a sleeping pad will ensure a comfortable night's rest. Given the fact that campfires are environmentally unfriendly, a lightweight stove for cooking is essential, and a backpacking cook kit will make meal preparation easy.

In addition to the above-mentioned clothing and equipment, you should always stash what are known as the "Ten Essentials" in your pack as well, even if you plan to be out only for the day.
1. Extra clothing—more than is needed for good weather
2. Extra food—so that something is left over at the end of the trip
3. Sunglasses—especially important for alpine areas
4. Knife—for first aid and emergency fire-starting
5. Fire starter—a candle or chemical fuel for wet wood
6. First-aid kit
7. Matches—in a weatherproof container
8. Flashlight—with an extra bulb and extra batteries
9. Map—topos are good, but also bring updated trail maps
10. Compass—be sure to know the declination, east or west

## A Note About Safety

Safety is an important concern in all outdoor activities. No guidebook can alert you to every hazard or anticipate the limitations of every reader. Therefore, the descriptions of roads, trails, routes, and natural features in this book are not representations that a particular place or excursion will be safe for your party. When you follow any of the routes described in this book, you assume responsibility for your own safety. Under normal conditions, such excursions require the usual attention to traffic, road and trail conditions, weather, terrain, the capabilities of your party, and other factors. Keeping informed on current conditions and exercising common sense are the keys to a safe, enjoyable outing.

*The Mountaineers*

# 1 PAWNEE BUTTES

**Distance: 3 miles round trip**　　**Management: Pawnee NG**
**Difficulty: Easy**　　　　　　　　**Wilderness status: none**
**Hiking time: 2 hours**　　　　　　**Season: Year-round**
**Elevation: 5,420 to 5,200 feet**　　**USGS map: Pawnee Buttes, Grover SE**

Rising a few hundred feet above the surrounding shortgrass prairie, the Pawnee Buttes are both the crowning jewel of the 193,060-acre Pawnee National Grassland and the destination of a short but rewarding hike. The trail passes some interesting plant communities and badlands formations, and offers the opportunity for hikers to enjoy a surprising variety of wildlife.

Reach the start of the Pawnee Buttes hike by driving 45 miles east from Fort Collins on Colorado Highway 14. After passing through Briggsdale, continue for another 13 miles and turn left toward the nearly abandoned town of Keota on County Road 103. Drive 4.5 miles north to Keota, then continue 3 miles north on County Road 105. Turn right onto County Road 104 and drive 3 miles to County Road 111,

*The Pawnee Buttes rise suddenly above the plains.*

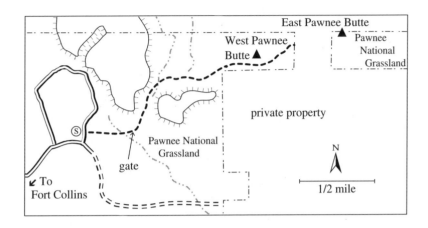

Turn left and drive 4.5 miles to where a secondary road turns north. Follow this route less than a mile to the signed trailhead.

The hike begins by dropping easily from the trailhead into a broad drainage. A popular route, this trail is well worn and easy to follow. Near the drainage bottom the route passes through a gate in a fence before reaching the next drainage north. On either side of the trail are low sandstone bluffs that look as if they might be fun to explore. These areas are off-limits from the beginning of March through June, however, to protect nesting birds of prey. An unfortunate incident in 1993 led to the abandonment of a prairie falcon nest and the death of some hatchlings. In addition to falcons, these grasslands are also home to golden eagles and hawks. Songbirds are plentiful, and you may glimpse some deer or pronghorn antelope.

As the trail winds its way into another shallow drainage, note the scattered juniper and squawbush, plus prickly pear cactus and yucca. Also growing in the vicinity of the buttes, but not right along the trail itself, are the easternmost stands of limber pines. Wildflowers grow in prodigious numbers along this trail during the late spring and summer months. After climbing easily out of the drainage bottom, the trail then continues on towards the imposing buttes, which are less than 0.5 mile to the northeast. The actual hiking route ends at a private property line marked by a fence. Formed from sedimentary rock deposited during the Oligocene and Miocene epochs, the Pawnee Buttes are actually remnants of a once-higher plain. The surrounding terrain was subsequently eroded away by runoff during the last glacial age. After enjoying the buttes up close, return to your car by the same route.

Obey all signs concerning the disturbance of nesting birds of prey and take care not to disturb other birds that may be nesting on the ground. Watch for flash floods in the wash bottoms and be wary of rattlesnakes, especially when exploring off-trail. Water is not available along this hike, so bring plenty. Be sure to respect the rights of private property owners in the area.

# *2* BARR LAKE

**Distance: 9 miles round trip**
**Difficulty: Easy**
**Hiking time: 6 hours**
**Elevation: 5,100 to 5,100 feet**
**Management: Barr Lake SP**

**Wilderness Status: None**
**Season: Year-round**
**USGS maps: Brighton, Mile High
Lakes**

Situated in the plains northeast of Denver, Barr Lake offers an interesting oasis for people and wildlife alike. With its 1,900-acre surface area when full, the lake serves as a stopover for a variety of migratory birds. It is also home to some interesting species of mammals. And in recent years, the lake has served as the only known bald eagle nesting site along the Front Range region of Colorado. This hike follows a 9-mile trail that circles the entire lake.

Barr Lake is reached by driving northeast from Denver on Interstate 76 to the Bromley Lane exit. Follow Bromley Lane east to Picadilly Road and turn south. The park entrance is a little over a mile down this road. The trail begins at the nature center and picnic area, which are at the end of the road within the park.

From the trailhead at the nature center, begin by turning left immediately after crossing the Denver & Hudson Canal. This canal parallels the trail along the lake's southeast shoreline. Because the trail actually follows the service road for the canal, the going is extremely easy.

*Cottonwoods growing along the shore of Barr Lake*

Immediately after crossing the canal, the Niedrach Nature Trail branches off to the right. By taking this short side route, you can access a boardwalk that leads to the lake's shoreline and penetrates the forest of cottonwoods that lines the lake. Besides breaking up the horizontal axis of the plains, these trees also add to the variety of the natural environment. The nature trail soon returns to the main trail, where the hike continues clockwise around the lake.

In addition to cottonwood stands, you also pass some small meadows where foxes and mule deer may be spotted, especially at dawn and dusk. Additionally, a few observation stations are accessed by following short side trails to the lake's shore. These small structures provide screening for the observation of birds. Included among the sightings that are possible at Barr Lake are Canada geese, a variety of ducks, grebes, great blue herons, egrets, and more.

At 1.5 miles the trail reaches the turnoff for an observation gazebo located at the end of a long boardwalk that extends far out into the lake. From this pleasant spot you can observe waterfowl up close—that is, when the water level is up. Because Barr Lake is used to store water for irrigation purposes, it can drop considerably during the late summer and fall. Under these circumstances the dropping lake level may leave the gazebo high and dry. Nevertheless, it is still a nice place to visit. A telescope there allows observation of distant birds as well as a glimpse of a bald eagle nest that sits in a large cottonwood to the

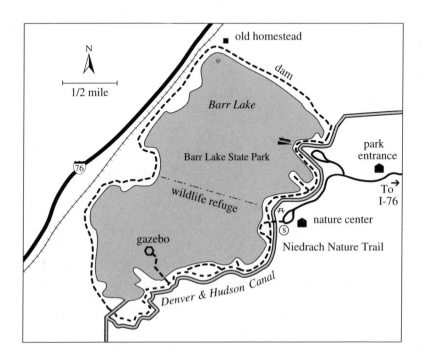

west. You may even see one or both parents perched in the branches nearby.

Although most visitors turn back after visiting the gazebo, the trail continues on around the southwest end of the lake, where it crosses the lake's inlet. Some interesting cattail marshes are encountered along the western portion of the lake's shoreline. As the route reaches the northwest side of the lake, the quiet solitude is washed away by noise from the nearby interstate highway and by an occasional passing train. An old homestead dating back to the 1880s is located along this section of the trail. The trail then reaches the dam, which spans more than a mile across the lake's northeast side. From the dam the trail continues along the eastern portion of the lake, passing a boat ramp and another observation boardwalk. After 9 miles the trail returns to the trailhead. Be sure to pay a visit to the nature center either before or after your hike.

Because the southern end of Barr Lake is included in a wildlife refuge, dogs are not permitted along this section of the hike. Fishing and boating are prohibited as well. Bring plenty of water to drink and binoculars for bird-watching.

# $\overline{3}$   CASTLEWOOD CANYON

**Distance: 5.9 miles round trip**
**Difficulty: Easy**
**Hiking time: 4 hours**
**Elevation: 6,600 to 6,200 feet**
**Management: Castlewood**
   **Canyon SP**

**Wilderness status: None**
**Season: Year-round**
**USGS maps: Castle Rock South,**
   **Russellville Gulch**

A recent addition to Colorado's state park system, beautiful Castlewood Canyon is located in the plains region southeast of Denver. Etched by Cherry Creek, this canyon includes several ecological communities that blend together in a relatively small area. These include surprisingly tall stands of timber, verdant riparian areas, fragile prairie grasses, and more. Add to these natural features a poignant lesson in man's attempt to control nature and you have a special place indeed.

To reach Castlewood Canyon State Park, drive 7 miles east from Castle Rock on Colorado Highway 86 to Franktown. Here, turn south onto Colorado Highway 83 and drive 5 miles to the park entrance. Stop at the visitor center to pick up a brochure that includes a detailed map of the park's trail system, then drive to the trailhead, which is located at the picnic area at Canyon Point.

The hike begins by following the Lake Gulch Trail northwest along a mesa top for a short distance before angling gently downward into the canyon bottom. As you descend from the rim you may note scattered ponderosa pines, along with thick patches of Gambel oak. The 0.9-mile Lake Gulch Trail drops a total of 200 feet before reaching the Inner

Canyon Trail at a creek crossing. At this intersection turn left and follow the Inner Canyon Trail for a short distance north to the site of an old dam. Built in 1890 to harness Cherry Creek for irrigation purposes, this cut rock dam had problems almost from the beginning. After springing leaks within its first years, the 65-foot-high, 630-foot-long dam finally burst after heavy rains in August of 1933. The wall of water created by the 200-acre reservoir killed two people and caused $1 million in damage. It is considered Denver's second worst flood. Today, only a small portion of the dam still stands, but the lessons are vivid just the same.

At the dam site the trail crosses the main wash bottom to reach a trailhead on the northwest side of Cherry Creek. Here it picks up the Creek Bottom Trail, which follows the canyon floor downstream for a little more than 1.5 miles. Along this section of the hike you will gain a

*Along the rim of Castlewood Canyon*

good feel for the riparian community supported by Cherry Creek's perennial flow of water. An important factor in the shaping of this riparian area is the occasional flash flooding, which precludes the growth of some species of plants but fosters others. Among the species of plants found along this corridor is poison ivy—watch out!

At the north end of the Creek Bottom Trail, the hike turns right at a trail intersection to take up the 1.9-mile Rim Rock Trail; the left-hand route leads less than 0.5 mile along the Homestead Trail to the park's west entry point. From this trail intersection the Rim Rock Trail climbs steeply—about 300 feet in less than 0.25 mile—to gain the east rim of the canyon. Perhaps the most interesting portion of the entire hike, the rim provides the best views of the canyon below and reveals an interesting mix of prairie grasslands and ponderosa pine forests as well. These forested areas are part of a much larger ecosystem known as the Black Forest. Stretching across a 40-mile-by-75-mile area of the eastern plains, the Black Forest features stands of ponderosa pine that take advantage of suitable growing conditions found along slightly higher reaches of the plains. As you follow the Rim Rock Trail, you can also enjoy the interesting cliff faces that drop into the canyon. Known as Castle Rock Conglomerate, this rock is composed of sands and coarse pebbles that were cemented together some 34 million years ago.

At its south end the Rim Rock Trail drops back into the canyon to meet with the 1.2-mile Inner Canyon Trail at the dam site. This hike then returns to the trailhead by way of the Inner Canyon route, which follows a side canyon upstream before climbing about 100 feet back up to Canyon Point. Along this last leg of the hike you will run across more riparian growth, and you can see how thick stands of Douglas firs take advantage of the north-facing canyon wall, which provides both protection from the elements and suitable ground moisture for the evergreens.

Although water is found along this hike, it is best to bring your own for drinking. Camping is prohibited within the state park and dogs must be kept on a leash. Watch for flash floods during rainy periods, and avoid wandering off the trail as the surrounding vegetation is quite fragile.

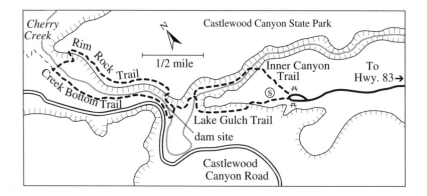

# 4    SANTA FE TRAIL

**Distance: 6 miles round trip**
**Difficulty: Easy**
**Hiking time: 3 hours**
**Elevation: 4,410 to 4,400 feet**

**Management: Comanche NG**
**Wilderness Status: None**
**Season: Year-round**
**USGS maps: Timpas, La Junta SW**

For some the thought of hiking across a nearly featureless prairie within sight of a highway does not sound appealing. For the committed history buff, however, such an excursion can be irresistible, especially if the hike follows the actual route of the Santa Fe Trail. Thanks to the trail's recognition as a national historic trail by Congress in 1987, it is now possible to visit and enjoy many different portions of the trail. One such place is found between the towns of La Junta and Trinidad along

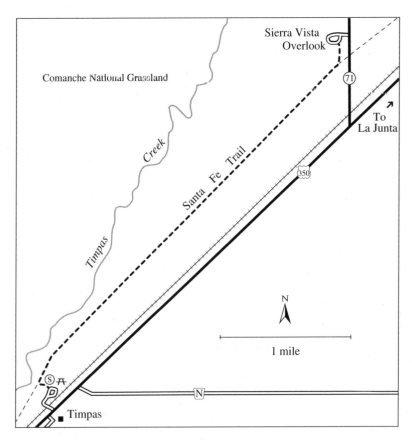

*A stone marker along the Santa Fe Trail*

US Highway 350. Here you can walk a stretch of the famed trail that is delineated by stone markers.

This hike begins at the Timpas Picnic Area, which is 16 miles south of La Junta on US Highway 350. Upon reaching the nearly deserted town of Timpas, turn right onto County Road 16.5 and drive across the railroad tracks to the newly constructed picnic facility. If you would like to have a shuttle at the other end, it can be reached by driving 3 miles northeast of Timpas on US Highway 350 to Colorado Highway 71. Follow this road north for 0.5 mile to the Sierra Vista Overlook, which is located on the only high point for many miles around.

Beginning along a short nature trail that heads west from the Timpas Picnic Area, the 3-mile stretch of the Santa Fe Trail running northeast to the Sierra Vista Overlook offers what may be the easiest hiking route you will ever find. This is because it traverses the short-grass prairie, a completely level land of ankle-high grass. As for the route itself, instead of being an actual tread, the way is marked every 0.25 mile or so by a waist-high, cut stone marker that is easily visible from a distance. Following these trail markers leads you in a virtually straight line from the Timpas Picnic Area to the Sierra Vista Overlook. In addition, you can see the overlook on the horizon. US Highway 350 is also visible less than 0.5 mile to the right.

While the hike itself may hold little challenge or intrigue, the fact that you are following the Santa Fe Trail is indeed of interest. A trade route rather than one of emigration, the Santa Fe Trail runs for 900 miles, from Independence, Missouri, to the city of Santa Fe in what is now New Mexico. Because trade with America was originally prohibited by the Spanish government, the Santa Fe Trail did not become a reality until Mexico gained its independence in 1821. Within just six weeks, the first trader, William Becknell, set out from Franklin, Missouri, to sell his wares in Santa Fe. Encouraged by the Mexican government, commerce quickly boomed as traders from both nations were eager to tap into a new market. Almost from the beginning the Santa

Fe Trail included two branches—the more direct Cimarron Route, which followed the normally dry Cimarron River from Dodge City through Oklahoma to Watrous, New Mexico, and the Mountain Route, which followed the Arkansas River west into Colorado and then south over Raton Pass. Initially desirable because of the availability of water, the longer Mountain Route became even more popular with the establishment of Fort Bent near the present-day town of La Junta in 1833. Commerce on the Santa Fe Trail continued after 1848, when the United States. seized control of the territory from Mexico, and did not end until the first train reached Santa Fe in 1880.

Visions of the Santa Fe Trail along this hikeable stretch must be conjured up more by your own imagination than by physical evidence. Look out across the prairie and get a feel for what it must have been like for those early traders headed to Santa Fe, with the seemingly ever-present winds buffeting your face and the numbing expanse of flat terrain stretching westward to the barely visible snowy summits of the Rockies (the Spanish Peaks, Sangre de Cristo Range, Greenhorn Mountain, and Pikes Peak are all visible on a clear day). If you still want physical evidence, drive 11 miles southwest from Timpas on US Highway 350 and 1 mile south on County Road 9 to the Iron Springs Historic Area. Here, wagon ruts are still visible.

Be sure to pack a quart of water per person as there is no potable water available on this hike. Also, watch for rattlesnakes, tarantulas, and scorpions while walking the prairie. Although rarely seen, these venomous creatures are, nevertheless, present. Keep in mind that all historic relics are protected by federal law.

# 5 PICKET WIRE CANYONLANDS

Distance: 17.4 miles round trip    Wilderness status: None
Difficulty: Moderate    Season: Year-round
Hiking time: 12 hours    USGS maps: Riley Canyon, Beaty
Elevation: 4,660 to 4,320 feet      Canyon, O V Mesa
Management: Comanche NG

For the first-time visitor to the plains region of eastern Colorado, the relatively deep and expansive canyon system carved by the Purgatoire River might come as quite a shock. Some 350 feet deep and rimmed by substantial cliff faces of sandstone, these canyons offer truly wonderful hiking opportunities where access is permitted. One such place is the Picket Wire Canyonlands area, located south of La Junta. Recently transferred to the Comanche National Grassland from the U.S. Army, this area offers not only some surprising canyon scenery but also a treasure chest of paleontological, prehistoric, and historic delights. The name Picket Wire originated with the way in which French trappers pronounced the Spanish-inspired name, Purgatoire. Locals have held on to the misnomer ever since.

To reach the trailhead, drive 13 miles south from La Junta on Colorado Highway 109 to County Road 802, turn southwest, and drive 8 miles to the intersection with County Road 25. Turn south onto this road and drive about 6 miles to the bulletin board for the Picket Wire Canyonlands. From this point the trailhead is 3.3 miles to the east along Road 500, a high-clearance two-wheel-drive (2WD) route that may be impassable when wet. A parking area and outhouse mark the trail's start. Be sure to close the wire gate behind you when making this approach drive and remember that all vehicles must stay on the roadway.

From the parking area this hike follows an old pasture road that is closed to motorized vehicles (managing agency trucks and other specially permitted vehicles are excepted) by a pipe gate. Beyond the gate, the road drops steeply into Withers Canyon, a side drainage of Picket Wire Canyon. Within this first 0.3 mile the route descends a total of 350 feet before reaching the mostly level canyon bottom. From there it continues following the old road south to where it reaches the wide open main canyon of the Purgatoire River, about 1 mile from the trailhead. At this junction is a trail register that is usually stocked with information on the Picket Wire Canyonlands. After turning right here, the trail follows the mostly level four-wheel-drive (4WD) road for the rest of the way.

In the few places where the trail runs directly adjacent to the Purgatoire River you can see that the waterway is not very large. It is, nevertheless, one of the more substantial streams that flow across the arid plains region of southeastern Colorado. In places where the river is out of sight, its meandering course is often marked by tall cottonwoods growing along its banks. Willows, tamarisks, and a variety of other water-loving plants are also common in the Picket Wire Canyonlands. Wildlife includes both mule and white-tailed deer, badgers, coyotes, antelope, bighorn sheep, and mountain lions.

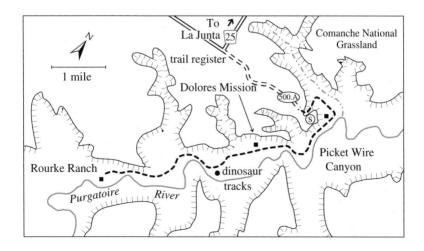

*An old homestead in the Picket Wire Canyonlands*

A short distance beyond the trail register are the crumbling remains of an adobe homestead. As one of a handful of old structures in the area, it serves as a reminder that the late 1800s saw some settlement activity in the Picket Wire Canyonlands. A second reminder comes 3.7 miles from the trailhead in the form of the Dolores Mission, which was established in the late 1800s. Today, remnants of the building, along with a nearby cemetery, are visible. In other stretches of the hike you may also happen upon prehistoric rock art that dates back between 300 and 4,500 years. Although little is known about the early Indian inhabitants of the area, it is thought that they were nomadic hunters who occasionally passed through these canyons while in search of game.

Farther on—a little over 5 miles from the trailhead—the hike takes you much farther back in time with the longest mapped and recorded dinosaur track site in North America. Continuing for 0.25 mile and containing over 1,300 individual footprints, these tracks were set 150 million years ago by enormous brontosaurs and smaller, meat-eating allosaurs as they walked across a muddy shoreline. Preserved in the Morrison Formation, these tracks are evidence of social behavior among younger brontosaurs—namely that they traveled as a pack in a single direction. Today, the tracks are visible in a shelf of bedrock that runs adjacent to the river.

Beyond the dinosaur track site, the trail continues for another 3.4 miles to reach the Rourke Ranch, which, like the Dolores Mission, dates back to 1871. Before being sold in 1971, this ranch grew from 40 acres to over 52,000 acres in size, making it one of the largest cattle operations in this part of the state. The buildings are in the process of being stabilized by the Comanche National Grasslands as part of their management plan for the Picket Wire Canyonlands. From the Rourke Ranch it is 8.7 miles back to the trailhead. If your time is limited you may wish to turn back sooner, perhaps at the dinosaur track site or the Dolores Mission. In any case, you will get a good feel for the wonderful scenery and the interesting natural history of the Picket Wire Canyonlands.

The Picket Wire Canyonlands are open to mountain bikes, but closed to all motorized vehicles. Because camping is prohibited in the canyonlands, you will have to complete your hike within a day. Bring plenty of water as water from the Purgatoire River is not drinkable. Watch for rattlesnakes, scorpions, and such. Keep in mind that flash floods have been known to occur within these stream bottoms. Also, it is important to note that all cultural resources—homestead sites, dinosaur tracks, Indian rock art, et cetera—within the Picket Wire Canyonlands are protected by law. Collecting artifacts is strictly prohibited.

# 6 VOGEL CANYON

**Distance: 2.25 miles round trip**      **Management: Comanche NG**
**Difficulty: Easy**                    **Wilderness status: None**
**Hiking time: 2 hours**                **Season: Year-round**
**Elevation: 4,400 to 4,300 feet**      **USGS map: La Junta SE**

While the nearby Picket Wire Canyonlands offer a stunning contrast to the expansive plains that stretch south of La Junta, considerably smaller Vogel Canyon provides a more intimate break. Graced by both natural beauty and relics of the past, this small canyon system is a real joy to visit. Four hiking trails have been established in Vogel Canyon; this hike follows the Canyon and Mesa trails to complete a nice 2.25-mile loop.

The hike begins at the Vogel Canyon Picnic Area, which is reached by driving 13 miles south from La Junta on Colorado Highway 109. Turn right at the sign for Vogel Canyon and drive southwest for 1 mile on County Road 802. Turn left at an intersection and continue south for less than 2 miles to the picnic area.

From the trailhead, follow the Canyon Trail through a V-shaped cattle guard (to the left of the gated fence crossing) and then south among scattered juniper trees. Stone cairns mark the way along this stretch. Within 0.25 mile this trail begins dropping into the head of a shallow side canyon. Well defined along this stretch, the Canyon Trail is easy to follow as it continues down the wash bottom for another 0.25 mile or so. Along this first segment of the hike you may note some old stone foundations near the canyon rim to the west. These are the remains of the Westbrook homestead, which dates back to the

*Recent vandalism to a rock art panel in Vogel Canyon*

Depression era. Farther on, at the base of the canyon's east wall, are petroglyphs (images carved into the rock) left behind by the prehistoric inhabitants of the area.

A little over 0.5 mile from the trailhead, the Canyon Trail reaches one of two springs found in Vogel Canyon. Crowded by a few cottonwoods, some cattails, and a tamarisk or two, this reliable source of water not only made it possible for ranchers to homestead in the canyon, but it has also attracted wildlife such as deer and antelope over the

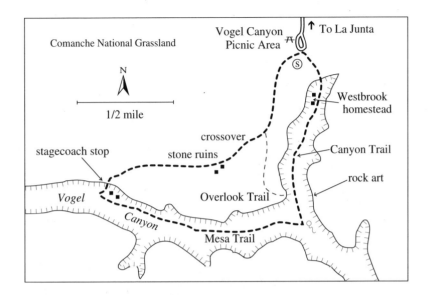

years. At the spring the Canyon Trail intersects with the Mesa Trail, which heads west up the main fork of Vogel Canyon. After turning right at this junction, continue along the Mesa Trail as it follows Vogel Canyon upstream. The trail begins to fade away, but because the route continues along the flat canyon bottom, and thanks to a few stone cairns, it is not difficult to follow.

Eventually, about 0.75 mile from the Canyon Trail–Mesa Trail intersection, the route climbs the canyon rim to the north to return to the trailhead. To find this short ascent out of Vogel Canyon, watch for some stone foundations to the right of the canyon floor. These are the remains of a stagecoach stop along the Barlow & Sanderson's Mail and Stage Line, which was active between 1872 and 1876. Less than 100 yards beyond these ruins, look for two stone cairns that lead north through some rocks. After reaching the top—a climb of less than 100 feet—continue north across the mesa top for a short distance until you find another cairn. From this one look eastward for additional markers that can be followed back to the trailhead area. This section of the route passes among scattered junipers and encounters some additional stone ruins. In sections where no stone markers exist, just keep heading east. As you near the trailhead, look for a wooden crossover that provides access over a fence running north to south. Soon after, you reach the Overlook Trail, which has been graveled for wheelchair access. Turn left on this trail to return to the trailhead.

Watch for rattlesnakes, tarantulas, and scorpions along this hike, especially when away from established trails. Bring drinking water, as the water in Vogel Canyon is not potable. Do not disturb rock art and other historic sites along the way.

# 7     PICTURE CANYON

| | |
|---|---|
| Distance: 4 mile round trip | Management: Comanche NG |
| Difficulty: Easy | Wilderness status: None |
| Hiking time: 2 hours | Season: Year-round |
| Elevation: 4,300 to 4,450 feet | USGS map: Tubs Spring |

As the name suggests, Picture Canyon is home to some well-known examples of Native American rock art. But this unexpectedly memorable place in southeastern Colorado also offers hikers some wonderful canyon scenery, many unusual geologic formations, and an interesting collection of flora and fauna. Hikers can explore Picture Canyon on a newly established 4-mile loop that visits its unique natural and cultural features.

To reach the beginning of this hike, drive 20 miles south from Springfield on US Highway 287 to the small town of Campo. Turn right onto County Road J and continue west for 10 miles to County Road 18. Turn left and drive 5 miles south to the signed right turn for Picture Canyon. Drive less than 2 miles south to the Picture Canyon Picnic Area at the road's end.

From the picnic area the route follows Picture Canyon downstream for about 0.3 mile along an old road that is closed to most vehicles. Upon reaching an area where the canyon begins to widen, you may want to pay a visit to the rock art panels scattered along the canyon's east wall. Although these pictographs and petroglyphs (pictographs are painted on the rock, petroglyphs are carved into the rock) have been badly vandalized over the years by modern-day visitors, they still present a fascinating collection of ancient images. Some drawings, such as one of a horse, cannot date back before the time that these beasts of burden were introduced to the West by the Spanish—sometime after A.D. 1600. Other images are far older, however, as archaeologists have unearthed camps in the area that date to A.D. 500 and earlier. One of the more unusual rock art images in Picture Canyon consists of a series of vertical lines crossed by a longer horizontal line. Found in several locations across southeastern Colorado and neighboring Oklahoma, these strange designs so closely resemble a form of Old World writing known as ogham that some scholars believe the region may have been visited by the ancient Celts of Ireland as long ago as 200 B.C. While most archaeologists doubt such a scenario, these carvings do pose one of the more mystifying questions about prehistoric America. When visiting these or any other rock art panels, be sure not to touch, trace, or disturb the images in any way.

After enjoying Picture Canyon's rock art, return to the trail and follow it north up a side canyon that feeds into Picture Canyon just around the corner. From this point the rest of the route is marked by both fiberglass and cedar signposts. Eventually all of the fiberglass posts will be replaced by cedar posts. Within 0.25 mile of entering this

*A natural arch along the Picture Canyon Trail*

side canyon, the trail turns west at a check dam that spans the wash bottom. From this point follow the side canyon for another 0.3 mile to an area of interesting rock formations known as Hells Half Acre. Here, look for a post that points the way up through a rocky area to the south and then west. While no tread exists along this stretch of the hike, the trail markers eventually lead you up to the canyon's rim and the flat mesa top above. Characterized by such plant species as blue grama grass, buffalo grass, cholla cactus, prickly pear cactus, and yucca, this prairie ecosystem contrasts with the trees, cattails, and thick shrubs found along portions of the canyon bottom below.

From the canyon's rim, head northwest for 0.5 mile before reaching a side canyon that drops into the next drainage to the west. From this point follow rock cairns down this side drainage. Upon reaching the main canyon, which is less than 0.25 mile west, turn right and follow the drainage upstream to a rock formation known as the Wisdom Tooth and a beautiful little natural arch. Beyond the arch the route follows an old road a little way before turning due east. It then takes up a

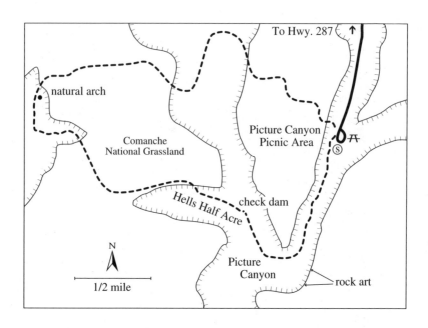

faded road, which it follows eastward along the head of a side canyon. From this portion of the route you get a great view of the surrounding prairie. You can also see Oklahoma to the south. Eventually, the hiking route reaches a graveled county road, which in turn drops back to the Picture Canyon Picnic Area, which is about 1.5 miles from the natural arch.

Watch for prairie rattlesnakes and other venomous creatures, especially when venturing beyond the established trails. Bring drinking water, as any water found along this hike must be treated. Be sure not to touch or deface in any way the fragile rock found within the canyon. Keep in mind that all historic and prehistoric artifacts are protected by federal law.

#  SOUTH BOULDER FOOTHILLS

**Distance: 4 miles round trip**  
**Difficulty: Easy**  
**Hiking time: 2 hours**  
**Elevation: 5,600 to 6,520 feet**  
**Management: City of Boulder Open Space**

**Wilderness status: None**  
**Season: Year-round**  
**USGS map: Eldorado Springs**

The city of Boulder has set the pace for open space preservation among Colorado's Front Range communities. In all, their aggressive program has set aside nearly 25,000 acres of prime foothills acreage. Not satisfied with simply acquiring the land, however, the program has also established many miles of hiking trails and numerous trailhead facilities. One of the most interesting of these hiking areas lies between Boulder and the Eldorado Springs area to the south. Known as the South Boulder foothills, this region encompasses a variety of ecosystems, plus some outstanding scenery. The hike described below follows a portion of the main Mesa Trail and some shorter secondary trails.

To reach the beginning of this hike, drive south from Boulder on Colorado Highway 93 to Colorado Highway 170 and the turnoff for Eldorado Springs. Turn right and drive 1.6 miles to the South Mesa trailhead on the right. The Doudy Draw trailhead on the left accesses more open-space land to the south.

From the trailhead, follow the Mesa Trail across South Boulder Creek and then immediately turn left at the first trail junction onto the Homestead Trail. A few feet beyond, turn right onto the Towhee Trail. These intersections, as well as all other trail junctions in the area, are well marked by small metal signs. Nearby stands a beautiful stone structure known as the Doudy-Debacker-Dunn House. First homesteaded in 1858 by Sylvester Doudy, the surrounding area was sold to John Debacker in 1869 for $500. The portion of the home that is still standing dates back to 1874. Debacker turned over the spread to his daughter and his son-in-law, John Dunn, in 1901.

Heading northwest from the homestead site, the Towhee Trail

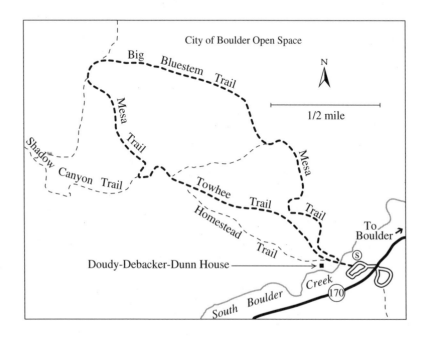

climbs easily for about a mile along the bottom of Shadow Canyon as it approaches the base of Bear Peak. Along this portion of the hike, be sure to note the different riparian species of plants that grow along the small stream flowing through the drainage. Included in this plant community are cottonwood trees, willows, wild plums, chokecherries, hawthorns, and a fair amount of poison ivy. Eventually, the Towhee Trail ends at a junction with a short connecting trail that leads to the Shadow Canyon Trail. After turning left at this point, continue for about 0.25 mile to the next intersection, where a right turn leads out of Shadow Canyon to the Mesa Trail. Upon gaining higher ground, the route enters scattered stands of ponderosa pines. These stately conifers are the last tree species to brave the windswept environs of the Great Plains beyond.

Following the Mesa Trail for a little more than 0.5 mile, the hike passes a turnoff for the Shadow Canyon Trail. Climbing to the highest reaches of Bear Peak, this trail gains a couple of thousand feet before reaching the Bear Peak and South Boulder Peak summits above. As part of the Flatirons, these rugged mountains are composed of the Fountain Formation, which was deposited as alluvial fans along the edge of the ancestral Rockies. These once-level deposits were subsequently tilted to their present aspect by the uplifting action of the Front Range some 65 million years ago. The most prominent feature in this portion of the Flatirons is the aptly named Devils Thumb.

Shortly after passing the turnoff for the Shadow Canyon Trail, this hike turns right onto the Big Bluestem Trail. Following a shallow drainage east, the Big Bluestem Trail drops easily. As it does it leaves the pine forests behind in favor of grasslands that typify the prairie beyond. This intermingling of two very different ecosystems is one of the most interesting features of this hike. Note how the pines give way, a few at a time, before surrendering completely to open meadows. Among the many species of plants that constitute this grassland community is the trail's namesake, big bluestem grass. After nearly a mile, the Big Bluestem Trail reconnects with the Mesa Trail. At this junction turn left and follow the Mesa Trail south for 0.9 mile to return to the trailhead. Keep a watchful eye out for some of the wildlife that lives here. Besides the Abert squirrels that favor the ponderosa pine forests, you may spot mule deer browsing in the brush or a coyote hunting in a meadow. Surprisingly, in an area so close to sprawling cities, black bears, bobcats, and mountain lions have also been seen here.

Be sure to bring drinking water on this hike as none is available. Currently dogs are permitted, but they must be restrained at all times. Be sure to check on current regulations posted at the trailhead. Because horses are commonly encountered along this trail system, be sure to allow plenty of room for passage.

*The Rocky Mountains tower above the South Boulder Foothills.*

# 9   FORGOTTEN VALLEY

**Distance: 2.4 miles round trip**
**Difficulty: Easy**
**Hiking time: 2 hours**
**Elevation: 8,000 to 8,200 feet**
**Management: Golden Gate**
   **Canyon SP**

**Wilderness status: None**
**Season: May to November**
**USGS map: Black Hawk**

Covering some 14,000 acres of the Front Range west of Denver, Golden Gate Canyon State Park harbors not only a number of beautiful natural areas but also some rather alluring historical secrets as well. One easy-to-reach destination within the park that offers hikers both scenery and a palpable taste of the past is Forgotten Valley.

To begin the hike into Forgotten Valley, drive north from Golden on Colorado Highway 93, then turn left onto the Golden Gate Canyon Road (Colorado Highway 46). Follow this road for 14 miles, turn right at the park visitor center, and drive 2.4 miles to the Bridge Creek trailhead. This hike begins by following the Burro Trail north.

Within the first 0.25 mile the Burro Trail crosses the normally dry Ralston Creek and then climbs steeply before leveling off to continue along a more moderate grade. As it climbs, the route encounters scattered stands of ponderosa pine, small meadows, and sporadic clumps of aspen. Later on you may note spruce and fir growing on the shaded north-facing slopes. Nearly 0.5 mile from the trailhead, the Burro Trail intersects with the Mountain Lion Trail. At this point the hike turns left onto the Mountain Lion Trail, which it then follows for the rest of

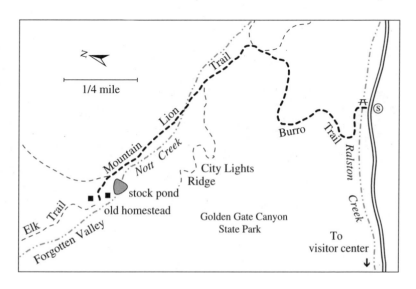

the way to Forgotten Valley. Shortly after this intersection a 0.5-mile side trail turns left to access City Lights Ridge, a high point with some nice vistas. From this trail junction it is 0.7 mile of mostly level hiking along the dry Nott Creek drainage to Forgotten Valley. Because the entire route into Forgotten Valley follows old roadbeds, it is quite easy to follow.

The site of some historical treasures, Forgotten Valley today features a stock pond plus a handful of antiquated buildings. First homesteaded in 1882 by a Swedish immigrant named Andes Tallman, this out-of-the-way meadow was occupied by his descendants until 1951. The state acquired the land in the 1970s. While the log structures were built in the 1880s, the larger frame structure replaced the original homesite prior to 1900. The center of the existing structure is actually an old schoolhouse that was moved here from another location. Testifying to a shadier side of the area's history is the fact that many locations throughout Golden Gate Canyon State Park served as hideaways for bootleggers during Prohibition. Ideal because of the availability of water and its proximity to a ready market in Denver, Forgotten Valley was an ideal location for a still. During the early 1920s the homestead was rented to some loggers who distilled alcohol on the side. Before revenue agents got to the valley, however, they were able to move out and escape capture. From Forgotten Valley the Mountain Lion Trail branches up a side drainage while the Elk Trail continues along Nott Creek.

Bring water on this hike as it is not available along most of the trail. Be aware that both mountain bikes and horses are permitted on this trail. It is possible to camp at Forgotten Valley by reserving one of several backcountry sites.

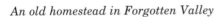

*An old homestead in Forgotten Valley*

# 10 MOUNT AUDUBON

**Distance: 7 miles round trip**
**Difficulty: Moderate**
**Hiking time: 4 hours**
**Elevation: 10,400 to 13,233 feet**

**Management: Roosevelt NF**
**Wilderness status: Indian Peaks WA**
**Season: July to September**
**USGS map: Ward**

Rising to an elevation of 13,233 feet, Mount Audubon is one of the more prominent summits within the Indian Peaks Wilderness. Despite its lofty stature, however, this gentle mountain pales when compared to its immediate neighbors in terms of ruggedness. Indeed, topped by a moderately difficult trail, Audubon poses little challenge to the discerning climber. On the other hand, for the hiker who is simply out to enjoy some incredible views, this peak cannot be beat. Not only does it reveal some upclose views of the surrounding mountains, but it affords incredibly far-reaching vistas in all directions as well.

This hike begins at Brainard Lake, which is located 5 miles west of Ward at the end of Brainard Lake Road (County Road 102). Ward is located along Colorado Highway 72, which runs from Estes Park to the Denver metropolitan area.

From the Mitchell Lake trailhead, located north of Brainard Lake, this hike follows the Beaver Creek Trail for 1.5 miles before turning left onto the Mount Audubon Trail. In this first 1.5-mile segment the route climbs about 1,000 feet along easy to moderate grades. Within the first mile the Beaver Creek Trail makes a few switchbacks as it pushes nearer to timberline. Not until the trail breaks out of the forest— mostly Engelmann spruce and subalpine fir along this hike—is the signed Mount Audubon–Beaver Creek Trail junction reached.

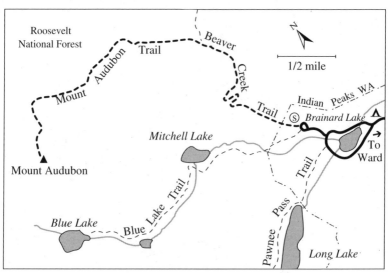

*The rugged Indian Peaks as seen from Mount Audubon*

After bearing left on the Mount Audubon Trail, the route climbs steadily westward to gain another 2,000 feet to the summit. This last segment of the hike ascends the east face of Mount Audubon before reaching a small saddle just north of the peak. It then climbs strenuously up the last pitch to the summit. Some scrambling among boulders and rocks can be expected in this section. From the summit you can look north past nearby Sawtooth Mountain into the southern end of Rocky Mountain National Park. The eastern horizon falls off among the foothills of the Rocky Mountains and the Great Plains beyond. To the west is a chain of mostly 12,000-foot peaks named after Indian tribes of the west—Paiute, Pawnee, Shoshoni, and Navajo. These especially rugged peaks carry the Continental Divide through the 73,000-acre Indian Peaks Wilderness. As part of the Front Range, the Indian Peaks were uplifted during the Laramide Orogeny, beginning 65 million years ago as a large block of Precambrian rock. The east faces of the Indian Peaks are characteristically more rugged than their backsides, in part because this mountain block was tilted along its length during its uplifting. Within the last 2 million years, glaciers subsequently etched away at these peaks, adding to their ruggedness in the process. Looking south from Mount Audubon, the view takes in the southern portion of the Front Range, which includes Mount Evans and Pikes Peak.

Thanks to its proximity to the Denver–Boulder area, and because of the relative easy access to the high country that the Brainard Lake area provides, the hike to Mount Audubon, like many other trails in the area, is very popular. Because of this the Forest Service prohibits backcountry camping in the Brainard Lake area. You may want to plan your hike for a less crowded time of the year. Water is not available along this hike, so be sure to bring your own. Lightning is an almost daily threat during the summer, especially in the afternoon. General weather conditions can deteriorate rapidly as well.

 # ARAPAHO GLACIER

**Distance: 7 miles round trip**          **Wilderness status: Indian Peaks WA**
**Difficulty: Moderate**                  **Season: July to September**
**Hiking time: 4 hours**                  **USGS maps: Monarch Lake,**
**Elevation: 10,121 to 12,700 feet**          **East Portal**
**Management: Roosevelt NF**

Nestled in a high alpine cirque in the south end of the Indian Peaks Wilderness, Arapaho Glacier is one of only a few glaciers still found in Colorado. Although geologists are not quite sure whether these perma-

*Arapaho Glacier lies in a cirque below South Arapaho Peak.*

nent ice fields are left over from the last ice age or if they formed within the last few thousand years, they do show signs of movement characteristic of glaciers. Because Arapaho Glacier falls within land set aside by the City of Boulder for its water supply, it is off-limits to hikers. It is possible, however, to hike to the south ridge of South Arapaho Peak for a good look at the geologic anomaly.

The hike to the Arapaho Glacier overlook begins at the Fourth of July trailhead, which is located northwest of Nederland. From downtown Nederland drive 0.6 mile south on Colorado Highway 72 to the signed turnoff for the Eldora Ski Area. Turn right onto County Road 130 and drive 8.6 miles to the trailhead and campground at road's end. The last 6 miles of this drive are rough and narrow but passable to most vehicles.

Setting out from the upper parking lot at the Buckingham Park Campground, the hike begins by climbing easily among the spruce and fir forests typical of the area. The first 0.5 mile or so of this trail was reconstructed by the Boy Scouts in 1981, so it is in good shape with an abundance of steps, log corridors across wet areas, and other improvements. Eventually, the trail steepens to climb along a more moderate grade. Within the first mile the route reaches the first of two trail junctions. The trail to the left continues 3.5 miles around the head of the

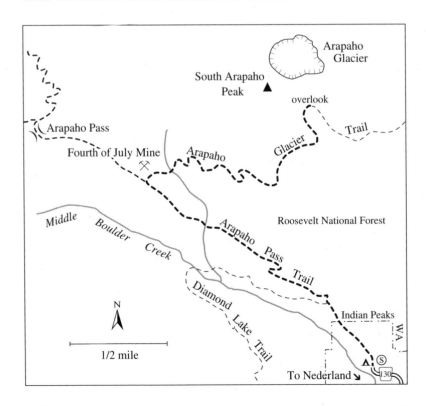

drainage to reach Diamond Lake, a popular destination for backpackers and day hikers alike. Take the trail to the right, which continues on for another mile to the Fourth of July Mine, which is set in an area of krummholz growth just below timberline. Dating back to the 1870s, this mine produced some silver before eventually petering out. Unscrupulous promoters of the mine then devised a scheme to convince investors that there was still a large deposit of copper to be unearthed. In all, millions of dollars in worthless stocks were sold to unsuspecting investors. Today, the Fourth of July Mine features some old machinery, a pile of decaying timbers, and a large tailings pile.

At the Fourth of July Mine is a second trail junction. The trail that continues northwest travels about 1 mile to 11,900-foot Arapaho Pass; take the trail that branches off to the right and continues on to the Arapaho Glacier overlook. Climbing steadily along a mostly moderate grade, the remaining 1.5 miles gain another 1,500 feet before reaching a high point of 12,700 feet. In short order, this route leaves the last vestiges of timber behind to enter alpine tundra. As you climb, vistas of the Front Range to the south come into view. Included in this panorama are Pikes Peak and Mount Evans.

Upon reaching the overlook, you can see the eastern plains stretching east of the foothills. From the overlook, you can also peer into the head of North Boulder Creek, where the Arapaho Glacier spans the rocky cirque below. You may note bluish ice in places, along with cracks and crevasses that stretch across some portions. These crevasses provide evidence that the glacier is actually in motion, albeit ever so slow. While this hike turns back at this point, it is possible to continue following this high alpine ridge eastward along what is sometimes called the Glacier Rim Trail. In 6 miles this route reaches the Rainbow Lakes trailhead. It is also possible to scramble up 13,397-foot South Arapaho Peak, which rises just north of the overlook.

Because much of this hike crosses highly exposed terrain, be wary of afternoon lightning storms. Water is available along the way, but it must be treated first. Keep in mind that the Fourth of July trailhead is an extremely popular entry point for the Indian Peaks Wilderness, especially on weekends.

# 12 EMERALD LAKE

**Distance: 3.6 miles round trip**
**Difficulty: Moderate**
**Time: 3 hours**
**Elevation: 9,475 to 10,080 feet**

**Management: Rocky Mountain NP**
**Wilderness status: None**
**Season: June to October**
**USGS map: McHenrys Peak**

With more than 350 miles of backcountry trails, Rocky Mountain National Park offers hikers an incredible variety of routes from which to choose. While some take several days to complete, others are comparatively short and easy. Regardless of the length of any of these wil-

*Hikers along the trail to Emerald Lake*

derness excursions, however, they all feature spectacular mountain scenery and a plentiful supply of natural wonders. One particularly short but popular hike climbs from Bear Lake Road to Emerald Lake in the eastern portion of the park. Because it is easy, this excursion makes a wonderful introduction to the splendor of Rocky Mountain National Park for hikers of nearly all abilities.

To begin this hike, drive west from Estes Park a short way on US Highway 36 to the park headquarters. Continue through the Beaver Meadows entrance station and turn left onto Bear Lake Road. The trailhead is located near the road's end. To help alleviate traffic

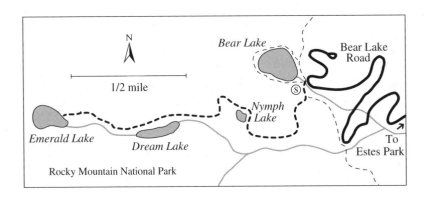

congestion, a free shuttle operates along the Bear Lake Road during the summer.

Climbing a little over 600 feet in 1.8 miles, the trail to Emerald Lake is not particularly difficult, nor is it hard to follow. From the trailhead the route sets out through a forest of lodgepole pine, Engelmann spruce, and subalpine fir. Before encountering diminutive Nymph Lake about 0.5 mile out, the route intersects a trail which heads southwest to Glacier Gorge. Beyond Nymph Lake, the route continues to climb before reaching larger Dream Lake 1.1 miles from the trailhead. Perfectly reflecting both Hallett Peak and Flattop Mountain, which rise to the west, Dream Lake is thought to be the most photographed lake in the park. It also marks the turnaround point for many hikers, especially those with small children.

From Dream Lake the trail climbs another 250 feet along the final 0.75 mile of the hike before reaching the east shore of Emerald Lake. Along this last segment of the hike some beautiful scenery opens up, especially to the east. And at Emerald Lake itself the stunning geology of Rocky Mountain National Park really unfolds. As part of the Front Range, the mountains of Rocky Mountain National Park serve as textbook examples of faulted anticlines—that is, elongated blocks of Precambrian rock that were uplifted between 40 million to 65 million years ago. What really shaped this mountain landscape, however, were the large glaciers that covered the region a million years ago. Not only were the many lakes of the park formed by glaciers, but the classic U-shaped valleys, the moraines, and the rugged east and north faces of such summits as nearby Hallett Peak all owe their existence to the sculpting action of these bygone sheets of ice. Several small glaciers still exist in the park above the 11,000-foot level.

Where the wildlife of the park is concerned, you may not spot such impressive creatures as bighorn sheep, elk, and moose along this busy trail, but you are likely to see marmots and pikas, both of which haunt the upper elevations of the park.

Water is found along this hike, but it must be treated. Lightning strikes are common in the area, especially during afternoon thunderstorms. To avoid the crowds that occasionally venture to Emerald Lake, you may want to try this hike after Labor Day.

## 13  LULU CITY

**Distance: 7.4 miles round trip**    **Management: Rocky Mountain NP**
**Difficulty: Easy**    **Wilderness status: None**
**Hiking time: 4 hours**    **Season: May to October**
**Elevation: 9,000 to 9,600 feet**    **USGS map: Fall River Pass**

Following the Colorado River upstream through the mountain-ringed Kawuneeche Valley in the west end of Rocky Mountain National Park, the hike to Lulu City reveals a surprising bit of the park's history while offering a look at the headwater area of the mighty Colorado River.

This hike begins at the Colorado River trailhead, which is located about 9.5 miles north of Rocky Mountain National Park's western entrance. The western entrance is located north of Grandby on US Highway 34, which inside the park is known as Trail Ridge Road. Because this is a popular hike, be prepared to see many other hikers, especially along the first few miles of this trail.

From the trailhead the hike follows the Colorado River Trail north to where it soon climbs a short, moderately steep switchback. After that it levels off to continue along level or easy grades the rest of the way. Near the 0.5-mile mark the trail reaches a junction. The trail to the left crosses the Kawuneeche Valley before climbing to the Grand Ditch, which traverses the slopes of the Never Summer Range to the west. Dug by hand around the turn of the century, the Grand Ditch still carries water across the Continental Divide to cities and farmlands on the Front Range. In so doing it saps the Colorado River of some of its strength, even before it really gets started. The right-hand trail leads to Lulu City.

Beyond this intersection, the trail continues due north for the remainder of the hike. Along this first portion of the hike, the route passes within a few feet of the fledgling Colorado River in places. While the Colorado is often thought of as a mighty river, here—only a few miles from its headwaters—it is a gently flowing stream. Among

*An interpretive sign at Lulu City*

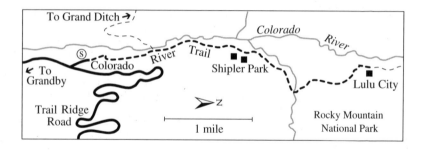

the trees growing along this portion of the hike are lodgepole pine, spruce, fir, and aspen. There are also some nice open meadows in which you might spy a moose or perhaps a small herd of elk. While such species of wildlife have lost much of their shyness in the park, they still prefer visiting these open areas in the early morning and late evening.

A little over 2 miles from the trailhead the route reaches Shipler Park, which features a pair of old cabins in disrepair. Like those at Lulu City, these structures represent a bygone era of get-rich-quick schemes and failed dreams. Beyond the Shipler cabins the trail continues another 1.2 miles before reaching Lulu City. Within this last stretch the trail climbs an easy grade among a forest of mostly lodgepole pine before dropping back to the river and the Lulu townsite.

Today, the remains of Lulu City are proof that the feverish search for gold and silver during the late nineteenth century touched nearly every corner of the Colorado Rockies. First established in 1879, Lulu City (named after the daughter of probable town founder Benjamin Franklin Burnett) soon grew to a "Saturday-night population" of 500. In all, 100 blocks were platted, and although not all were developed, the town did boast four lumber mills, an elegant hotel, a post office, and more. Of course, Lulu City was as lively a scene as nearly any boomtown of the day. Although some gold, silver, and lead were unearthed in the nearby mountains, the boom turned to bust in only a few short years. By 1884 the town was virtually abandoned. Amazingly, all that is left of this once-bustling city are a few rotting log foundations and some old stories.

While this hike turns around at Lulu City, it is possible to continue farther up the Colorado River drainage. About a mile north of Lulu is Little Yellowstone, a severely eroded section of white and yellow rock reminiscent of Yellowstone Canyon in Yellowstone National Park. This colorful substrata dates back to a volcanic eruption that occurred some 28 million years ago. It is also possible to climb beyond Little Yellowstone to reach the Continental Divide at La Poudre Pass. La Poudre Pass is about 3.7 miles beyond Lulu City.

Although water is plentiful along this hike, it must be treated. Regulations for hiking within a national park prohibit pets in the backcountry. In addition, an overnight stay does require a backcountry permit.

# 14 MIRROR LAKE

**Distance:** 12.2 miles round trip
**Difficulty:** Moderate
**Hiking time:** 8 hours
**Elevation:** 10,070 to 11,025 feet
**Management:** Roosevelt NF, Rocky
Mountain NP

**Wilderness status:** Comanche
Peak WA
**Season:** July to September
**USGS maps:** Chambers Lake,
Comanche Peak

Nestled in the isolated northwest corner of Rocky Mountain National Park, Mirror Lake is an exceptionally memorable destination for day hikers and backpackers alike.

From Fort Collins, drive west on Colorado Highway 14 toward Cameron Pass. About 5 miles before the pass, turn left onto Long Draw Road (Forest Road 156) and drive 8.5 miles to the signed Corral Creek trailhead. Across the road from the trailhead is an information center administered by both the Forest Service and the Park Service.

From the trailhead this hike follows the Corral Park Trail for 0.25 mile before entering the Comanche Peak Wilderness. In another 0.75 mile it reaches the southern end of the Big South Trail, which heads north

*Mirror Lake offers hikers a scenic reward.*

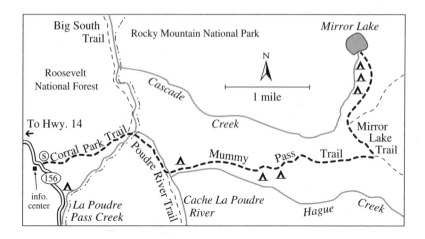

to follow the Cache La Poudre River downstream to a trailhead on Colorado Highway 14. Within this first mile, the hike drops about 300 feet in all. After turning right at the junction, follow the Poudre River Trail across La Poudre Pass Creek, which is usually swollen by waters carried across the Continental Divide by the Grand Ditch. Up to this point the hike traverses lands administered by the Roosevelt National Forest. Beyond this creek crossing, the remainder of the hike falls within Rocky Mountain National Park.

About 0.5 mile beyond the park boundary the Poudre River Trail reaches the start of the Mummy Pass Trail. While the Poudre River Trail turns right to follow the Cache La Poudre River south for 9 miles to Milner Pass along the Continental Divide, the Mummy Pass Trail crosses the Cache La Poudre River before heading east toward its namesake and the destination of this hike, Mirror Lake. Just east of the Cache La Poudre River is the Hague Creek campsite. Overnight campers in Rocky Mountain National Park must spend the night in one of several designated backcountry sites, most of which include a primitive privy. Beyond the campsite the trail climbs slightly before reaching the west end of an expansive open park. Located at the edge of this park are two more backcountry campsites, Desolation and Flatiron.

After skirting the edge of the meadow, the Mummy Pass Trail begins ascending along a more moderate grade. It is within the next 2.5 miles that the hike completes the lion's share of its 1,300-foot climb. This section of the hike, which travels among pristine stands of lodgepole pines, is quite beautiful. Nearly 3 miles beyond the Cache La Poudre River crossing, the Mummy Pass Trail connects with the Mirror Lake Trail. From this junction a right turn leads nearly 2 miles to Mummy Pass, while a left turn takes you 1.6 miles north to Mirror Lake. Although there are a few small climbs along this last stretch, most of it is level. As the trail nears the lake, a number of signs add some confusion to the hike. Each sign points left to different backcountry campsites, all of which are named Mirror Lake. Since these signs do not mention that they are campsites, it is easy to think that they are pointing the way to Mirror Lake itself. To find the actual lake, keep right at each of these junctions.

Nestled near timberline, Mirror Lake is surrounded by stunted spruce forests along with some areas of krummholz trees. Rising some 1,200 feet above the lake to the northwest is a rugged beautiful but unnamed peak, while 12,702-foot Comanche Peak sits off to the northeast. A steep trail branches off from the Mirror Lake Trail and eventually accesses Comanche Peak, which rises along the border between the park and Roosevelt National Forest. Trout fishing is good at Mirror Lake, but as with the streams and rivers encountered along the first section of this hike, anglers are allowed to use flies and artificial lures only.

Although lightning can pose a danger along this high-country hike, the route does not cross any particularly exposed areas. All water should be treated before drinking, and overnight visitors must first obtain a permit from Rocky Mountain National Park. Because fires are prohibited in the park's backcountry, be sure to bring a stove for cooking.

# 15   MOUNT McCONNEL

**Distance: 5 miles round trip**
**Difficulty: Moderate**
**Hiking time: 3 hours**
**Elevation: 7,520 to 8,010 feet**
**Management: Roosevelt NF**

**Wilderness status: Cache La Poudre WA**
**Season: March to November**
**USGS map: Big Narrows**

At 9,380 acres, the Cache La Poudre Wilderness is one of the smallest wilderness areas in the state. Nevertheless, hikers who reach the summit of the wilderness area's Mount McConnel will be rewarded with breathtaking views and pristine timberlands.

This hike begins at the Mountain Park Recreation Area, which is located about 26 miles west of Fort Collins off Colorado Highway 14.

From the trailhead, this hike begins by following the 2-mile-long Kruetzer Trail. Built by the Civilian Conservation Corps (CCC) in 1936, this trail is named after William Kruetzer, the first official forest ranger in the United States. Working in a forest preserve in the central part of the state, Kruetzer became the supervisor of the Colorado National Forest, which is now known as the Roosevelt National Forest. The Kruetzer Trail climbs 800 feet as it winds its way up the north slope of Mount McConnel. Interpretive signs along the way identify and describe some of the area's flora, including lodgepole and ponderosa pine. Some interesting outcrops of igneous rock are also encountered along the way. Views of the Cache La Poudre River below add to the hike's pleasurability.

From the upper end of the Kruetzer Trail turn left on the Mount McConnel Trail, which continues on to the summit. Because the remaining 0.5 mile to the top ascends another 500 feet, grades along this climb are moderate to strenuous in difficulty. Upon reaching the 8,010-foot summit of Mount McConnel, you can enjoy incredible views of the Mummy Range to the south. The most distant visible mountains fall within Rocky Mountain National Park. From the summit, return to the Kruetzer Trail by way of a steep and rocky route that drops north. After reconnecting with the Kruetzer Trail the route is better defined.

No water is available along the hike to Mount McConnel. Lightning strikes are possible, given the fact that the mountain is a high point in this region of the Roosevelt National Forest.

*Pine-covered mountains surround Mount McConnel.*

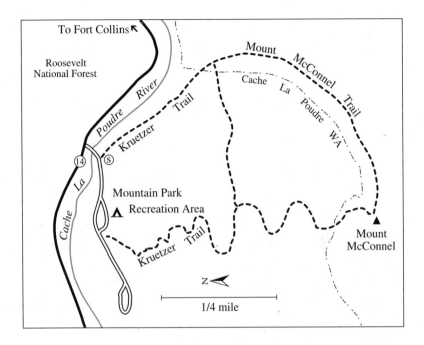

# 16    EMMALINE LAKE

**Distance: 10 miles round trip**
**Difficulty: Moderate**
**Hiking time: 6 hours**
**Elevation: 8,800 to 11,000 feet**
**Management: Roosevelt NF**

**Wilderness status: Comanche**
    **Peak WA**
**Season: July to October**
**USGS maps: Comanche Peak,**
    **Pingree Park**

Stretching across the northern border of Rocky Mountain National Park, the Mummy Range holds both rugged granite faces and gently

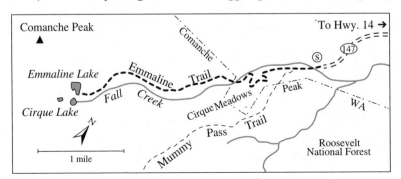

rolling alpine terrain. This dichotomy of landscapes resulted from both the geologic makeup of the range and the persuasive carving action of past glaciers. A good place to enjoy this picturesque topography is at Emmaline Lake, located at the eastern foot of Comanche Peak.

To begin this hike, drive 35 miles west from Fort Collins on Colorado Highway 14 to Pingree Park Road. Turn south and continue for another 15.8 miles to Forest Road 145. Turn right and drive 0.3 mile to a small parking area. It is possible to continue for another 0.5 mile on a 4WD road before reaching the road's end.

From the trailhead follow the road for a little over a mile to where it ends at the north end of the highly scenic Cirque Meadows. Along this first segment of the hike you encounter the turnoff for the Mummy Pass Trail, which heads southwest into the park and over its namesake. From the end of the road the Emmaline Trail crosses Fall Creek and then continues upstream the rest of the way to Emmaline Lake. Within the first 1.25 miles following the creek crossing, the trail climbs along mostly easy grades through forests of lodgepole pines, spruce, and firs. Eventually, however, the trail takes up a moderately difficult grade as it gains the upper reaches of the Fall Creek drainage. Around the 10,800-foot level the Emmaline Trail leaves the taller timber behind in favor of stunted krummholz growth. Soon after, it passes by a beautiful waterfall. A short distance farther, the trail climbs one final pitch before reaching its destination—Emmaline Lake. In the 3 miles from the road's end to the lake, the Emmaline Trail gains 1,200 feet.

At Emmaline Lake you can enjoy a nice view of a classic glacial cirque. Rimmed by high cliffs to the south and west, this circular escarp-

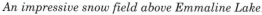

*An impressive snow field above Emmaline Lake*

ment of granite was etched out by large mountain glaciers that covered the higher terrain of the Rocky Mountains about a million years ago. Contrasting with the rugged cliffs are the much gentler western slopes of these same peaks. Named for their resemblance to reclining mummies, the Mummy Range formed as the result of faulted anticlines that were uplifted about 65 million years ago. Rising east of Emmaline Lake is the tallest summit in the area, 12,702-foot Comanche Peak. Although Emmaline Lake is the largest lake in the basin, nearby Cirque Lake is equally beautiful.

Although not particularly exposed, this trail can see lightning activity in July and August, when afternoon thunderstorms are common. All water found along the hike must be treated before drinking.

# 17 RAWAH LAKES

**Distance: 18.5 miles round trip**
**Difficulty: Moderate**
**Hiking time: 3 days**
**Elevation: 8,560 to 11,220 feet**
**Management: Roosevelt NF**

**Wilderness status: Rawah WA**
**Season: July to September**
**USGS maps: Boston Peak,**
  **Rawah Lake**

Encompassing the southern portion of the Medicine Bow Range, the Rawah Wilderness includes some memorable mountain areas. At the heart of this wilderness is the Lakes District—an area of sky-blue lakes strung along the crest of the range. By following several different trails it is possible to visit many of these lakes in one multiday hike.

From Fort Collins drive west on Colorado Highway 14 along the Cache La Poudre River to Chambers Lake. Turn right onto Laramie River Road (Forest Road 190), a well-maintained gravel road that is passable to all vehicles, and continue 6 miles north to the developed West Branch trailhead, which is 0.25 mile north of the Tunnel Campground. As the large parking lot at the trailhead indicates, this hike is very popular.

From the trailhead, follow the West Branch Trail for 3 miles as it continues upstream along the West Branch of the Laramie River. About 2 miles in, this route reaches the lower end of the Camp Lake Trail, which is the return leg for this hike. In another mile the West Branch Trail reaches the south end of the Rawah Trail. From the trailhead to this junction, the West Branch Trail has climbed about 1,000 feet along mostly easy grades. Several stands of aspen dot the first 2 miles of this hike, but expect to see mostly lodgepole pines, Engelmann spruce, and subalpine firs as you gain elevation.

After turning right at the West Branch–Rawah Trail intersection, the route continues to climb along a mostly easy grade for another 0.5 mile before reaching a set of switchbacks. Taking up a more strenuous ascent at this point, the route climbs 700 feet in a mile before reaching the next trail junction. A left turn at this intersection leads 1.5 miles up the North Fork Trail to Twin Crater Lakes. Situated at the 11,000-foot mark, the Twin Crater Lakes area features extensive krummholz growth. Clearly visible to the northwest is 12,644-foot South Rawah Peak. From Twin Crater Lakes, South Rawah Peak is a relatively easy, nontechnical climb.

Beyond the Rawah–North Fork Trail intersection, the Rawah Trail continues to climb northwest toward 11,220-foot Grassy Pass. At first this ascent is easy, but within the last 0.5 mile leading up to the pass the trail climbs through a couple of steep switchbacks. After reaching the top, the route descends slowly before reaching the Rawah Lakes area. Numbering four in all, the Rawah Lakes are scattered along the northeastern base of 12,473-foot North Rawah Peak. Two of these lakes are located at trailside, and the other two are easily accessible via short side hikes. In the vicinity of the Rawah Lakes, the Rawah Trail intersects the McIntyre Lake Trail, which heads north. About

*The trail leading to Twin Lakes in the Rawah Wilderness*

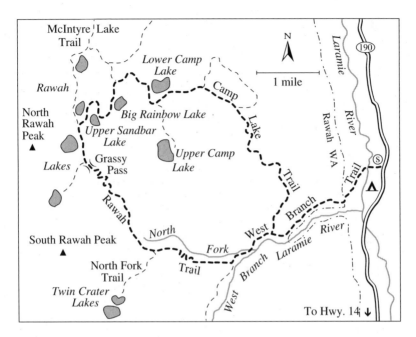

4 miles from the turnoff for Twin Crater Lakes, the Rawah Trail reaches the upper end of the Camp Lake Trail. While the Rawah Trail continues northeast for another 9 miles to a trailhead on Laramie River Road, this hike bears right to follow the Camp Lake Trail east and south before eventually rejoining the West Branch Trail. From the Rawah–Camp Lake Trail junction it is 2 miles to Lower Camp Lake—a nice place to camp. A side trail climbs a couple of hundred feet in about 1 mile to reach Upper Camp Lake to the south. While Lower Camp Lake is situated among the trees, Upper Camp Lake is closer to timberline and features some interesting subalpine growth.

From Lower Camp Lake the Camp Lake Trail soon begins following an old water ditch that is no longer used. About a mile from the lake the trail cuts southeast from the ditch to cross a low ridge before reuniting with the ditch on the far side. This shortcut saves about a mile and, while the trail in this section may be somewhat faint in places, it is not difficult to find your way, especially with the help of a topographic map. From where it rejoins the ditch, the Camp Lake Trail continues for another couple of miles south along a steady grade before dropping nearly 1,000 feet back into the West Branch of the Laramie River drainage. From the intersection with the West Branch Trail, it is 2 miles back to the trailhead. Fishing is good in many of the lakes along this hike, and, given some added time, you may want to bag a peak or two.

Water is readily available along this hike, but must be treated. Lightning may present a hazard in the higher terrain. Forest Service regulations require that dogs be kept on a leash at all times.

# 18 MONTGOMERY PASS

**Distance: 3.6 miles round trip**
**Difficulty: Moderate**
**Hiking time: 3 hours**
**Elevation: 10,040 to 11,000 feet**
**Management: Roosevelt NF,**
  **Colorado SF**

**Wilderness status: None**
**Season: July to September**
**USGS map: Clark Peak**

This short hike offers easy access to a high mountain pass from which it is possible to look out in all directions across many miles of northern Colorado.

The hike to Montgomery Pass begins at the Zimmerman Lake trailhead, which is located about 65 miles west of Fort Collins, 1.5 miles north of Cameron Pass, on Colorado State Highway 14. Although the trailhead is on the east side of the road, the Montgomery Pass Trail begins west of the highway, directly across from the north end of the parking area.

*Montgomery Pass is marked by this sign.*

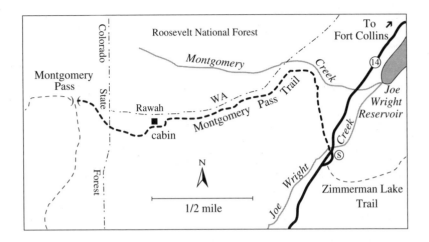

For the first 0.25 mile the trail roughly parallels the highway north before reaching an old jeep trail, which it then follows the rest of the way to the summit. Although wider than most backcountry trails, enough years have passed since it was closed to vehicles that it is now a pleasurable route to follow. Upon reaching the old road, the route parallels Montgomery Creek for a short distance before bending left to climb the mountain slope along easy to moderate grades. For most of the way, the trail travels amid a forest mix of Engelmann spruce and subalpine fir. As it nears the top, however, small forest openings provide suitable habitat for a variety of wildflowers. Also encountered along the upper end of the hike is a small cabin that has fallen into disrepair. This abode once housed miners who worked the nearby mines.

After crossing a small stream the trail breaks out of the timber before reaching Montgomery Pass a short distance beyond. Although this hike began in Roosevelt National Forest, the pass itself is located on Colorado State Forest lands. From the pass, it is possible to continue hiking in a few different directions. Heading west, a faint trail drops into the Colorado State Forest, which encompasses the west slope of the mountain range. Hikers could also choose to follow the alpine crest of the mountains in either direction. To the north rises 12,951-foot Clark Peak, the high point of Colorado's share of the Medicine Bow Mountains. And heading south a faint trail continues a couple of miles to 10,276-foot Cameron Pass. From the pass itself vistas take in the flat-topped mountains of the Neota Wilderness and the Mummy Range to the east, and the expansive North Park to the west. Rising on the western horizon beyond the park is the Mount Zirkel Wilderness.

Water is available along this hike, but it must treated. Lightning storms crop up frequently in the area, especially on summer afternoons. Because the Montgomery Pass Trail is wide and gentle, it is a popular cross-country ski route in the winter.

# 19 LAKE AGNES

**Distance: 1.6 miles round trip**
**Difficulty: Moderate**
**Hiking time: 2 hours**
**Elevation: 10,200 to 10,663 feet**
**Management: Colorado SF**

**Wilderness status: None**
**Season: July to September**
**USGS maps: Mount Richthofen,**
**Clark Peak**

A mere 1.6 miles, the round-trip hike to scenic Lake Agnes is ripe with rewards. Nestled beneath both the Nokhu Crags and Mount Richthofen, this sparkling lake promises both incredible photo opportunities and good high-country fishing for those who make the steep but short climb.

The trailhead for the Lake Agnes Trail is reached by driving west on Colorado Highway 14 over Cameron Pass (approximately 68 miles from Fort Collins) to the signed turnoff on the south side of the highway. This turnoff is 2.4 miles south of Cameron Pass and 7 miles east of the small village of Gould. From the highway drive 1.9 miles south to the Crags Scenic Area. Although this road is steep and rough for the last mile, it is passable to most carefully driven cars. Visitors must pay a day-use fee charged by the Colorado State Forest.

From the parking lot at the Crags Scenic Area, the trail begins by crossing a stream; shortly beyond it takes up the 400 foot climb to the lake. Although much of this ascent is steep, the trail is well marked and easy to follow. After 0.3 mile the route splits. The trail to the right reaches the lake after climbing for another 0.5 mile through the Engelmann spruce and subalpine fir forest, while the left-hand route follows a rocky, avalanche-swept creek bottom for 0.4 mile to the lake. The creek route is usually impassable for a longer period of time due to snowbanks that tend to linger in the protected drainage.

Although talus slopes drop down to the water's edge along the east and south shores, it is possible to circle the lake given enough time. An interesting tree-covered island rises near the west shore. Because the lake is located just below timberline, krummholz growth is evident on the island and in different places around the lake. Fishing is said to be

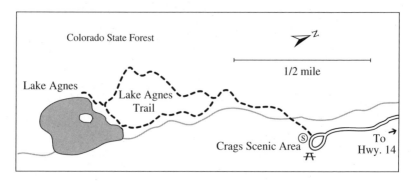

*Hikers visiting Lake Agnes*

good, but anglers are restricted to artificial flies and lures only. Wildlife in the area includes mule deer, elk on occasion, marmots, pikas, and an occasional band of bighorn sheep. The rugged profile of the 12,485-foot Nokhu Crags soars to the southeast and the bulk of 12,940-foot Mount Richthofen, the highest summit within the Never Summer Range, rises to the south.

All water found along the hike must be treated before drinking. Watch for lightning on summer afternoons. Camping along this hike is prohibited, and pets should be kept on a 6-foot or shorter leash. You may want to check with the Colorado State Forest concerning other regulations.

## 20 BAKER PASS

**Distance: 12 miles round trip**
**Difficulty: Moderate**
**Hiking time: 8 hours**
**Elevation: 8,940 to 11,253 feet**
**Management: Arapaho NF, Rocky Mountain NP**

**Wilderness status: Never Summer WA**
**Season: July to September**
**USGS maps: Bowen Mountain, Mount Richthofen, Grand Lake**

Nestled up to the western border of Rocky Mountain National Park, the Never Summer Mountains got their name from the Arapaho Indian word *Ni-chebe-chii* or "No Never Summer." Although the range does seem to be gripped by winter for much of the year, it is probably no more so than other comparable mountain ranges in northern Colorado. Nevertheless, the name does have a certain mystique, as do the mountains themselves. A nice day hike, or perhaps an overnight excursion, into the Never Summers follows the Baker Gulch Trail for 6 miles to the drainage's headwaters at 11,253-foot Baker Pass. Because the pass lies at the heart of the range, and because the Never Summers are not well known, the chances of finding solitude along this hike are great.

The Baker Gulch Trail begins on the west side of Rocky Mountain National Park. From the park's west entrance drive 6.4 miles north on Trail Ridge Road to the turnoff for the Bowen–Baker trailhead.

Although this hike follows a dirt road for its first 0.5 mile, it takes up a foot trail once it reaches a camp for park employees. Shortly beyond this point the route begins climbing out of the Kawuneeche Valley along Baker Gulch Creek. Ascending along an easy to moderate grade most of the way, this first half of the trail includes some switchbacks as it passes through forests of lodgepole pine, aspen, spruce, and fir, plus some open areas. As you climb, you may note what looks like a road across the mountain slope above. That is the Grand Ditch. Constructed in the 1890s, this water development enjoys a permanent easement across the northwest corner of the park so that it can siphon water from the west side of the Continental Divide to cities and farms along Colorado's Front Range. About 4 miles from the trailhead the Baker Gulch Trail crosses the Grand Ditch and its service road Shortly after, the trail heads in a more northerly direction as it rounds 12,397-foot Baker Mountain. About 0.5 mile north of the ditch is the signed turnoff for the trail to Parika Lake. The lake, situated at an elevation of 11,400 feet, lies a mile or so west and is 1,000 feet higher than this point.

Continuing north from the trail junction, the Baker Gulch Trail maintains a mostly easy ascent as it heads toward the pass. In the last 2-mile stretch from the ditch to the pass, the route climbs about 800

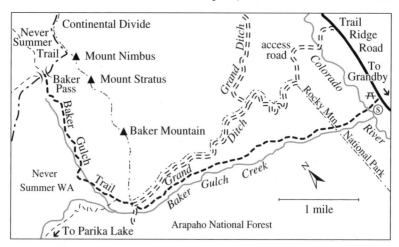

feet, spending much of the time in open meadows that span the valley's bottom. Exposed areas such as these are good places to spot deer, elk, and other fauna that inhabit the Never Summers. One species of note is the Rocky Mountain bighorn sheep, which prefers the higher terrain above.

Upon arriving at the pass, admire the view of the Cloud Range—a trio of peaks (Mount Stratus, Mount Nimbus, and Mount Cumulus) that carry the Continental Divide along the western border of the park. Heading north from the pass is the Never Summer Trail—a 9-mile route that runs the length of its namesake mountains. And, now that you have hiked 6 miles to get to this remote pass, you should know that a side trail leads 1 mile west to the end of the 4WD Jack Creek Road. While this alternate route does allow for quick and easy access

*The views from the head of Baker Gulch are superb.*

to Baker Pass, you would have missed the beauty of Baker Gulch had you taken that trail instead.

Because the Never Summers are wracked by lightning throughout much of the summer, plan to be off the higher terrain by noon or shortly after. Be prepared for deteriorating weather conditions. Water is available along this hike, but it must be treated.

# 21 RED DIRT PASS

**Distance: 15 miles round trip**  **Management: Routt NF**
**Difficulty: Moderate**  **Wilderness status: Mount Zirkel WA**
**Hiking time: 2 days**  **Season: July to September**
**Elevation: 8,480 to 11,400 feet**  **USGS map: Mount Zirkel**

Beginning at the Slavonia trailhead, this hike takes you past the popular destination of Gold Creek Lake to access a beautiful mountain valley and a high pass beyond. The rewards of this 2-day trip include the historic remains of an old mine, some wonderful flower-filled meadows, and that top-of-the-world feeling that 11,400-foot Red Dirt Pass provides. Add to all this the opportunity to climb nearby Mount Zirkel and you have all the makings for a memorable overnight trip.

To reach the Slavonia trailhead, drive 2 miles west from Steamboat Springs on US Highway 40 to the Airport Road (County Road 129). Turn right and drive 20 miles north to Seedhouse Road (Forest Road 400). Turn right again and follow this route for 14 miles to its end. Although graveled, Seedhouse Road is well maintained and passable to all vehicles. Upon arriving at the Slavonia trailhead, do not be surprised to see a lot of cars in the parking lot. Accessing the most popular area of the Mount Zirkel Wilderness, this trailhead is used by hikers intent on following the 10-mile Gilpin Lake–Gold Creek Lake loop.

From the trailhead, begin by following the Gold Creek Lake Trail

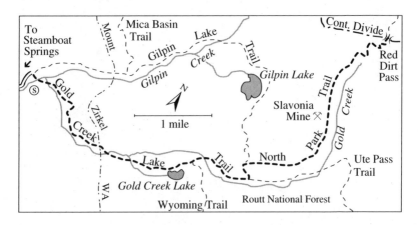

*A lively waterfall along the Gold Creek Lake Trail*

past its namesake to the turnoff for the North Park Trail. In the 5 or so miles from the trailhead to where the North Park Trail turns right, the Gold Creek Lake Trail climbs 1,700 feet along easy to moderate grades, with a few sections that could be considered strenuous. At the 4-mile mark, Gold Creek Lake serves as the turnaround point for many day hikers. The Forest Service restricts camping within 0.25 mile of this extremely popular destination. Fishing at the lake is fair to good. Beyond Gold Creek Lake, the trail intersects the Wyoming Trail (see the Wyoming Trail hike) and then the Ute Pass Trail as it continues for another mile to where it meets the lower end of the North Park Trail. In the last 0.3 mile leading up to this junction, the route climbs about 400 feet. At the intersection the Gilpin Lake Trail turns left to cover 5.6 miles before arriving back at the Slavonia trailhead. The chief at traction along this route is Gilpin Lake, which, like Gold Creek Lake, is very popular. Similar camping restrictions apply there, as well.

From the Gold Creek Lake–Gilpin Lake–North Park Trail junction, the North Park Trail continues east and then north, following the Gold Creek drainage toward its headwaters, which are located just below Red Dirt Pass. Contouring along the west face of this classic, glacially carved canyon, the North Park Trail passes the old Slavonia Mine about 1 mile beyond the trail junction. Today the Slavonia Mine is little more than scattered piles of lumber, a few pieces of machinery, and some rotting log foundations. Beyond the mine, the trail eventually breaks out of the Engelmann spruce–subalpine fir forest to continue above timberline for the remainder of the hike. Watch for wildflowers in these open meadows. Although some marshy areas may be encountered along this portion of the trail, the route is fairly evident.

As the trail approaches the head of the Gold Creek drainage, it begins climbing the final 1,000 feet of this hike in a series of moderate to strenuously steep switchbacks before reaching Red Dirt Pass. Situated on the Continental Divide, Red Dirt Pass does provide some wonderful views—especially those of the Gold Creek drainage and Ute Pass to the south, and Frying Pan Basin, which opens up beyond the pass. While this hike turns around at Red Dirt Pass, it is a relatively easy traverse northwest to reach 12,180-foot Mount Zirkel. Not only is this summit the namesake of this wilderness, but it is also the highest point in the Park Range. Mount Zirkel was named for a geologist who visited the area as part the King Survey, which explored the 40th Parallel in 1871. The climb from Red Dirt Pass to the summit ascends 800 feet in slightly less than a mile.

Although this hike returns to the trailhead by way of the Gold Creek Trail, it is also possible to return to your car via the Gilpin Lake Trail. This side excursion would add 1 mile and 700 feet of climbing to your trip.

Water is found along this hike, but you must treat it. Lightning can pose a hazard on Red Dirt Pass and in other high locations. Be mindful of Forest Service regulations concerning camping near lakes in the area. If crowds are a concern, you may want to plan your hike for a weekday.

# 22  WYOMING TRAIL

**Distance: 20 miles one way**
**Difficulty: Moderate**
**Hiking time: 3 days**
**Elevation: 10,300 to 11,880 feet**
**Management: Routt NF**

**Wilderness status: Mount Zirkel WA**
**Season: July to September**
**USGS maps: Buffalo Pass, Mount Ethel, Mount Zirkel**

Following the Continental Divide for most of its 20-mile length, this hike along the Wyoming Trail offers a memorable multiday excursion

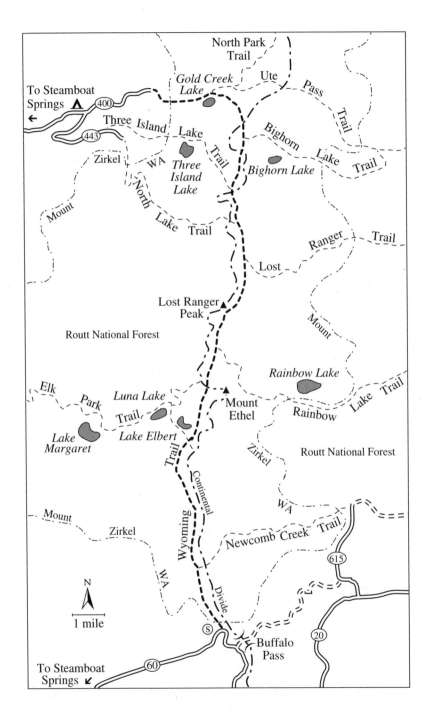

across some beautiful alpine terrain. Running north from Buffalo Pass to the Wyoming border, the Wyoming Trail covers nearly 50 miles in all. This hike takes in the highest portion of the route as it traces the Divide along the southern half of the Mount Zirkel Wilderness. This segment of the Wyoming Trail is also part of the interstate Continental Divide Trail.

The hike begins at Buffalo Pass, which is located east of Steamboat Springs. From downtown Steamboat, turn north on Seventh Street and follow the signs for Buffalo Pass through town. Outside of the city turn right onto County Road 38 (Forest Road 60). Follow this road 11.3 miles to the trailhead, which is located on top of the pass. Forest Road 60 is gravel, but passable to most vehicles. For directions to an alternative starting point at the north end of this hike, see the Red Dirt Pass hike.

From Buffalo Pass the Wyoming Trail begins by following an old jeep road for 4 miles along the crest of the Park Range. Traversing mostly rolling terrain, this portion of the hike includes a few short descents and climbs, but the grades are mostly easy. The beauty of the area is greatly enhanced by the many open parks the trail crosses along the way. Such areas are good places to spot deer, elk, and other species of wildlife that call the Mount Zirkel Wilderness home. These meadows become quite colorful in July and early August when a variety of alpine wildflowers are in full bloom. Tree species of the area include Engelmann spruce and subalpine fir. As the Wyoming Trail continues north, some nice scenery opens up. The expansive North Park stretches to the east, and rising in the southeast are the Rabbit Ears and Never Summer mountain ranges.

About 2 miles from Buffalo Pass the Wyoming Trail intersects the

*Gently rolling alpine terrain along the Wyoming Trail*

upper end of the Newcomb Creek Trail, a secondary route that climbs up from the eastern side of the range, gaining some 2,000 feet in 5 miles. Nearly 7 miles in, the Wyoming Trail picks up the upper end of the Luna Lake Trail, which climbs from the Elk Park Trail, which runs along the west side of the mountains. A side excursion of less than 2 miles along this route leads to Lake Elbert and Luna Lake.

Beyond this trail intersection the Wyoming Trail passes just west of 11,924-foot Mount Ethel. Bagging this summit would involve very little energy as it is less than a mile away and only 300 feet higher than the Wyoming Trail itself. Beyond Mount Ethel, the route continues north along the crest of the Park Range for another 2 miles before reaching the upper end of the 7.5-mile Rainbow Lake Trail, which climbs from a trailhead that lies at the eastern base of the range. About 2 miles past the Rainbow Lake–Wyoming Trail intersection, the Wyoming Trail reaches its high point of 11,880 feet as it skirts a short distance east of 11,932-foot Lost Ranger Peak. The Lost Ranger Trail connects with the Wyoming Trail about 1.5 miles north of the peak; the North Lake Trail is intersected a mile north of that. While the Lost Ranger Trail approaches the Wyoming Trail from the east, the North Lake Trail ascends the west side of the range.

In the next few miles two more trails encounter the Wyoming Trail. The first of these, the Three Island Lake Trail, begins near Seedhouse Campground to the west. The second route—the Bighorn Lake Trail— climbs up from the North Park side of the wilderness. A short distance beyond the Bighorn Lake–Wyoming Trail intersection, the Continental Divide veers northeast while the Wyoming Trail continues due north and eventually drops into the upper end of Gold Creek. Because sections of this portion of the trail may be difficult to find, a topographic map would be helpful when searching for the route. Generally speaking, the Wyoming Trail descends due north to reach the Gold Creek Lake Trail, which is a short distance northeast of the lake. Upon reaching the Gold Creek Lake Trail, turn left and continue 4.5 miles west to the Slavonia trailhead.

Because much of this hike is near timberline, the threat of lightning is very real, especially in the summer. Water is found along the way, but it must be treated. Expect to see a lot of other hikers near both ends of this route.

## 23 FISHHOOK LAKE

**Distance: 3 miles round trip**      **Management: Routt NF**
**Difficulty: Easy**      **Wilderness status: None**
**Hiking time: 2 hours**      **Season: June to October**
**Elevation: 10,000 to 9,800 feet**      **USGS map: Rabbit Ears Peak**

A short but enjoyable excursion, the hike to Fishhook Lake not only accesses a fine fishing hole but it also reveals some interesting timbered areas as well.

This hike begins in the Rabbit Ears Pass area of the Park Range. To reach the trailhead, drive 20 miles east from Steamboat Springs on US Highway 40 to the left turn for Dumont Lake. Drive 1.5 miles to a monument that honors nearby Rabbit Ears Peak. Turn left at the monument and drive 4.3 miles north on Forest Road 311. This road can be rough in places, but it is passable to most vehicles when dry. The trailhead is on the right, about 0.25 mile from the road's end.

Following the south end of the Fish Creek Trail for 1.5 miles, the hike to Fishhook Lake is relatively easy. From the trailhead the route enters the timber—Engelmann spruce and subalpine fir mostly— where it begins to descend along an easy to moderate grade. Within this thick forest are occasional small openings in which such wild-

*Deadfall litters the shore of Fishhook Lake.*

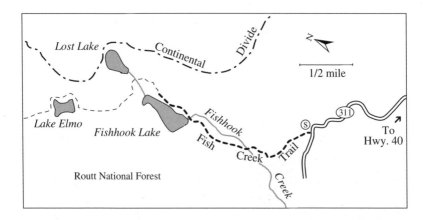

flowers as Richardson's geranium, mountain bluebell, and lupine grow. After 0.75 mile the trail levels off just before reaching an open park that follows Fishhook Creek. In the next 0.25 mile the trail parallels the creek before crossing to the left bank, where it then enters the timber on the far side. Once among the trees, the route climbs a few easy grades as it continues to parallel the creek. From the stream crossing it is another 0.5 mile to Fishhook Lake and the turnaround point for this hike.

Surrounded by timber, Fishhook Lake is actually one of several lakes in the area. A short distance beyond is Lost Lake, followed by Lake Elmo, Round Lake, and Lake Percy. All of these lakes, plus Fishhook Creek, are favored fishing spots among local anglers. The relatively level terrain in this part of the Park Range belies the fact that these lakes are actually strung along the Continental Divide. Because this is an easy hike it can be enjoyed by young children as well as adults.

Water from the creek and lake must be treated before drinking. Besides hikers, mountain bicyclists also enjoy the route. Watch for the occasional out-of-control rider.

# 2A SERVICE CREEK

**Distance: 11.6 miles one way**
**Difficulty: Moderate**
**Hiking time: 8 hours**
**Elevation: 7,000 to 9,240 feet**
**Management: Routt NF**

**Wilderness status: Sarvis Creek WA**
**Season: June to October**
**USGS maps: Blacktail Mountain,**
**Walton Peak, Lake Agnes**

Spanning the width of the newly established Sarvis Creek Wilderness Area, the Service Creek Trail offers an excellent introduction to the northern portion of the Gore Range. Gentle in comparison to the southern half of the range, this end of the Gores manifests as gently rolling mountains covered with ubiquitous timberlands. The Sarvis Timber Company logged portions of this region between 1912 and 1916. The names "Service" and "Sarvis" have both been used to describe the creek and the wilderness area. The 47,140-acre Sarvis Creek

*A small meadow along the Service Creek Trail*

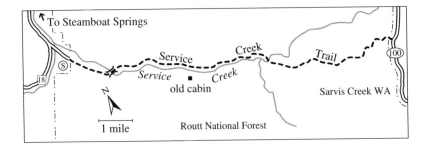

Wilderness Area was established as part of the Colorado Wilderness Act in 1993.

Because this hike description follows the Service Creek Trail one way, a shuttle is required. (It is, of course, possible to return to your car by hiking back the way you came.) To reach the upper trailhead at the end of the hike, drive south from Rabbit Ears Pass (which is on US Highway 40) on Forest Road 100 to Buffalo Park. The hike begins at the lower end of the Service Creek Trail, which is located west of the wilderness boundary. To reach this trailhead drive south from Steamboat Springs on US Highway 40 to Colorado Highway 131. Turn right and drive 4.25 miles to County Road 18 (watch for the sign for Lake Catamount). Turn left onto County Road 18 and drive 6.7 miles south to the signed left turn for the Service Creek trailhead. It is another 0.4 mile to the end of the road and the start of this hike.

The Service Creek Trail begins by following the right side of its namesake. Along this lower end, the creek has cut an interesting little canyon. Spruce and fir trees are common, as are lodgepole pines. Some aspens are also encountered. Within the first 1.5 miles the Service Creek Trail gains about 800 feet along easy to moderate grades. After this point the route levels off a bit before crossing a bridge at 2 miles. For the next several miles the route follows the north side of the creek. In one rocky area the creek actually disappears for a few hundred yards. Farther on are the remains of the Sarvis Timber Company's operations, including an old logging flume. Beyond that is a dilapidated cabin on the south side of the creek. The trail then crosses a series of small meadows. Up to this point the trail has covered 6 miles.

A little more than 7 miles from its start, the trail begins heading southeast, away from Service Creek. From here the route climbs another 500 feet over the next 1.5 miles before leveling off again. Along the last portion of the hike, beautiful forests of lodgepole pine are a real treat to walk through. Eventually the Service Creek Trail reaches a dirt road that continues east for less than a mile before intersecting with Forest Road 100 at Buffalo Park.

Water is available along much of this hike, but it must be treated first. Although the Service Creek Trail is never greatly exposed, the threat of lightning exists. Also keep in mind that camping is prohibited with 100 feet of streams and trails.

# 25 FLAT TOPS TRAVERSE

**Distance: 7 miles one way**
**Difficulty: Moderate**
**Hiking time: 4 hours**
**Elevation: 9,720 to 11,400 feet**
**Management: White River NF,**
  **Routt NF**

**Wilderness status: Flat Tops WA**
**Season: July to September**
**USGS maps: Trappers Lake,**
  **Devils Causeway**

At 235,230 acres, the Flat Tops Wilderness features expansive headlands that are high enough to be considered alpine tundra. Uncharacteristically level, this treeless terrain is a real joy to explore—if for no other reason than because it is very easy to hike. Of course, the Flat Tops also feature many forested valleys, numerous lakes, and miles of mountain streams. This hike east from Trappers Lake to Stillwater Reservoir is a wonderful way to experience the Flat Tops, as it traverses Colorado's second-largest wilderness area in a moderately difficult day hike.

Although you can follow this hike in either direction, this description begins at Trappers Lake in the White River National Forest and ends at Stillwater Reservoir in the Routt National Forest. To reach the Stillwater Reservoir trailhead, drive 17 miles west from Yampa on County Road 7 (Forest Road 900) to its end. To reach Trappers Lake from Meeker, drive 2 miles east on Colorado Highway 13 to County Road 8. Turn right and follow this road 39 miles east to its junction with Forest Road 205. Turn right again and drive 10 miles to the Trappers Lake outlet parking lot.

From the Trappers Lake trailhead, hike south around the east side of Trappers Lake for 0.75 mile to where the Stillwater Trail begins. After turning left at this junction continue eastward along Cabin Creek

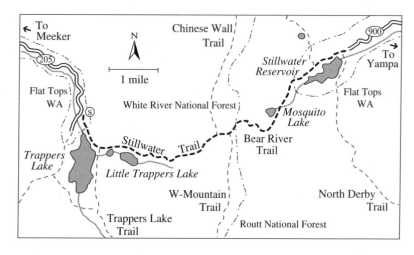

*Backpackers along the Bear River Trail in the Flat Tops Wilderness*

for the next mile. Along this stretch of the hike you first pass Coffin Lake and then—at the 1-mile mark—Little Trappers Lake. Situated at an elevation of 9,926 feet, Little Trappers Lake is a mere 200 feet higher than the start of this hike. In the vicinity of the lake you can enjoy views of the impressive Chinese Wall—a grand escarpment that rises to the northeast. An area of great beauty, Trappers Lake was spared development thanks largely to the efforts of Arthur H. Carhart, the first landscape architect to be employed by the U.S. Forest Service. When directed to investigate the possibilities of developing homesites at Trappers Lake in 1919, Carhart strongly recommended that the area instead be left as is. His advice planted some of the first seeds for the concept of wilderness preservation.

Beyond Little Trappers Lake, the Stillwater Trail continues to climb eastward along occasionally steeper grades. As it gains in elevation the route passes through a mixed forest of spruce and fir that was devastated by a spruce bark beetle invasion in the 1940s. This forest, along with many others in the Flat Tops, today features countless dead snags. In all, the epidemic affected 68,000 acres of timber. At about the 2-mile mark the trail reaches the 11,000-foot level and the top of the Flat Tops plateau. Leaving the trees behind, the trail continues across alpine tundra for the next 3 miles or so. Although you still have to climb 400 feet before reaching the high point of this hike, the going is nevertheless easy. A little over 3.5 miles from the trailhead the Stillwater Trail intersects the Chinese Wall Trail, which runs north to south (see Hike 26, Lost Lakes–Devils Causeway), and shortly beyond this connects with the north end of the W-Mountain Trail. About 0.5 mile beyond the Chinese Wall–Stillwater Trail intersection, the Stillwater Trail crosses into the Routt National Forest, where it becomes the Bear River Trail. This change of forest jurisdiction also marks the 11,400-foot high point of this hike.

From where the route begins following the Bear River Trail, it is another 3 miles to the Stillwater Reservoir and the end of this hike. Once the trail drops off the plateau it enters more forest that was affected by the beetle invasion of the 1940s. The grades drop easily along this last segment of the hike and the scenery is nonstop, especially to the east where the Bear River drainage and 12,354-foot Flat Top Mountain (the wilderness area's highest point) come into view. Should you not have a shuttle you can turn back at the boundary between the two national forests and return to Trappers Lake.

Because of its high elevation, much of this hike is exposed to lightning. You may want to complete this hike early in the day if you go in July or August. Bring drinking water along as there is none available above timberline. Water from all other sources must be treated. Because the Stillwater and Trappers Lake trailheads are the two most popular entry points for the Flat Tops Wilderness, expect to see other hikers.

# 26 LOST LAKES–DEVILS CAUSEWAY

**Distance: 19.5 miles**
**Difficulty: Moderate**
**Hiking time: 3 days**
**Elevation: 10,280 to 11,928 feet**
**Management: Routt NF, White River NF**

**Wilderness status: Flat Tops WA**
**Season: July to September**
**USGS maps: Devils Causeway, Trappers Lake**

With 167 miles of trails, the Flat Tops Wilderness is quite conducive to long-distance hiking excursions. One particularly nice trip that accesses some of the most memorable topographical features of the area heads north from the Stillwater Reservoir to Lost Lakes. It then climbs west to pick up a high route that continues south toward the trailhead. Within the last few miles, the hike crosses one of the most dramatic and unusual landmarks in the northern mountains of Colorado—the Devils Causeway. This 3-foot-wide, 1,500-foot-high gangplank is a real thrill to traverse.

The hike begins at the Stillwater Reservoir trailhead. To reach it, drive 17 miles west of Yampa on County Road 7 (Forest Road 900), all the way to its end.

From the trailhead follow the East Fork Trail southwest for 0.8 mile to the first trail intersection. The Bear River Trail continues straight at this junction to eventually climb up and over to Trappers Lake (see the Flat Tops Traverse hike), while this hike turns right to follow the East Fork Trail in a more northerly direction. Less than 0.5 mile past the junction the route enters the Flat Tops Wilderness, and shortly beyond this boundary it passes close to Little Causeway Lake. From the lake the trail ascends along mostly moderate grades before reaching an 11,600-foot saddle that is situated between the Bear River drainage and the Williams Fork drainage to the north. From the trailhead to this point, the route ascends 1,300 feet in 1.6 miles.

At the saddle a steep trail climbs a few hundred feet to the left before reaching the Devils Causeway about 0.25 mile west. Hikers who are not particularly bothered by heights can save the visit to this unusual feature for the end of the trip. If you do suffer from acrophobia and you think you might want to forgo crossing the causeway, leave your pack at the saddle and make the quick side trip up now. Whether or not you cross it, this interesting landform should not be missed.

From the saddle the East Fork Trail continues north to drop into the head of the East Williams Fork drainage. As the route descends it returns to the spruce and fir forests typical of the drainages of the Flat Tops. Here as in many places across the wilderness, you can see countless spruce trees that died as a result of a beetle infestation during the

*A hiker crossing the Devils Causeway*

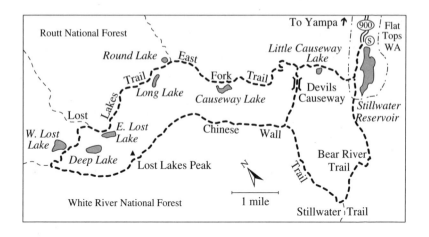

1940s. A little over 5 miles from the trailhead, the East Fork Trail reaches Causeway Lake. After that—near the 6.5-mile mark—the route reaches Round Lake, where the next trail junction is encountered. While the East Fork Trail bears right to continue for another 7.5 miles to a trailhead north of the wilderness, this hike turns left onto the Lost Lakes Trail. Within the next mile it passes Long Lake, after which it makes a steep but short ascent to the top of a 10,720 foot divide. From there the Lost Lakes Trail drops to reach East Lost Lake. The forest along this segment of the hike still bears scars from a severe fire at the turn of the century.

After reaching East Lost Lake this hike encounters another trail junction, 2.6 miles beyond the turnoff at Round Lake. Keeping left on the West Lost Lakes Trail, the route climbs 700 feet in 1.4 miles to reach the divide that separates the Williams Fork drainage from the White River drainage. (This divide also forms the boundary between the Routt and White River national forests.) The climb ascends along moderate to strenuous grades; within the last 0.5 mile there are several switchbacks as well. Where it tops out at an elevation of 10,720 feet, the West Lost Lakes Trail intersects the Chinese Wall Trail, which runs north to south. Turn left at this junction to begin the return leg of this hike.

Beyond the West Lost Lakes–Chinese Wall Trail junction, the route climbs some more before continuing southeast for 6 miles along broad headlands of alpine tundra. There is something special about hiking across this treeless terrain as it constantly seems as if you are looking down upon the rest of the world. Although this segment of the hike crosses 11,928-foot Lost Lakes Peak (the high point of the entire hike), the grades are easy throughout. Because the trail is faint or nonexistent in places as it crosses this alpine terrain, you will need keep to an eye out for the widely spaced rock cairns and trail posts that mark the way.

After 6 miles of following the Chinese Wall Trail this hike reaches the turnoff for the Devils Causeway. If you would like to cross the causeway, turn left here and continue northeast for a mile to the narrow passage; if you wish to avoid the causeway, follow the directions given in the next paragraph. Epitomizing the unusual geology of the Flat Tops, the Devils Causeway resulted from a protective cap of volcanic rock that has prevented the erosion of material underneath. The Flat Tops as a whole were formed in this manner as volcanic activity some 35 million years ago spread lava across the White River Plateau. From the causeway continue east for 0.25 mile to the East Fork Trail and follow it south for 1.6 miles to the trailhead.

If you decide not to cross the Devils Causeway, continue south on the Chinese Wall Trail for another 2 miles to the Stillwater Trail. Turn left and follow it a short distance east to where it becomes the Bear River Trail at the White River–Routt national forest boundary. From this point it is 3 miles to the Stillwater Reservoir trailhead. Bypassing the causeway adds a little more than 2 miles to the hike's total distance.

Bring plenty of water, especially for the section of the hike that follows the Chinese Wall Trail. Water drawn from lakes and streams along the rest of the hike must be treated. Because of the inevitability of lightning along the higher reaches of this route, you may want to plan your hike so that you will traverse the higher alpine areas early in the day. The Devils Causeway is a popular destination for day hikers, and most of the lakes along this route are popular camping sites.

# 27 VASQUEZ PEAK

**Distance: 10 miles round trip**  **Management: Arapaho NF**
**Difficulty: Moderate**  **Wilderness status: Vasquez Peak WA**
**Hiking time: 7 hours**  **Season: July to September**
**Elevation: 11,315 to 12,947 feet**  **USGS map: Berthoud Pass**

After crossing Berthoud Pass a few miles north of Interstate 70, the Continental Divide continues due west among the surprisingly gentle Vasquez Mountains. This interesting hike follows the Continental Divide Trail to 12,947-foot Vasquez Peak. As he highest summit in the area, Vasquez Peak is the namesake of the 12,300-acre Vasquez Peak Wilderness, which was established as part of the Colorado Wilderness Act of 1993.

Although some people begin this hike at the Mary Jane Ski Area near Winter Park, the route is more easily accessed by way of a service road at the Berthoud Pass Ski Area. To reach this access point, take Interstate 70 to US Highway 40, turn north, and drive to the top of Berthoud Pass. Parking is provided on the east side of the road, but the hiking route follows a ski-area road that begins west of the highway.

From 11,315-foot Berthoud Pass, follow the ski-area service road (it is closed to public traffic) uphill along mostly moderate grades for nearly a mile to the top of the ski lift, gaining 535 feet in elevation. The route then heads west for nearly a mile along a mostly treeless ridgeline, gaining another 500 or so feet before reaching the Continental Divide and a junction with the Mount Nystrom Trail, which begins at the Mary Jane Ski Area. A right turn here would take you down a gently descending ridge for 7 miles to the ski area. Instead, turn left and continue along the broad alpine ridges that carry the Continental Divide through the Vasquez Mountains. For the rest of this hike the Mount Nystrom Trail and the interstate Continental Divide Trail follow the same route across the crest of the mountains.

Because the hike has already attained an elevation of 12,300 feet, it is an easy matter to continue along the Continental Divide for at least the next 1.5 miles. In this segment the grade changes are slight, despite the fact that the trail eventually draws to within a few feet of the 12,521-foot summit of Stanley Mountain. The views from this high route are impressive. Winter Park and Fraser lie directly north, though out of sight, while to the south yawns the West Fork Clear Creek drainage. and spilling down the south side of Stanley Mountain is the Stanley Slide—an avalanche path that regularly plagues US Highway 40 below. Along the Divide itself you can plainly see the effects that glaciers have had on this mountain terrain as glacial cirques line the north- and east-facing slopes of the peaks.

West of Stanley Mountain the Continental Divide Trail drops steeply—800 feet in 0.5 mile—to reach 11,700-foot Vasquez Pass. Beyond the pass the trail climbs strenuously—about 1,000 feet in 0.75 mile—to regain all the elevation it just lost, and then some. After

*A stone cairn marks the Continental Divide Trail near Vasquez Peak.*

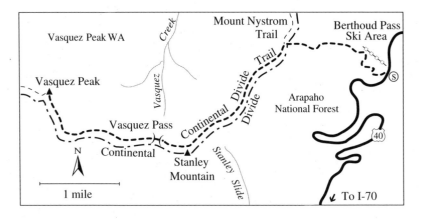

reaching an unnamed summit just beyond Vasquez Pass, the route continues west and north for a little over 1 mile before reaching the 12,947-foot summit of Vasquez Peak. In this last mile leading up to the peak the route climbs a total of 500 feet. Beyond Vasquez Peak the Continental Divide Trail continues another 3.5 miles before reaching 12,652-foot Mount Nystrom and the western end of the Vasquez Peak Wilderness Area. As you return to Berthoud Pass, keep in mind that you have a 800-foot climb up the east side of Vasquez Pass.

Water is not available along this hike, so pack a couple of quarts. Watch for lightning, a frequent phenomenon on these high ridges.

# 28 UPPER CATARACT LAKE

| | |
|---|---|
| **Distance: 10.2 miles round trip** | **Management: Arapaho NF** |
| **Difficulty: Moderate** | **Wilderness status: Eagles Nest WA** |
| **Hiking time: 8 hours** | **Season: July to October** |
| **Elevation: 8,600 to 10,756 feet** | **USGS map: Mount Powell** |

Although by no means the highest of Colorado's mountain chains, the Gore Range is considerably more rugged than many. As a faulted anticline range, these mountains rise abruptly to form an impressive collection of jagged peaks. Exploring these mountains is surprisingly easy, however, given the plentiful number of trails that penetrate it from the east and west. Add to this the fact that a mining boom never really materialized in the Gores, and you have a Colorado mountain range that is virtually untouched by pick and shovel. This nice all-day hike into the Gore Range begins near Lower Cataract Lake and climbs steadily to Upper Cataract Lake in the northeast portion of the mountains.

To reach the start of this hike, drive 16 miles north from Silverthorne on Colorado Highway 9. Turn left onto Heeney Road (County

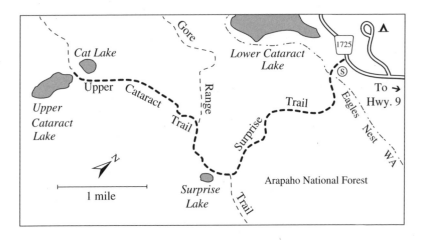

Road 30) and continue 5.3 miles northwest to Cataract Creek Road (County Road 1725). Turn left again and drive 2.3 miles to the Surprise trailhead.

This hike begins by following the 2.6-mile Surprise Trail to Surprise Lake. Climbing steadily in places, this trail winds its way up through both aspen groves and spruce–fir forests. Just prior to reaching Surprise Lake, the Surprise Trail intersects the Gore Range Trail. Covering 54.5 miles in all, this route runs the length of its namesake mountains, mostly along the eastern foot of the range. If you are looking for a nice week-long hike, the Gore Range Trail would be ideal as it accesses several side trails that, in turn, climb higher into the mountains. The hike to Upper Cataract Lake turns right onto the Gore Range Trail and follows it for 0.5 mile before turning left onto the Upper Cataract Trail. Shortly after taking up the Gore Range Trail, the route reaches Surprise Lake, which, in comparison to other lakes in the Gore Range, is small and somewhat uneventful.

Shortly beyond Surprise Lake turn onto the Upper Cataract Trail and follow it another 2 miles to Upper Cataract Lake. A much larger body of water than Surprise Lake, Upper Cataract Lake is nestled just below beautiful 13,432-foot Eagles Nest Peak. Rising just south of Eagles Nest Peak is Mount Powell, named for Major John Wesley Powell, who climbed the summit in 1868. The Gore Range itself was named after Sir Saint George Gore, a rich nobleman who traveled west in 1855 on a hunting safari. It was reported that he bagged 2,000 bison, 1,600 deer and elk, 100 black bears, and untold numbers of smaller game.

Although Upper Cataract Lake is the turnaround point of this hike, the Upper Cataract Trail does continue for another 1.5 miles to Mirror Lake. True to its name, Mirror Lake reflects an impressive cirque of rocky summits, including Eagles Nest Peak. The Upper Cataract Trail then passes by Mirror Lake and eventually crosses Elliot Ridge to the west side of the range.

Water is available along this hike but must be treated. Lightning is a potential hazard, although the hike to Upper Cataract Lake does not encounter any greatly exposed terrain.

# 29 ECCLES PASS

Distance: 10 miles round trip
Difficulty: Moderate
Hiking time: 5 hours
Elevation: 9,1400 to 11,900 feet

Management: Arapaho NF
Wilderness status: Eagles Nest WA
Season: July to October
USGS maps: Frisco, Vail Pass

Located in the southern end of the Gore Range, 11,900-foot Eccles Pass makes a great destination for hikers who set out along the Meadow Creek Trail, both for the scenery and for the sheer pleasure of reaching this high point.

The hike to Eccles Pass begins at a trailhead just north of Frisco. After turning off Interstate 70 at the Frisco exit (Exit 203), turn northwest and drive a short distance to the pavement's end. Turn left onto a gravel road and continue another 0.5 mile to the signed trailhead. Camping is not permitted within 0.25 mile of the interstate.

The Meadow Creek Trail begins by climbing moderate to strenuous grades along an old jeep road. Near the 2-mile mark the route levels off a bit and begins to parallel Meadow Creek as it breaks into more open terrain. Up to this point it has passed mostly through thick stands of lodgepole pine and glades of aspen. Beyond this point, however, the trail continues through a series of subalpine meadows until it reaches timberline less than a mile from the pass. Occasionally soaked by run-off from melting snows in early summer, some sections of the trail can be boggy in places, but the plethora of wildflowers that grows here is well worth the trouble. Be sure to stay on the trail to avoid damaging fragile meadow areas.

Within the last mile of the hike the Meadow Creek Trail intersects

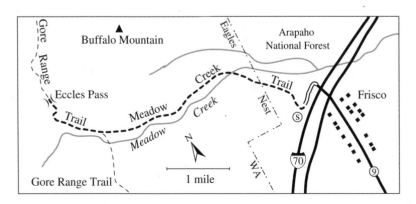

*An old stump along the hike to Eccles Pass*

the Gore Range Trail, which runs along the eastern side of the Eagle Nest Wilderness. Turn right onto the Gore Range Trail and continue north up a short series of switchbacks to reach Eccles Pass, where you are treated to wonderful views in all directions. To the south the Gore Range continues for a few more miles before giving way to the Ten Mile Creek drainage and the Mosquito Range beyond. To the east rise the Williams Fork Mountains. Looking north the vista takes in the South Willow Creek drainage, Red Peak, and Buffalo Mountain.

From Eccles Pass the Gore Range Trail drops into the South Willow Creek drainage. About 1 mile north of the pass, the Gore Creek Trail branches west to climb up and over Red Buffalo Pass before dropping down Gore Creek to a trailhead east of Vail. Red Buffalo Pass was once considered as a possible route for Interstate 70. Fortunately, the freeway was instead built around the southern tip of the Gore Range.

Water is plentiful along this hike, but must be treated before drinking. Watch for lightning in open areas and on the pass itself, and be prepared for rapidly deteriorating weather conditions, even in midsummer.

# 30  HANGING LAKE

**Distance: 2.4 miles round trip**   **Management: White River NF**
**Difficulty: Strenuous**   **Wilderness status: None**
**Hiking time: 2 hours**   **Season: Year-round**
**Elevation: 6,100 to 7,250 feet**   **USGS map: Shoshone**

True to its name, Hanging Lake is tucked away on a high ledge in a narrow canyon. Scenic, to say the least, this precious jewel of a lake offers a just reward for all who hike the steep but short trail up.

This hike begins at the Hanging Lake rest stop along Interstate 70 in Glenwood Canyon, through which the Colorado River flows. Westbound travelers must exit a few miles farther west at the Grizzly Creek exit and double back on the eastbound lane to the Hanging Lake exit. Eastbound travelers can drive east from Glenwood Springs directly to the Hanging Lake exit. The return access to Interstate 70 from Hanging Lake is westbound only, so drivers who wish to continue east on Interstate 70 must travel west to the Grizzly Creek exit to get back on track after the hike.

From the newly completed Hanging Lake rest area, the hike begins by following the paved bicycle path east, or upstream, for about 0.25 mile to a narrow side canyon. Upon turning left up this drainage, the route climbs a mile up a mostly strenuous grade that does not quit until it reaches the lake. Such a steep ascent is understandable since this segment of the trail ascends some 1,000 feet. The trail is also rocky in most places. About a third of the way up, the trail intersects the Dead

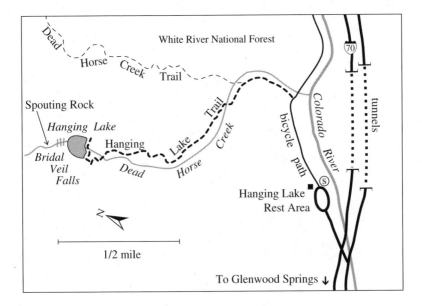

89

Horse Creek Trail. Within the last 0.3 mile leading up to the lake, the trail steepens as it climbs through a cliff area. Along this last stretch of the hike, metal handrails provide some safety as a drop-off of 100 feet or more is encountered. The trail in this portion also climbs up a roughed-in staircase that is extremely steep but short.

While the hike to Hanging Lake is strenuous, it is also quite beautiful and well worth the effort. As the trail climbs along Dead Horse Creek, it passes a wonderful riparian plant community. In addition to such shady deciduous trees as box elders and cottonwoods, an interesting variety of undergrowth can be found at trailside. Perhaps most alluring are the many ferns that grow along the streambed. Their presence, along with moss-clad boulders, attests to the humid conditions of this ecological niche. Benches along most of the route provide nice rest spots from which to enjoy the canyon.

Upon reaching 1.5-acre Hanging Lake, hikers are immediately rewarded with its secretive, Eden-like ambience. Walled in by limestone cliffs and leafy cottonwoods, Hanging Lake resulted from the collection of water in a geologic fault. Because the lake's fragile shore has been built up from carbonate deposits, visitors are required to stay on the boardwalk that rings the south shore. Dropping into the north end of the lake is Bridal Veil Falls, a small but beautiful cascade of water. Of special interest are the schools of trout that teem in the lake's clear waters. Because of the fragile nature of this lake, both swimming and fishing are prohibited. Follow a short side trail just west of the lake to visit nearby Spouting Rock, a waterfall that has cut a passage through solid limestone.

Water along this hike must be treated before drinking, and treat the dangerous drop-offs at the top of the trail with respect. You can expect to see many other hikers making the trip up from the popular rest stop.

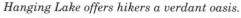

*Hanging Lake offers hikers a verdant oasis.*

# 31 ROXBOROUGH STATE PARK

**Distance: 2.25 miles round trip**  **Management: Roxborough SP**
**Difficulty: Easy**  **Wilderness status: None**
**Hiking time: 2 hours**  **Season: Year-round**
**Elevation: 6,200 to 6,000 feet**  **USGS map: Kassler**

Given Roxborough State Park's wealth of geologic features, its ecological diversity, and its scenic beauty, you might find it hard to believe that this unique area can be so close to Denver. But Roxborough
State Park proves that natural wonders and large metropolitan areas
can coexist. Not only has it been designated as a Colorado Natural
Area, but it is a National Natural Landmark as well. Of the park's five
different hiking trails, the Fountain Valley Loop Trail cuts to the chase
where these natural wonders are concerned.

To reach Roxborough State Park from Denver, drive south on US
Highway 85 to Titan Road, which is about 4 miles south of Colorado
Highway 470. Turn right and drive west for 3.4 miles to where the
road turns south and becomes the North Rampart Range Road. Continue south for a little over 3 miles to Roxborough Park Road. Turn
left, then make a right soon after at the Roxborough Community Center.
Follow this road south for about 2 miles to the park's visitor center.

Begin at the visitor center, where you can purchase or borrow a trail
guide that corresponds to numbered features along the route. From
there, the Fountain Valley Loop heads north along a wide, graveled
trail. The going is very easy throughout, with very little grade change.
Within a short distance you can take in a view of the terrain ahead
from a vista point located just off the trail. Looking north from here,
you see several geologic formations angling upward. The most colorful
of these is the red sandstone that constitutes the Fountain Formation.
This layer of rock was deposited some 300 million years ago in a
streambed that carried sand and gravel down from the ancestral Rocky

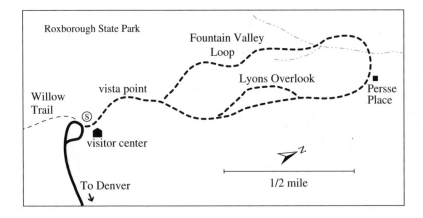

Mountains. Next in line is the yellowish sandstone of the Lyons Formation, which resulted from sand dunes and stream deposits along the shoreline of an ancient sea. Farther east is the Dakota Hogback, a pronounced formation of gray and buff-colored rock that was deposited along flood plains 135 million years ago. Sedimentary in origin, these three formations were once horizontal but were subsequently tilted upward when the present-day Rockies were uplifted beginning 65 million years ago. The oldest rocks in the area are the gneisses and granites that make up the foothills of the Rockies along the western end of the park. Igneous in nature, they date back 1.2 billion years to Precambrian times.

From the overlook continue north to where the loop splits. Stay right here to follow the loop counterclockwise. A bit farther north is an expanse of grasslands. In addition to its unique geology, Roxborough State Park encompasses an interesting ecological transition zone. Touted as a place where the plains and the mountains meet, the park features both the grassland community of the Great Plains, which spread eastward, and the shrub and forest communities of the Rocky Mountains to the west. This interface is easily noted: prairie grasses grow in many open areas, while Gambel oak, ponderosa pines, and Douglas firs inhabit the foothills and nearby summits.

Because of this ecological variety and the fact that Roxborough State Park has remained quite pristine, a wide variety of wildlife inhabits the area. Among the smaller creatures that live here are pocket

*Impressive rock formations along the Fountain Valley Loop in Roxborough State Park*

gophers, rock squirrels, raccoons, and prairie rattlesnakes. The larger species include mule deer, elk, coyotes, black bears, and mountain lions. And, if you are lucky, you might spot a golden eagle soaring along on the thermals above.

As you continue north along the east side of the loop, a short side trail climbs easily to the left to reach the Lyons Overlook. From this vantage point you gain nice views to the north and west, plus an upclose look at the Lyons Formation, upon which you are standing. This side trip is less than 0.5 mile in length, but because it drops back to the Fountain Valley Loop it adds very little to the hike's overall length.

At the north end of the Fountain Valley Loop is an old homestead known as the Persse Place. Dating back to the turn of the century, this soon-to-be-restored stone abode was built by Henry S. Persse, who lived here in the summer. His dream was to turn this area into a resort, but fortunately the scenario never materialized.

From the Persse Place, the Fountain Valley Loop heads south to double back to the visitor center. This final stretch of the hike encounters a number of small ecosystems the trail guide describes in some detail. These include a riparian community of cottonwood trees, a sedge meadow community, an aspen grove, and more. Eventually, after the trail passes some pinnacles of Fountain Formation sandstone, it reaches the close of the loop and the short return trip to the visitor center.

Bring water as none is available along the hike. Watch for rattlesnakes and keep in mind that park regulations prohibit leaving the trail, collecting any natural materials, rock climbing, pets, and bikes.

# 32 RESTHOUSE MEADOWS

**Distance: 13 miles round trip**
**Difficulty: Moderate**
**Hiking time: 8 hours**
**Elevation: 10,600 to 11,200 feet**
**Management: Arapaho NF**

**Wilderness status: Mount Evans WA**
**Season: June to October**
**USGS maps: Idaho Springs,**
   **Harris Park**

Thanks to its proximity to Denver, the Mount Evans Highway is a very popular driving route, especially on the weekends. While this road is often heavily utilized, hikers can leave the crowds behind in favor of a quiet trail through the forests and alpine areas of the Mount Evans Wilderness. One of these backcountry routes is the 6.5-mile-long Resthouse Meadows Trail, which leads to an isolated park surrounded by stunning mountain scenery.

The Resthouse Meadows Trail begins at the Echo Lake Campground, which is reached by driving 14 miles south from Idaho Springs on Colorado Highway 103 to Highway 5. The trailhead is located just past the campground fee station. Parking is available on the left side of the road.

From the trailhead, the Resthouse Meadows Trail climbs steadily up an easy grade through a beautiful forest of Engelmann spruce and sub-alpine fir for the first mile. At the 1-mile mark the route tops a ridge, then begins dropping along an easy to moderate grade into the Vance Creek drainage. Because this section of the trail crosses a south-facing slope, the added exposure to the sun allows for the addition of lodge-pole pine to the spruce–fir mix.

*This stone chimney is all that remains of the Mount Evans Shelter House, which was destroyed in a forest fire.*

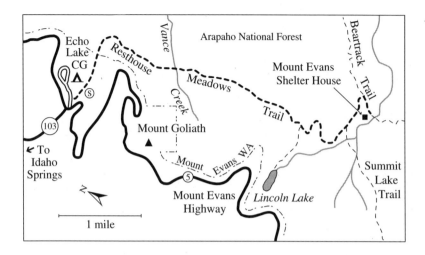

About 1.5 miles out, the Resthouse Meadows Trail crosses perennially flowing Vance Creek. A small meadow in the vicinity provides a nice place to stop for lunch. Beyond Vance Creek, the trail begins the first of several easy climbs that it makes over the next 1.5 miles. Like the first portion of the hike, this section travels through a forest of mostly spruce and fir trees. About 4 miles from the trailhead, the route reaches a large burn area. Thought to have been ignited by a careless camper's fire in September 1962, the Resthouse Fire swept across 1,000 acres before it was finally extinguished. In the decades since, grasses, wildflowers, and some shrubs have taken hold in the burn, but the forest itself is still just a ghostly collection of sun-bleached tree trunks. where the trail first enters this area the dead snags are mostly the tall, straight trunks of spruce and firs, but in another 0.25 mile the twisted and gnarled remains of bristlecone pines are also apparent. Years of weathering have made these old trunks quite picturesque.

Nearly 0.5 mile into the burn area the trail reaches this hike's high point of about 11,400 feet, and the turnoff for Lincoln Lake. Situated at 11,700 feet, Lincoln Lake lies at timberline less than a mile up the side trail that turns right. If you visit the lake be sure to scan the rocky slopes above for mountain goats. The Resthouse Meadows Trail turns left at this signed intersection, and soon begins dropping toward the route's namesake below. In this last 0.5-mile segment of the hike, the trail descends nearly 1,000 feet. As you hike down to the meadows, you can see a number of beaver ponds strung along the creek bottom. You may also note large patches of willows and some aspen groves, which turn bright yellow in the fall.

While the Resthouse Fire scorched timber on all sides of Resthouse Meadows, scattered stands of trees within the meadows area were spared from the flames. Within the Resthouse Meadows area, you first pass the turnoff for the 4-mile Summit Lake Trail, which climbs west to its namesake, located on the upper end of the Mount Evans Highway,

The Resthouse Meadows Trail then intersects the Beartrack Trail. Turn right at this junction and continue less than 0.25 mile to reach the ruins of the Mount Evans Shelter House, the turnaround point for this hike. Like the surrounding forests, this structure perished in a fire some years ago. All that remains today is a stone chimney and some of the foundation.

Dogs must be on a leash while in the Mount Evans Wilderness. Water is available along this hike, but must be treated. Some weekends see heavy use along the first couple of miles of the trail. Although this hike is not very exposed, lightning poses an occasional hazard.

# 33 MOUNT GOLIATH NATURAL AREA

**Distance: 3 miles round trip**
**Difficulty: Easy**
**Hiking time: 2 hours**
**Elevation: 11,550 to 12,150 feet**

**Management: Arapaho NF**
**Wilderness status: None**
**Season: July to September**
**USGS map: Idaho Springs**

This short and mostly easy hike accesses one of the more interesting ecological features of the Colorado Rockies: an extensive forest of bristlecone pine. Given this forest's uniqueness, it is now the centerpiece of the 1-square-mile Mount Goliath Research Natural Area.

The 1.5-mile Mount Goliath Trail begins at the lower end of the Mount Goliath Research Natural Area. To reach this trailhead, drive 14 miles south from Idaho Springs on Colorado Highway 103 to Echo Lake. Turn right onto the Mount Evans Highway (Colorado Highway 5) and drive another 2.9 miles to a large parking area on the left. The Mount Goliath Trail begins at the south end of the parking lot. While this hike description includes the return hike on the trail, you can

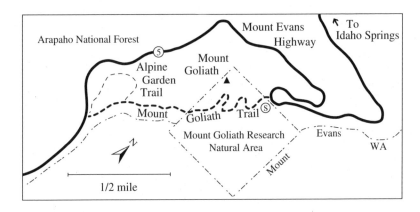

arrange for a shuttle to pick you up at the upper trailhead, which is a few miles farther up the Mount Evans Highway.

From the parking area the Mount Goliath Trail climbs through some patches of willow before angling up a somewhat steeper grade along the east face of Mount Goliath. Within the first 0.5 mile the trail completes most of its 600-foot climb in a few moderately steep switchbacks. The trail then levels off for the next 0.5 mile or so, giving hikers incredible views that stretch east across the Front Range and to the Great Plains beyond. Visitors also encounter some nice examples of this natural area's premier attraction. The bristlecone is a member of the limber pine family, and some specimens elsewhere in the country are as old as 5,000 years. While the oldest of the Mount Goliath trees dates back a "mere" 1,600 years, many of these larger ones are nevertheless quite picturesque. Sculpted over the years by the elements, these trees have been framed in the viewfinders of many a camera. Given this stand's extensive size, it is no wonder that scientists regularly conduct studies here. You may also note some Engelmann spruce intermingled among the bristlecones.

Eventually, the Mount Goliath Trail contours around a more southerly facing slope where it leaves the last of the bristlecones, and a few final krummholz stands of spruce, behind. It then climbs a bit through arctic-alpine tundra to reach the upper trailhead. A stark contrast to the forests below, this tundra ecosystem features plants that are only a few inches high. Among the animals that live in this extremely cold and windy region are pikas, marmots, ptarmigans, bighorn sheep, and mountain goats. The upper end of the Mount Goliath Trail connects

*An old bristlecone pine in the Mount Goliath Natural Research Area*

with the 0.5-mile Alpine Garden Trail. Unless you have a shuttle to pick you up at the trail's upper end, return to your car by doubling back on the Mount Goliath Trail.

Bring water on this hike as none is available along the way. Watch for the frequent lightning storms that cross this exposed area, and keep in mind that gathering wood, rocks, or any other natural material is prohibited within the Mount Goliath Research Natural Area.

# 34    WIGWAM PARK

**Distance: 13.2 miles round trip**    **Wilderness status: Lost Creek WA**
**Difficulty: Moderate**    **Season: June to October**
**Hiking time: 9 hours**    **USGS maps: Windy Peak, Topaz**
**Elevation: 9,500 to 10,250 feet**    **Mountain**
**Management: Pike NF**

Spanning the Kenosha and Tarryall mountains, the 120,000-acre Lost Creek Wilderness Area encompasses an interesting mix of forests, open meadows, creek bottoms, and alpine ridges. Because of its size and the fact that no 14,000-foot peaks are found within its boundaries, this wilderness offers a considerable amount of solitude throughout. One seldom-used route—the Wigwam Trail—follows the area's namesake creek east for a couple miles before continuing on to beautiful Wigwam Park, one of several natural parks found within the Lost Creek Wilderness.

To reach the beginning of this hike, drive 13 miles northeast from Fairplay on US Highway 285 to Lost Park Road (Forest Road 127). Turn right and follow this good dirt road east for 20 miles to its end. The trailhead is located just east of the Lost Park Campground.

From the trailhead the Wigwam Trail heads southeast across an open marshy area before reaching a short stretch of narrow canyon. About 1 mile out the trail enters East Lost Park, where it stays for 2 more miles. This naturally treeless area is partly the result of deep, finely textured soils more suitable for grasses, sedges, and willows than for the lodgepole pines, Engelmann spruce, and subalpine firs that constitute the nearby forests. Of course, other influences, such as moisture levels, also contributed to the formation of such meadows. The end result is a beautiful open park where deer and elk may be spotted during the early morning and evening.

About halfway through East Lost Park, and 3 miles from the trailhead, Lost Creek turns south, away from the trail, to eventually reach an area where it occasionally disappears from view and instead flows beneath boulder fields. The Wigwam Trail continues east to reach the far end of East Lost Park. It then begins an easy climb of about 300 feet to cross into the Wigwam Creek drainage. From this low saddle the Wigwam Trail drops about 600 feet in the next mile to reach Wigwam Park, which features a number of beaver dams, some nice

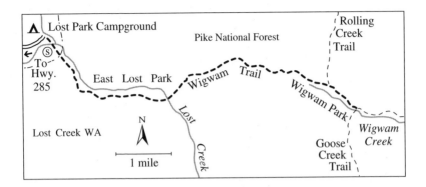

camping spots, and two trail intersections. The first is with the Rolling Creek Trail, which heads 6.4 miles north to the Wellington Lake area; the second is with the Goose Creek Trail, which continues nearly 10 miles south along the eastern end of the Lost Creek Wilderness Area.

While Wigwam Park is the turnaround point for this hike, you can extend your hike for many miles. You could follow the Wigwam Trail east for another 3.5 miles to a trailhead just beyond the wilderness boundary. You might explore the above-mentioned Rolling Creek and Goose Creek trails, which access their respective trailheads on the eastern side of the wilderness. If you're interested in a 3- to 5-day loop hike, you could follow the Goose Creek Trail south to the McCurdy Park Trail, turn right, and go west to the Brookside–McCurdy Trail. After turning right again you could then continue north to return to your car at the Lost Park Campground.

All water found along this hike must be treated before drinking. Lightning is not too prevalent, but be mindful of it just the same.

# 35   WALDO CANYON

**Distance: 7 miles round trip**      **Management: Pike NF**
**Difficulty: Easy**                           **Wilderness status: None**
**Hiking time: 4 hours**                 **Season: April to November**
**Elevation: 7,050 to 8,100 feet**   **USGS map: Cascade**

In the vicinity of Pikes Peak (and along its entire eastern face), the Front Range abruptly rises from the Great Plains as a wall of rugged mountains. Exploring a portion of this beautiful area is the Waldo Canyon Trail, an easy and highly rewarding hike that begins just a few minutes from downtown Colorado Springs. Because of its accessibility and its considerable beauty, the Waldo Canyon Trail is quite popular. In fact, Pike National Forest statistics show that this is the most heavily used trail in the Pikes Peak region.

To reach the start of this hike, drive west from Colorado Springs on

US Highway 24 for about 9 miles to the signed trailhead and large parking area on the north side of the road. The trailhead is about 3.5 miles west of Manitou Springs.

From the trailhead the route climbs immediately up a number of stairs before leveling off to ascend a mostly easy grade. A short distance in, the trail reaches a registration box from which it contours along the mountainside toward the east for about 1 mile. The trail then heads north into Waldo Canyon itself. Along this first segment of the hike, the trail is wide and well worn, and the grades are mostly easy. Views are also quite nice, especially those of Fountain Creek Canyon (through which US Highway 24 runs) and the Colorado Springs area down-canyon. At one point you can see the handful of tall buildings in the downtown section of the city. Because the first mile of trail traverses warm and relatively dry south-facing slopes, vegetation along the way includes junipers and pinyon pines, Gambel oaks,

*Along the Waldo Canyon Trail near Colorado Springs*

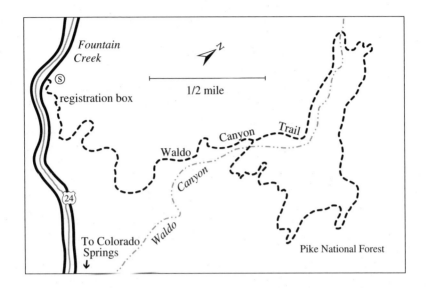

mountain mahogany shrubs, some yuccas and grasses, and a few ponderosa pines scattered about. In the second mile, the route encounters more Douglas firs as the canyon becomes more sheltered. Within the first 2 miles the trail climbs a total of 450 feet.

Nearly 2 miles from the trailhead the Waldo Canyon Trail drops slightly into the main portion of the canyon. Here it enters a small meadow that was once home to the Waldo Hog Ranch. Some camping sites are found in this meadow. Although the stream that usually flows through Waldo Canyon occasionally dries up after periods of no rain, there is sufficient ground moisture to support a variety of trees, including large ponderosa pines and Douglas firs, some Colorado blue spruce, a few cottonwoods, and even some aspens.

A short distance above the meadow area, the trail reaches a fork where the two ends of a 3-mile loop join together. From this junction you can travel in either direction to complete the loop. If you turn left, you will follow along the Waldo Canyon bottom for about a mile before reaching the 8,000-foot level. The trail then contours to the east and south to reach a ridgeline. After following this ridge for a short distance, the trail begins dropping back into the canyon by way of a series of short switchbacks. From the bottom of the loop portion to its high point, this section of the trail climbs about 600 feet. Turning left at the junction and following the trail clockwise allows you to encounter easy to moderate grade changes. No matter which way you turn, however, you will enjoy a number of nice vistas, especially those taking in Pikes Peak to the south. And you may even spot some of the wildlife that inhabits the canyon, such as mule deer, elk, and bighorn sheep.

Water is not always available along this trail, so bring your own. Watch for mountain bikes. Because of the hike's popularity, you may want to plan your visit for a weekday.

# 36 THE CRAGS

**Distance: 5 miles round trip**
**Difficulty: Easy**
**Hiking time: 3 hours**
**Elevation: 10,100 to 10,800 feet**
**Management: Pike NF**

**Wilderness status: None**
**Season: June to October**
**USGS maps: Pikes Peak, Woodland Park**

Rising more than 14,000 feet, Pikes Peak has managed to capture the imaginations of all who have spied its impressive summit. Among its more interesting features are the many pink-colored outcrops of Pikes Peak Granite found throughout the massif. Dating back to Precambrian times, Pikes Peak Granite formed as part of a batholith, a large intrusion of molten rock deep within the earth. The rock then cooled very slowly. Perhaps nowhere are these formations more fascinating than in the area known as the Crags. Located on the back, or west, side of the mountain, these fantastical spires of rock are accessible via a short, easy trail.

To reach the trailhead, drive 24 miles west of Colorado Springs on US Highway 24 to the small town of Divide. Turn left and drive 4.3 miles south on Colorado Highway 67 to County Road 62, which becomes Forest Road 383. Turn left and drive 3.2 miles on this somewhat rough but passable road to the Crags Campground. The trail starts at the upper loop.

From the trailhead the Crags Trail travels northeast for most of the way as it follows Fourmile Creek to its headwaters. For the first 2 miles the trail is in very good condition and grade changes are either nonexistent or easy. Along the way, the route encounters forests of Engelmann spruce and subalpine fir, aspen glades, and a few nice natural meadows. These open areas make for good wildlife watching in the early morning and evening hours. Some picturesque pools and cascades may also be enjoyed along Fourmile Creek. After the first mile a number of nearby granite outcrops add interest to the hike. These are but a taste of what is to come, however.

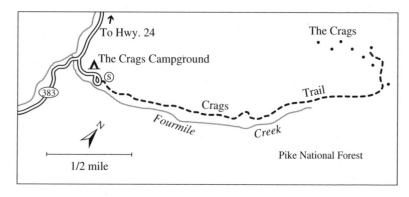

*One of many granite outcrops at the Crags near Pikes Peak*

Within the last 0.5 mile the trail begins to climb along a more moderate grade. Upon reaching the head of Fourmile Creek, the trail picks its way northwest for about 0.25 mile along a rocky ridge. While interesting rock formations are scattered along this last segment of the hike, the Crags themselves are best enjoyed from the trail's end, which is located at a high point along this ridge. From this vantage point the striking pinnacles of Pikes Peak Granite are visible in almost all directions. Well worn after countless centuries of erosion, these formations exude an organic quality, much like abstract sculptures. From this vista you can also enjoy some fine scenery. To the north is the Rampart

Range, while a look west reveals nearby Florissant Fossil Beds National Monument. And rising abruptly to the east are the treeless reaches of Pikes Peak itself. You might also note a number of interesting bristlecone pines growing in the immediate vicinity. Some are still alive, while others have died to become snags of wildly twisted wood.

Although water is available along this trail, it must be treated before drinking. Watch for lightning at the exposed top end of the Crags Trail.

# 37 THE CAVES

**Distance: 4 miles round trip**
**Difficulty: Easy**
**Hiking time: 3 hours**
**Elevation: 8,400 to 8,550 feet**
**Management: Florissant Fossil**
   **Beds NM**

**Wilderness status: None**
**Season: Year-round**
**USGS map: Lake George**

Known for its fossilized tree stumps, insects, and such, Florissant Fossil Beds National Monument also features a variety of nice hiking routes, all of which may be enjoyed by hikers of any age. This hike heads west from the visitor center past some interesting ecological

*Petrified tree stumps in Florissant Fossil Beds National Monument*

communities to an area incorrectly named the Caves. (The Caves are not caves at all, but rather short passageways through which a stream flows.) The name originated with locals. Perhaps out of respect for its folkloric significance, the Park Service has kept the title.

To reach Florissant Fossil Beds National Monument, drive 32 miles west from Colorado Springs on US Highway 24 to the small town of Florissant. Turn south onto County Road 1 and drive 2.4 miles to the signed turnoff for the national monument visitor center.

Like all routes within Florissant Fossil Beds National Monument, the hike to the Caves begins at the visitor center—the facility's back door, to be exact. From here walk a short distance—less than 0.25 mile—on the Walk Through Time Loop in a counterclockwise direction. This short stretch of the monument's main interpretive trail passes a selection of fossilized stumps, the remnants of giant sequoia and coastal redwood trees that once grew along an ancient stream. These stumps, like a variety of other plants and insects, were eventually buried by volcanic dust and ash that spewed from several volcanic eruptions that took place over a period of 700,000 years. The end result of this process is an unusually well-preserved look at what life was like some 35 million years ago. While this hike description departs from the Walk Through Time soon after these stumps, be sure to complete the 0.5-mile loop at some point during your visit.

Shortly after passing the fossilized tree stumps, this hike turns left at the first trail intersection, then right at the second one, which follows shortly after. The sign at this second turn points the way to the Caves. From this junction the route heads west along a level grade for 0.2 mile before reaching a third trail junction. Here, turn right again before dropping gently into a broad valley to the north. Upon entering this drainage, note how the ponderosa pines that grow in the vicinity of the visitor center give way to open meadows. Parks like this are ideal places to spot deer, elk, coyotes, and other species of wildlife that

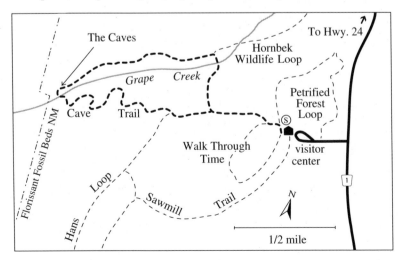

105

inhabit the area. Covering much of the monument, these meadows are also filled with flowers in the summertime. Appropriately, florissant is French for "flowering."

After crossing Grape Creek, the Caves Trail turns left at yet another intersection to continue west for 0.8 mile along a meadow's edge. Besides passing a small stock pond along the way, this segment of the hike encounters some fragile wetlands found along the stream to the left. Growing along the edges of this meadow are some scattered aspens and Colorado blue spruce trees. At the head of this valley, the trail finally reaches the Caves themselves, located in a pile of house-size granite boulders. Visitors can explore the passageways here, and picnicking is permitted.

From the Caves it is 1.75 miles back to the visitor center by way of the Cave Trail, which climbs a low ridge to the east. This last stretch of the hike encounters forests of Douglas firs, as well as more ponderosa pines, blue spruces, and aspens. About 1 mile from the Caves the trail intersects with the Hans Loop, where you turn left. (The right-hand route follows the Sawmill Trail, which loops south through the woods before eventually returning to the visitor center.) In another 0.5 mile the route rejoins the first segment of the hike, thereby completing a loop. From here it is about 0.5 mile back to the visitor center.

Because any water found along this hike must be treated, it is best to bring your own. Keep in mind that fossil collecting in Florissant Fossil Beds National Monument is strictly prohibited.

## 38  BEAVER CREEK

**Distance: 8 miles round trip**
**Difficulty: Strenuous**
**Hiking time: 5 hours**
**Elevation: 6,120 to 7,480 feet**
**Management: BLM**

**Wilderness status: Beaver**
    **Creek WSA**
**Season: Year-round**
**USGS maps: Phantom Canyon,**
    **Mount Pittsburg**

The incredibly beautiful Beaver Creek drainage is somewhat unusual in that it features an extensive low-elevation canyon system within Colorado's mountainous Front Range. A nice loop hike through this area heads up Beaver Creek before climbing out of the canyon bottom to top a high ridge. The route then drops into Trail Gulch and eventually returns to the trailhead. As one of the last undeveloped tracts of wildlands in the Colorado Springs area, the Beaver Creek canyon system is currently included within a 26,150-acre wilderness study area managed by the BLM.

To reach the start of this hike, drive 6 miles east from Canon City on US Highway 50 to Phantom Canyon Road (County Road 67). Turn left and drive 1.7 miles to County Road 123. Turn right, drive 0.25 mile to the Beaver Creek Road, turn left, and drive 11 miles north to the trailhead at road's end.

*Dramatic cliffs rise above Beaver Creek Canyon.*

From the trailhead follow the Beaver Creek Trail upstream for 0.75 mile to where the Beaver Creek and Trail Gulch trails connect. Keep left at this junction and continue up Beaver Creek Canyon for another 2.25 miles to where the east and west forks of Beaver Creek divide. Within the first 1.5 miles of following Beaver Creek, the trail stays well above the creek bottom along the east wall of the canyon. Farther on, however, it drops to a level much closer to the canyon floor. Within the first 3 miles of the hike you can expect some grade changes, although none is very steep or long. While hiking along Beaver Creek, be sure to note the different plant communities found within the canyon.

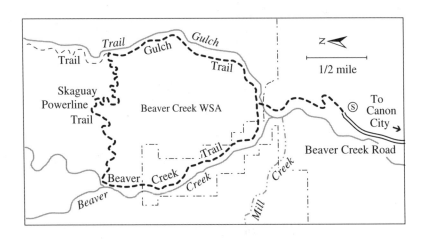

Growing across the drier hillsides and canyon faces is a woodland mix of pinyon pine and juniper. Some canyon walls, especially those that face north, feature Douglas firs as well. You may also see a few ponderosa pines scattered here and there. Along the perennial streambed below grows a nice riparian community of cottonwoods, willows, and other water-loving plants. Wildlife in the Beaver Creek area covers a wide range of species—mule deer, mountain lions, back bears, bighorn sheep, wild turkeys, and even peregrine falcons. Because Beaver Creek itself is a substantial stream, the waterway is quite popular among anglers.

Just above the point where the east and west forks of Beaver Creek branch off, this hike turns east to take up the considerably more rugged Skaguay Powerline Trail. About 2 miles in length, this route climbs more than 1,000 feet in a little over a mile, with several switchbacks, to reach the crest of a ridge that divides Beaver Creek and Trail Gulch. It then drops significantly—about 1,000 feet—with several more switchbacks, before reaching the Trail Gulch Trail. Grade changes range from moderate to strenuous, and the going can be rocky and rugged. In addition to connecting the Beaver Creek and Trail Gulch drainages, the Skaguay Powerline Trail offers impressive vistas of both canyons. Adding considerably to the beauty of the Beaver Creek area are the rugged outcrops of colorful Pikes Peak Granite that constitute the canyon's walls. (Beaver Creek is located at the southern end of the Pikes Peak batholith.) As for the powerline after which this trail is named, only a few scattered poles are left.

Upon reaching the bottom of Trail Gulch, this hike turns south to follow the drainage downstream for a little over 2 miles to where it empties into Beaver Creek. (It is also possible to continue upstream along Trail Gulch for a few additional miles.) The well-used route through Trail Gulch is in good shape and easy to follow. At the intersection with the Beaver Creek Trail, turn left and go 0.75 mile to return to the trailhead.

Although water is found along portions of this hike, bring your own as the traverse over the Skaguay Powerline Trail is dry. All creek water must be treated before drinking. Watch for flash floods in the canyon bottoms.

# 39 MOUNTS DEMOCRAT, LINCOLN, AND BROSS

**Distance: 6 miles round trip**  
**Difficulty: Strenuous**  
**Hiking time: 6 hours**  
**Elevation: 12,000 to 14,286 feet**

**Management: Pike NF**  
**Wilderness status: None**  
**Season: July to September**  
**USGS maps: Climax, Alma**

Hiking to the top of three of Colorado's elite "Fourteeners" in one day seems like a major undertaking, suitable only for a seasoned

*Peak baggers descend Mount Cameron on their way to Mount Lincoln.*

mountaineer. The summits of this lofty trio, however, are close enough to one another so that a hiker of average strength and ability can do just that. Linked together by relatively straightforward ridge walks, Mount Democrat, Mount Lincoln, and Mount Bross are the crowning jewels of the Mosquito Range, which rises between the towns of Fairplay and Leadville.

The hike begins at Kite Lake. To reach the lake from Fairplay, drive nearly 6 miles north on Colorado Highway 9 to the town of Alma. Turn left in downtown Alma at the sign for Kite Lake and County Road 8, and follow this gravel road for 5.5 miles to the lake. The last 0.25 mile is steep enough that some cars may not make it.

Because Kite Lake is situated at 12,000 feet, hikers have a jump on this hike before they even leave their vehicle. From the trailhead, a well-used trail heads around the east side of the lake toward an alpine basin to the north. Within the first 0.5 mile the route climbs past an old miner's shack that is still fairly intact. It then angles northwest to begin switchbacking up to a saddle that connects Mount Democrat and Mount Cameron. After a mile of climbing the route reaches the 13,400-foot saddle, where it turns south to climb along the northeast ridge of Democrat. Many routes ascend this ridgeline—the result of thousands of climbers who have tackled the peak—so choose the one that looks best to you. They will all get you to the top. Within the 0.5 mile from the saddle to the 14,148-foot summit of Mount Democrat you first reach a false summit, from which it is a short climb west to the top.

As evidenced by the remains of a fallen-down building near Democrat's summit, the Mosquito Range has been subject to heavy mining activity for many decades. Beginning in the 1870s, miners have poked and prodded at these mountains in search of gold, silver, and other metals such as molybdenum, which is used to toughen steel alloys and in fertilizers, dyes, and enamels. From the summit you can plainly see

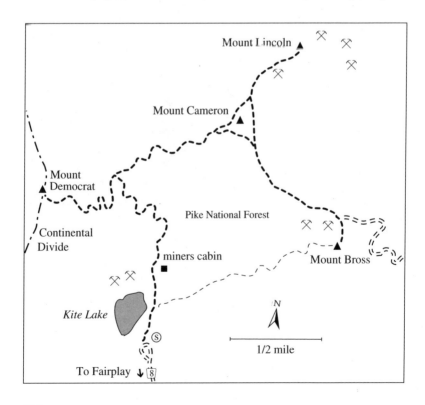

the giant Climax Mine to the northwest, which has, over the past seventy years, produced more than half of the world's supply of molybdenum. Other sights include nearby 14,036-foot Mount Sherman, the Sawatch Mountains, and even the distant Maroon Bells to the west. To the north is 14,264-foot Quandary Peak and the Gore Range. Two more Fourteeners—Grays and Torreys peaks—are visible to the northeast. And, rising beyond the expansive South Park to the southeast, is 14,110-foot Pikes Peak.

After you've had your fill of the views from Mount Democrat, backtrack down to the saddle before climbing some 800 feet to the 14,238-foot summit of Mount Cameron. Along this ascent the route follows a well-defined trail that picks its way up the southwest ridge of the peak. Because Mount Cameron is considered part of Mount Lincoln, it does not count as an official Fourteener. It is an interesting peak, however, simply for its broad and relatively smooth summit. From Cameron the route drops a short distance to the north before making an easy climb of only a few hundred feet to the summit of 14,286-foot Mount Lincoln. Home to plenty of mining activity, the slopes of Lincoln are dotted with old excavations, tailings piles, a few roads, and even some structures clinging to the mountain's south and east faces. The name, of course, reflects nineteenth-century praise for our sixteenth president. It is believed that Mount Democrat gained its name from miners from the South who didn't care much for the Republican Lincoln. Nearby Mount Bross—the third summit of this hike—was named after William Bross, a mine owner from nearby Alma.

To reach the 14,172-foot summit of Mount Bross from Lincoln, return to Mount Cameron and follow the trail that skirts along its east face to the saddle connecting Cameron and Bross. You may note a 4WD road that nearly tops this saddle before climbing up to the summit of Bross. Yes, this Fourteener is still accessible by vehicle, but you probably won't see many drivers making the attempt. After climbing 300 feet from the saddle to the top of Bross, you can enjoy the very broad and level countenance of this summit.

The quickest way to return to your car is to descend directly from Bross to Kite Lake by way of a very steep trail that drops down a gully on the mountain's west face. Quite dramatic in its vertical descent—2,200 feet in 1 mile—this loose and rocky route may be too difficult for some, and the Forest Service discourages its use. The Forest Service advises that you circle back around to Cameron and hike back down to the saddle that accesses Democrat. This milder descent adds a little more than a mile to your hike, but bypasses the really steep terrain.

Although all three mountains are accessed by trails, this hike is not without hazards. First and foremost is the weather—watch for lightning and incoming precipitation. It is best to simply begin your hike at dawn so that you are off the peaks by early afternoon. Second, bring plenty of water as none is available along the way. Altitude sickness can pose a problem for some, especially since a lot of the route is above 13,000 feet. And finally, although these summits are relatively gentle, there are still drop-offs in some places. Exercise caution in these areas.

# 40 BUFFALO PEAKS LOOP

**Distance: 11.5 miles round trip**
**Difficulty: Moderate**
**Hiking time: 8 hours**
**Elevation: 9,950 to 11,500 feet**

**Management: Pike NF**
**Wilderness status: Buffalo Peaks WA**
**Season: July to September**
**USGS maps: South Peak, Jones Hill**

Since the passage of the Colorado Wilderness Act of 1993, the Buffalo Peaks have become the centerpiece of the 43,410-acre Buffalo Peaks Wilderness Area. Following a pair of scenic drainages across the north slope of these prominent 13,000-foot mountains, the Rich Creek and Rough & Tumbling Creek trails can be combined to create one memorable loop hike.

To reach the start of this hike, drive 4.8 miles south from Fairplay on US Highway 285 to Weston Pass Road (County Road 5). Turn right on this good gravel road and drive 7 miles to its intersection with County Road 22. Bear right and drive another 2.9 miles to the signed trailhead. This description follows the loop counterclockwise.

From the trailhead, the Rich Creek Trail immediately crosses the South Platte River, after which it intersects with the lower end of the Rough & Tumbling Creek Trail. After turning right at this trail intersection, continue following Rich Creek upstream for nearly 6 miles. In its first mile the trail crosses the stream three times. At about 1.25 miles it intersects an 0.8-mile side trail that turns right to access

*An old snag along the Rich Creek Trail*

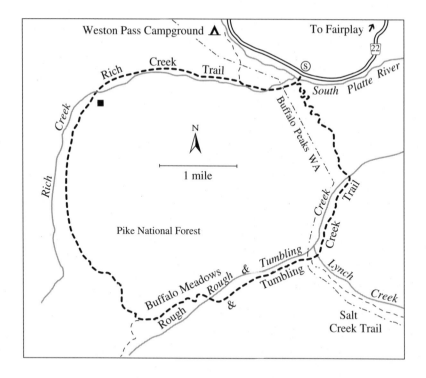

the Weston Pass Campground, and near the 2-mile mark it reaches the remains of an old cabin. Along this first segment of the hike the surrounding forest includes a mix of lodgepole pine, Engelmann spruce, subalpine fir, and aspen.

After climbing along an easy grade for the first 2 miles, the Rich Creek Trail begins to ascend more steeply during the third mile. Along this section some interesting vistas look back down the drainage. After 3 miles the route levels off again as it reaches an open park that follows the creek for the next couple of miles. Characterized by waist-high willows, this area provides vistas of nearby treeless ridges leading up to the higher Buffalo Peaks. This open area is a good place to spot deer and elk in the early hours of the day. Other wildlife of the Buffalo Peaks area includes bighorn sheep, which may occasionally be sighted around the higher reaches of the peaks. After nearly 2 miles of easy climbing through this scenic valley, the Rich Creek Trail reaches the high point of this hike at an 11,500-foot saddle. From here, the trail drops easily into the upper portion of the Rough & Tumbling Creek drainage (named for a number of cascades and waterfalls found farther downstream), where it takes up the expansive Buffalo Meadows. Just before reaching Rough & Tumbling Creek, the Rich Creek Trail ends at the junction with the Rough & Tumbling Creek Trail. While this hike turns left at this point, a right turn leads a couple of miles to a pass just west of the Buffalo Peaks.

Heading east from the Rich Creek Trail intersection, the Rough & Tumbling Creek Trail begins descending gently along its namesake drainage. Eventually the open environs of Buffalo Meadows give way to timbered areas. About 2 miles past the Rich Creek Trail–Rough & Tumbling Creek Trail intersection, the Salt Creek Trail turns right to follow Lynch Creek upstream. After keeping left at this junction, the route continues down Rough & Tumbling Creek before turning away from the stream to climb over a ridge to the north. In this ascent the trail climbs moderately to gain about 400 feet in 1 mile. The trail then drops about 600 feet before intersecting with the start of the Rich Creek Trail and the trailhead.

Water is available along this hike but must be treated. Watch for lightning along the higher portions of this hike.

# 41 MOHAWK LAKES

**Distance: 7.8 miles round trip**
**Difficulty: Moderate**
**Hiking time: 5 hours**
**Elevation: 10,400 to 12,200 feet**

**Management: Arapaho NF**
**Wilderness status: None**
**Season: July to September**
**USGS map: Breckenridge**

A popular hiking trail just south of the resort town of Breckenridge, the Spruce Creek Trail accesses some beautiful forested and alpine terrain. Climbing easily for most of the way, this route eventually makes a final push past some old mining cabins before reaching the Mohawk Lakes, which are situated near timberline in a scenic mountain valley.

To reach the Spruce Creek trailhead, drive south from Breckenridge on Colorado Highway 9 for 2.5 miles to Spruce Creek Road. Turn right and continue for another 1.2 miles to the signed trailhead and parking on either side of the gravel road. If you are in a hurry and you have a 4WD vehicle, you can shave a few miles off the hike by driving to the upper trailhead at road's end. In doing so, however, you will miss out on some scenic old-growth forest.

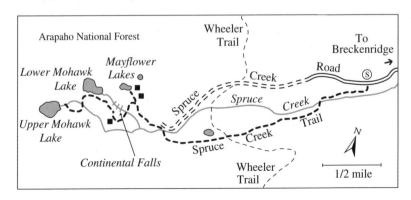

From the lower trailhead the Spruce Creek Trail sets out in a mixed forest of lodgepole pine, spruce, fir, and some aspen. Maintaining a mostly level grade for the first mile, the trail crosses its namesake creek (via a narrow bridge) at about 0.75 mile. After the stream crossing the route continues west to climb easily through beautiful forestlands. The trail itself is well developed and easy to follow throughout. At about 1.8 miles from the trailhead the Spruce Creek Trail intersects the Wheeler Trail, which runs north for several miles to the Gore Range beyond Interstate 70. Just beyond this intersection, the Spruce

*Continental Falls drains from the Mohawk Lakes.*

Creek Trail skirts around a scenic meadow with a nice view of the surrounding scenery. After another 0.25 mile or so the route reaches the upper trailhead.

Beyond the upper trailhead parking area, the trail begins to climb more steeply as it approaches the turnoff for the Mayflower Lakes less than 0.5 mile beyond. Situated in the timber at about 11,300 feet, the Mayflower Lakes are the site of several old log structures that date back to mining operations during the late 1880s. Shortly past the Mayflower Lakes, the trail encounters more miners' cabins, one of which is still in decent shape. Nearby you can take in a close-up view of Continental Falls. From this point the trail climbs steeply—500 feet in 0.5 mile—to reach the top station of an old aerial tramway and, a short distance beyond, Lower Mohawk Lake. Situated just below timberline, at an elevation of 11,800 feet, Lower Mohawk Lake is spectacularly scenic, to say the least.

After another climb of 400 feet in 0.5 mile, the Spruce Creek Trail reaches Upper Mohawk Lake. From here you can enjoy views of Pacific Peak to the west and Mount Helen to the north, and gaze east over the Blue River drainage to the Boreas Pass area. Rising to the south but out of view from the Mohawk Lakes area is 14,265-foot Quandary Peak. Upper Mohawk Lake marks the end of the Spruce Creek Trail and the turnaround point for this hike.

This trail sees heavy use by both hikers and mountain bikers, especially on weekends. Water is available along much of this hike, but it must be treated first. Watch for lightning, especially along the higher reaches of this hike.

 NOTCH MOUNTAIN

Distance: 10.6 miles round trip
Difficulty: Strenuous
Hiking time: 7 hours
Elevation: 10,320 to 13,100 feet
Management: White River NF

Wilderness status: Holy Cross WA
Season: July to September
USGS maps: Minturn, Mount of
    the Holy Cross

Few, if any, of Colorado's high mountain peaks are as fabled as Mount of the Holy Cross. Featuring an enormous cross formed by two intersecting crevasses that remain filled with snow for much of the year, this mystical mountain has attracted considerable interest for more than a century. While the 14,003-foot peak is a popular climb for many, the best place to actually view the cross is nearby 13,224-foot Notch Mountain, which rises to the east.

The hike to Notch Mountain begins at the Fall Creek trailhead, which is adjacent to the Half Moon Campground. To reach this trailhead, drive west from Vail on Interstate 70 to Minturn. Exit south onto US Highway 24, drive 4 miles to Tigiwon Road (Forest Road 707), turn right, and drive 8 miles to the trailhead at the dirt road's end.

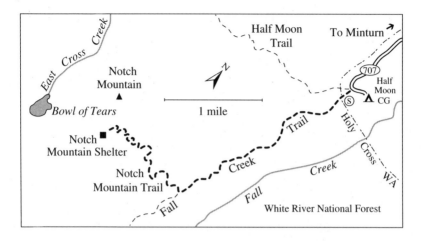

Because the Half Moon Trail (the route to the summit of Mount of the Holy Cross) also starts at this point, the parking lot can be crowded.

This hike begins by heading south along the Fall Creek Trail, which traverses the eastern end of the Holy Cross Wilderness. Climbing along easy to moderate grades, this first segment of the hike encounters nice forests of Engelmann spruce and subalpine fir. At the 2.5-mile mark the Fall Creek Trail intersects the Notch Mountain Trail. After turning right at this junction, the route soon reaches timberline, beyond which it breaks into alpine tundra and continues up the east slope of Notch Mountain. Along this final segment of the hike, the route climbs strenuously to gain some 1,900 feet in 2.8 miles. As you might expect, several switchbacks are encountered along the way. Be sure not cut these switchbacks—damage to the fragile tundra can result.

Awaiting hikers at the trail's end is an unobstructed view of the east face of Mount of the Holy Cross. This singular scene has stirred all who have made the climb up Notch Mountain. From the time the first white men explored the Colorado Rockies, stories of this snowy cross spread. It was not until 1873, however, that excitement over the mountain really began to build. That was when nineteenth-century photographer William Henry Jackson reached the summit of Notch Mountain. The weather was cloudy that evening, so it was not until the following morning that he got his first glimpse of the cross. After snapping a now-famous photo, Jackson returned with concrete evidence that this incredible geologic feature actually existed. His photo has since spurred thousands to visit Notch Mountain, and religious pilgrimages and even tales of miraculous healings have continued into this century. A stone shelter was built in 1924 to accommodate visitors, and in 1929 the mountain gained national monument status. That designation was withdrawn in the 1950s, however, as interest in the mountain dropped off. While the scene's natural beauty is an inspiration to all visitors, regardless of their religious beliefs, the views to the north, south, and east are equally stunning. Within this grand panorama you can see the rugged Gore Range, the Vail Ski Area (from this high point it looks puny), the Mosquito Range beyond the Leadville area, and the Sawatch Mountains as they stretch south through the Holy Cross Wilderness and on toward the Mount Massive and Collegiate Peaks wilderness areas beyond.

Lightning is a frequent hazard along the upper reaches of this hike. Very little water is available along this hike, so be sure to bring plenty.

# 43   FANCY PASS

**Distance: 8 miles round trip**
**Difficulty: Strenuous**
**Hiking time: 6 hours**
**Elevation: 10,000 to 12,380 feet**
**Management: White River NF**

**Wilderness status: Holy Cross WA**
**Season: July to September**
**USGS maps: Mount of the Holy**
   **Cross, Mount Jackson**

Located in the southern end of the Holy Cross Wilderness Area, the hike over Fancy Pass accesses some wonderful mountain terrain as well as a handful of pristine alpine lakes. Adding both miles and interest to this trip is a continuation of the route over nearby Missouri Pass. The end result is a 10-mile loop trip that connects two nearby trailheads.

This description begins at the Fancy Pass trailhead. To get there, drive 12 miles north from Minturn on US Highway 24 to Homestake Road. Turn right and continue 7.8 miles to Missouri Lakes Road (Forest Service Road 704). Turn right again and drive 2.6 miles to the signed trailhead. Slightly less than 0.5 mile before reaching the Fancy

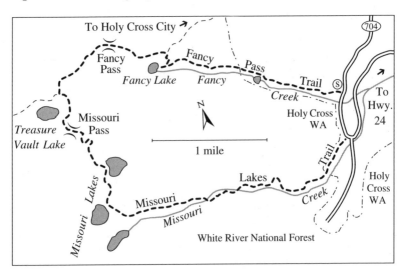

*Fancy Lake is the first of several alpine jewels reached along the hike over Fancy Pass.*

Pass trailhead you pass the Missouri Lakes trailhead, which marks the end of the trail portion of this hike.

The Fancy Pass Trail begins by climbing strenuously along an old 4WD road that leads past a small man-made pond. While this is a rough way to begin a hike, the initial ascent does get some climbing out of the way early. After 1.5 miles the route becomes a foot trail and levels off for a bit as it parallels Fancy Creek. Timber in the area includes lodgepole pines that grow side by side with Engelmann spruce and subalpine firs. Higher up the forest becomes a strictly spruce–fir mix. At 1.75 miles the trail crosses a small meadow, after which it begins a rather strenuous 0.25-mile climb to Fancy Lake. Located at timberline, Fancy Lake offers a scenic respite before you tackle Fancy Pass above.

From Fancy Lake, the Fancy Pass Trail climbs a short distance to join an old road that heads over the pass itself. The old route to nearby Holy Cross City, this road is littered with the remains of nineteenth-century cabins, wagons, nd an old mill. The road was built by the Gold Park Milling and Mining Company around the turn of the century. From the lake to 12,400-foot Fancy Pass is a climb of about 800 feet in 0.75 mile. Beyond the pass the trail drops easily over the next 0.75

mile to the head of Cross Creek and the Treasure Vault Lake area. Here the route picks up the upper end of the 4-mile-long Missouri Lakes Trail, which in turn climbs a short distance—300 vertical feet in 0.3 mile—to 11,986-foot Missouri Pass.

From this second pass the Missouri Lakes Trail drops steeply over the next 0.5 mile to reach the Missouri Lakes, which are scattered along the head of Missouri Creek. From here the route drops down Missouri Creek along a mostly moderate grade. On the lower end of the trail some interesting cliff faces add to the beauty of this hike. The route also passes several diversion pipelines. As part of the Homestake I water project, this development transfers water from Fancy and Missouri creeks, as well as other streams, across the Continental Divide and on to thirsty residents of Front Range cities. Phase II of the Homestake project would tunnel farther west under the Holy Cross Wilderness to tap into the Cross Creek and Fall Creek drainages. It is thought that such a plan would dry up many wetland areas within the Holy Cross area, thereby compromising its wilderness characteristics. The Holy Cross Defense Fund is now actively opposing phase II of the Homestake project. Upon reaching the Missouri Lakes trailhead you must walk 0.6 mile up the road to return to your car.

Water is available along this hike, but treat it before drinking. Watch for lightning in the higher reaches, and be aware that snow fields often linger well into August along some stretches of trail. Use caution when crossing these places.

# 44 HAGERMAN TUNNEL

| | |
|---|---|
| Distance: 5.5 miles round trip | Wilderness status: None |
| Difficulty: Easy | Season: June to September |
| Hiking time: 3 hours | USGS maps: Homestake Reservoir, |
| Elevation: 10,940 to 11,530 feet | Mount Massive |
| Management: San Isabel NF | |

For all their ruggedness, the Sawatch Mountains were far from impervious to man's endeavors during the nineteenth century. A good example of this is the old railroad grade that crosses the Continental Divide by way of the 2,161-foot-long Hagerman Tunnel. Representing the labor of hundreds of immigrant laborers, this tunnel was the highest railroad tunnel in the world at the time of its completion n 1887.

This hike starts on Hagerman Pass Road, which is near Turquoise Lake. From downtown Leadville drive a few blocks west on US Highway 24. Turn right onto a paved road directly across from the entrance to the Colorado Mountain College. Follow this road west for 7.5 miles, past Turquoise Lake, to a rough but passable gravel road that bears left. This is Hagerman Pass Road (Forest Road 105); follow it 4.8 miles to the trailhead. Parking is available on the right and the trail takes off on the left.

*Hagerman Tunnel was built in the 1800s to accommodate train travel over the Continental Divide.*

At the trailhead be sure to read the interpretive sign, which describes the Colorado Midland Railroad and its successful attempt to cross the Continental Divide. Begun in the early 1880s, this was the first standard gauge railroad to traverse the Colorado Rockies. With only 350 miles of track, however, the venture never made money. The trail to the tunnel follows the old railroad grade for part of the way. At the start this means hiking through a lengthy cut in the bedrock. Old ties are strewn about, some still in place and others discarded to the side. A little over a mile from the start the grade reaches the first of two ravines that were once crossed by lengthy trestles. The Hagerman Trestle is no longer standing, but it is possible to visualize the 1,100-foot-long, 84-foot-high structure as if it were still in place.

Where the trestle originally began the main trail drops down to continue along the railroad route. Instead of following the trail, take a sharp right onto an old road that provides a shortcut to the next curve above. In 0.25 mile this shortcut trail crosses the railroad grade and then reaches the old townsite of Douglass City. Once a camp for the mostly Italian workers who built the railroad and tunnel, Douglass City was as lively a community as any in the Rockies. Of course, it had its share of saloons—eight in all—and a dance hall, plus a post office. Today all that remains are some fallen-down log structures and scattered debris. From Douglass City climb directly to the railroad route above. In this next 0.5 mile you pass Opal Lake before reaching the final stretch of railroad, which approaches the tunnel entrance.

Like the trailhead and the Douglass City townsite, Hagerman Tunnel is accompanied by an interpretive sign which explains the excavation's

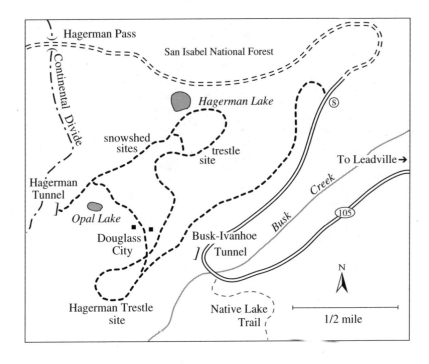

engineering and historical significance. Completed in 1887, the 2,161-foot-long Hagerman Tunnel was actually in service for only a few years. In 1891 it was replaced by the much longer Busk–Ivanhoe Tunnel, whose entrance you drove past on the way to the trailhead. Interestingly, the Busk–Ivanhoe Tunnel was converted to auto traffic in 1922 and did not close until 1943. Vehicles now cross the Divide by way of Hagerman Pass, which is located a few miles beyond the trailhead. The Hagerman Tunnel entrance is partially blocked by rock slides, but it is still possible to enter. *It is not advisable to do so, though,* due to safety concerns. Looking in from the outside you can see that snow and ice linger year-round in the tunnel's cool darkness.

So as not to miss other features of this hike, be sure to follow the railroad grade back down instead of taking the shortcut trail through Douglass City. Along the way the trail passes not only beautiful Hagerman Lake, but also the sites of thirteen different snowsheds. These structures fell down long ago, and very little evidence of their existence remains. Farther on, the trail passes the site of a second trestle that, like the Hagerman Trestle, has disappeared over the years. Within the next mile the railroad grade meets the shortcut trail below Douglass City. Turn left and follow it down to the start of the Hagerman Trestle. At this point turn left again to return to the trailhead.

Water is available along this hike, but must be treated before consuming. Lightning can be a problem, although this hike does not cross exposed terrain.

# 45     MOUNT MASSIVE

**Distance: 14 miles round trip**
**Difficulty: Strenuous**
**Hiking time: 8 hours**
**Elevation: 10,100 to 14,421 feet**
**Management: Pike–San Isabel NF**

**Wilderness status: Mount**
**Massive WA**
**Season: July to September**
**USGS map: Mount Massive**

Although Mount Massive is Colorado's second highest summit, with an elevation of 14,421 feet, it is readily accessible to hikers, thanks to a 7-mile hiking route that climbs all the way to the summit. Like its neighbor, 14,433-foot Mount Elbert, the summit of Mount Massive provides some of the most impressive vistas to be found anywhere in the Lower Forty-eight states. The hikes up both peaks begin at the same trailhead on Halfmoon Creek Road.

To begin this hike, drive 3 miles southwest from Leadville on US Highway 24. Turn right onto County Road 300, then left onto Halfmoon Creek Road (Forest Road 110). Drive another 7 miles to the signed trailhead.

The hike starts by following the much-touted Colorado Trail north for 3 miles. Along this first segment of the hike, the route climbs 1,100 feet along mostly easy grades. As the trail contours around to Mount Massive's east slope, it crosses a few minor drainages. At the lower elevations, timbered areas of lodgepole pine are common. As the trail

*Mount Massive as seen from timberline*

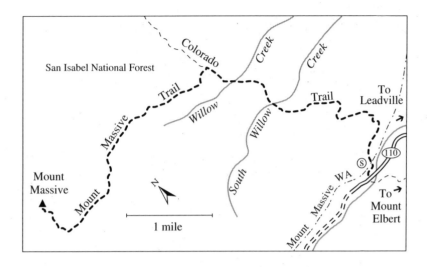

climbs, however, the forest changes to a mix of Engelmann spruce and subalpine fir. Shortly after reaching the 11,000-foot level, the Colorado Trail meets the 4-mile-long Mount Massive Trail, which this hike follows west to complete the final ascent to the top. Well defined after years of heavy use, the Mount Massive Trail climbs steeply, especially as it nears the top. In all, this second segment of the hike gains 3,200 feet, mostly above timberline. Be sure to note the variety of low-profile plants that grow in these alpine tundra areas. Stay on the trail, as these areas are very fragile. As you near the top, it may be difficult to pick out the actual summit. Stretching across 3 miles, Mount Massive's crest includes several false summits. By sticking to the trail, however, you will eventually wind up on the tallest point of the mountain.

While nearby Mount Elbert is taller than Mount Massive, the two peaks were once at the center of a controversy that questioned their rankings as the state's tallest and second tallest peaks. Elbert eventually won out, but by only 12 feet. From Massive's summit the views are commanding, to say the least. To the east lies Leadville and the Mosquito Range with its 13,000 and 14,000-foot peaks. The Arkansas River Valley stretches south, as does the Collegiate Range. North is the Holy Cross Wilderness Area, and west is the Hunter–Fryingpan Wilderness. Of course, the vistas extend far beyond the above-mentioned landmarks as well.

Water is found in places along the first half of this hike, but it must be treated before drinking. Watch for lightning on the peak, especially on summer afternoons. To best avoid hazards, plan to complete your hike early. As is true for all Fourteeners in Colorado, weather conditions can deteriorate rapidly on Mount Massive. Because this hike is quite popular, you may want to plan your trip for a weekday or after the Labor Day weekend.

# 46 ELKHEAD PASS

**Distance: 9 miles round trip**
**Difficulty: Strenuous**
**Hiking time: 6 hours**
**Elevation: 9,660 to 13,220 feet**
**Management: San Isabel NF**

**Wilderness status: Collegiate**
**Peaks WA**
**Season: July to September**
**USGS maps: Mount Harvard,**
**Winfield**

Elkhead Pass, the state's second highest saddle, is a real grunt of a hike—but worth every bit of the effort. Located on the north end of the Collegiate Peaks Wilderness, this route climbs to the head of Missouri Gulch, where it reveals some spectacular views. Additionally, three Fourteeners are located within the vicinity of the pass. While the round-trip distance listed in the information block above covers only the hike to the pass, it would be a relatively simple matter to scramble up the nearest of these elite peaks, Mount Belford.

This hike follows the Missouri Gulch Trail, which begins near the historic townsite of Vicksburg. To reach the trailhead, drive 19 miles south from Leadville on US Highway 24 to the turnoff for County Road 390, which becomes Forest Road 120. Follow this good graveled road west for 7.8 miles to the signed trailhead.

After crossing Clear Creek a short distance from the trailhead, the Missouri Gulch Trail begins climbing strenuously up a series of switchbacks. In this first 1.25 miles the route climbs 1,300 feet in all. The surrounding forest is a patchy mix of aspen, lodgepole pine, Engelmann spruce, and fir. Eventually, the trail levels off to climb along more moderate grades, and about 2 miles in it crosses a creek where a trail sign points the way to the creek's left bank. The route then climbs up the bottom of the gulch, which has been regularly scoured by avalanches, and enters a thick stand of spruce and fir forest. As timberline draws closer, the trail encounters an old cabin. A relict of the region's mining heritage, this structure has fallen into disrepair. Nearby, you may spot some bristlecone pines.

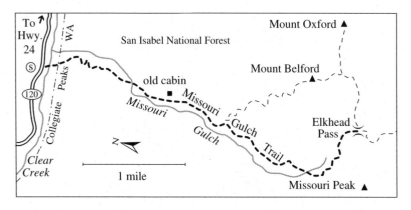

Beyond the cabin the trail soon breaks out into an open basin. While a few scattered pockets of krummholz trees lie ahead, the trail from here on out mostly crosses alpine tundra. After climbing easily through the first basin, the trail forks. While this hike turns right to continue up to Elkhead Pass, a left turn heads directly to the summit of Mount Belford. If your only goal is to bag the Fourteener and you do not mind extremely steep climbing, then take this route and forget about Elkhead Pass. However, most hikers who are intent on climbing the peak find it easier to first get to the pass and then head toward the summit from there.

*Elkhead Pass (center left) as seen from the summit of Mount Belford*

From the above-mentioned trail junction, the Missouri Gulch Trail makes a short and somewhat strenuous climb to access the next basin above. After this climb the grade levels off for a while as the trail continues south toward the pass. It then climbs again, and again levels off for a bit. In this stair-step manner, the pass is eventually reached. In one rocky area you must look for cairns that mark the way, but otherwise the route is clearly visible.

Situated at 13,220 feet, Elkhead Pass separates Missouri Gulch to the north from Missouri Basin to the south. From the pass you gain a commanding view not only of Missouri Basin, but also of a host of tall peaks to the south of the basin and north of the Clear Creek drainage. The Missouri Gulch Trail continues into the basin, where it turns east to drop down Pine Creek.

Despite its lofty altitude, Elkhead Pass is actually the low point of a ridge that includes three 14,000-foot peaks: 14,067-foot Missouri Peak just west of the pass; 14,197-foot Mount Belford less than a mile east; and 14,153-foot Mount Oxford, which is connected to Mount Belford by a ridge that runs to the east. While climbing Missouri Peak from Elkhead Pass involves some scrambling, the climb up Mount Belford is a relatively easy endeavor: from the pass the route climbs about 1,000 feet to reach the summit in only 1 mile. The breathtaking views from the summit take in the Maroon Bells–Snowmass Wilderness far to the west and Pikes Peak to the east.

Lightning poses a danger at both the pass and on the nearby summits, so plan to complete your hike earlier in the day during the summer. Water is available along most of the Missouri Gulch Trail, but it must be treated before drinking. As evidenced by the summit register on Mount Belford, this hike is very popular, especially on holiday weekends.

# 47   BROWNS CABIN

**Distance: 8.8 miles round trip**
**Difficulty: Moderate**
**Hiking time: 5 hours**
**Elevation: 9,900 to 12,040 feet**
**Management: San Isabel NF,**
    **Gunnison NF**

**Wilderness status: Collegiate**
    **Peaks WA**
**Season: July to September**
**USGS map: Mount Yale**

The hike to Browns Pass and nearby Browns Cabin offers a pleasurable way to enjoy the southern portion of the Collegiate Mountain Range. In addition to the incredible scenery you would expect to find among this collection of peaks, this excursion offers a vivid taste of Colorado's mining history.

The hike to Browns Cabin begins at the Denny Creek trailhead on Cottonwood Pass Road (County Road 306). From downtown Buena Vista, drive 12 miles west to the trailhead, which is located about 1 mile beyond the Collegiate Peaks Campground.

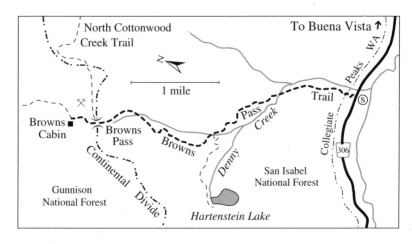

Following the Browns Pass Trail for the entire way, this hike climbs steadily north for 4 miles to the 12,040-foot pass, then drops for a short distance into the Texas Creek drainage where it reaches Browns Cabin. Small but beautiful Denny Creek runs alongside the trail for the first mile. Beyond the 1-mile mark the route crosses the stream to continue north, while the creek itself bends to the northwest. For the first 2 miles the trail climbs along easy to moderate grades. Forests at this elevation include lodgepole pine, Engelmann spruce, and subalpine fir, along with a few stands of aspen. About 2 miles in, a side trail branches left to continue for another mile to Hartenstein Lake, a nice destination in its own right. Located at an elevation of 11,451 feet, the lake is close to timberline.

Beyond the turnoff for Hartenstein Lake, the Browns Pass Trail continues to climb—first at an easy pace, but soon along a moderately steep ascent. In the 2-mile stretch from the Hartenstein Lake Trail junction to the pass, the route climbs a total of 900 feet. Having reached timberline around the 11,600-foot level, much of this portion of the hike traverses alpine tundra. Many species of wildflowers grow here in late July and early August.

Once on top of the pass, which is on the Continental Divide, you can enjoy a grand view, especially to the north. Rising along the far side of the Texas Creek drainage are the Three Apostles—a trio of summits that top 13,900 feet. Also to the north is 14,420-foot Mount Harvard. Although it rises 2.5 miles southeast of Browns Pass, 14,196-foot Mount Yale is not visible from the hike. Heading east from Browns Pass is the North Cottonwood Creek Trail. After climbing some 500 feet above the pass, this route drops down the North Cottonwood Creek drainage. In a little over 2 miles it passes Kroenke Lake, which is situated at 11,500 feet. About 6 miles from the pass the North Cottonwood Creek Trail ends at a trailhead just east of the wilderness.

From Browns Pass, the Browns Pass Trail crosses north into the Gunnison National Forest, then drops easily—about 300 feet in less than 0.5 mile—to reach Browns Cabin. Nestled in the trees just below

*Browns Cabin provides shelter for overnight hikers.*

timberline, this two-story structure dates back to the mining boom of the late nineteenth century. Because it's been maintained over the years, the building still provides shelter for overnight hikers. Although this hike turns around at the cabin, the Browns Pass Trail does continue northward for a little more than a mile to reach the Texas Creek Trail, which follows its namesake west to east.

Water is available along this hike, but must be treated. Watch for lightning in the vicinity of the pass and in other exposed areas.

# 48 WATERDOG LAKES

**Distance: 4 miles round trip**
**Difficulty: Moderate**
**Hiking time: 3 hours**
**Elevation: 10,200 to 11,475 feet**

**Management: San Isabel NF**
**Wilderness status: None**
**Season: June to September**
**USGS map: Garfield**

For a short but sweet hike in the Monarch Pass area, try the 2-mile trail to Waterdog Lakes. Located near timberline, these two lakes are surrounded by scenic alpine ridges. In addition, they offer some good fishing opportunities. While Waterdog Lakes are regularly stocked with Mackinaw trout, brook trout are caught there as well.

The Waterdog Lakes Trail starts a few miles below Monarch Pass on

*A log jam along the shore of Lower Waterdog Lake*

US Highway 50. From the town of Poncha Springs, drive west on US Highway 50 for 15 miles. Park in a large pull-off area on the left and look for the signed trailhead located in the woods on the right side of the road. The trailhead is about 0.25 mile east of the turnoff for the Monarch Park Campground.

The trail sets out by following a small creek upstream for a short distance before bearing left to contour along the hillside above the highway. The creek is lined by some beautiful old-growth spruce and fir trees. Upon turning onto the drier hillside, however, the trail enters a mix of lodgepole pine, Engelmann spruce, and fir. After paralleling the highway for about 0.3 mile, the trail turns right onto an old 4WD road that is now closed to vehicles. Originally, the start of the trail to Waterdog Lakes was reached by following this road from the Monarch Park Campground turnoff, but it was recently moved to prevent erosion.

Once the route turns onto this old road, it climbs along a mostly moderate grade for the next 0.5 mile or so before leveling off. In this middle portion of the hike the trail passes beneath a small powerline that is still in use. Eventually, within its last 0.5 mile, the trail climbs a strenuous grade that is loose and rocky in places. Soon after, the trail reaches the first of the two Waterdog Lakes. Upper Waterdog Lake is located about 0.3 mile beyond Lower Waterdog Lake. Because it is slightly higher, the upper lake features some krummholz growth along

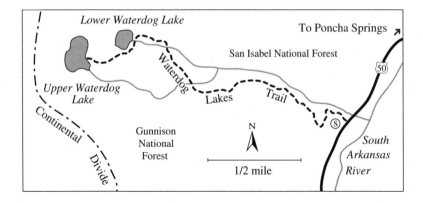

portions of its shore. At this elevation of nearly 11,500 feet, the forest mix is strictly spruce and fir, with no lodgepole pine in sight. Forming the western and northern skylines above the lakes are some treeless alpine ridges that carry the Continental Divide northward.

Although water is available along this hike, it must be treated before drinking. Lightning can pose a threat, although this route is not too exposed.

# 49  LOST MAN LAKE

**Distance: 8.8 miles one way**
**Difficulty: Moderate**
**Hiking time: 6 hours**
**Elevation: 10,570 to 12,800 feet**
**Management: White River NF**

**Wilderness status: Hunter–**
**Fryingpan WA**
**Season: July to September**
**USGS maps: Mount Champion,**
**Independence Pass**

Picking up where the Collegiate Peaks and Mount Massive wilderness areas leave off, the Hunter–Fryingpan Wilderness encompasses an 82,580-acre parcel of high mountain terrain along the western slope of the Sawatch Range. In addition to a number of 13,000-foot peaks and some nice timberlands, this wilderness includes many beautiful streams and lakes. The Lost Man Trail visits two of these lakes while exploring a pair of drainages. Stretching between two trailheads located along the highway leading over Independence Pass, this highly scenic route covers 8.8 miles as it circles north through the heart of the Hunter–Fryingpan Wilderness.

To reach the beginning of this hike, drive 14 miles east of Aspen on Colorado Highway 82. The upper trailhead is located 4.5 miles farther east on Colorado Highway 82, at the last switchback where the road crosses the Roaring Fork River.

From the lower trailhead, the Lost Man Trail crosses a bridge and then heads north along the left bank of Lost Man Creek before reaching Lost Man Lake 6 miles out. Along this first portion of the hike, the

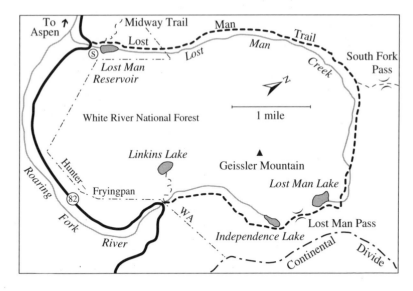

route climbs moderately as the trail's total elevation gain of 2,000 feet is spread evenly throughout. Along the way, two other trails intersect the Lost Man Trail to access different reaches of the wilderness. The first of these is the Midway Trail, which begins a short distance from the trailhead and heads northwest over 11,841-foot Midway Pass before dropping to Midway Creek. Midway Creek in turn feeds into

*Lost Man Lake as seen from Lost Man Pass*

Hunter Creek in the western portion of the wilderness. The second junction, with the South Fork Pass Trail, is located 4 miles in. This route climbs a couple of hundred feet to the top of South Fork Pass, then drops north to follow the South Fork of the Fryingpan River before reaching Deadman Lake 2 miles from the junction. Situated near the 11,000-foot level, Deadman Lake is a nice destination should you want to extend your hike a bit. From there, the South Fork Pass Trail continues for another 3.5 miles before ending at a trailhead north of the wilderness.

Situated at an elevation of 12,450 feet, Lost Man Lake is nestled in an exceptionally scenic glacial cirque that is entirely above timberline. Several suitable camping sites can be found here, but remember to camp at least 100 feet away from both the lake and the stream. To avoid ecological damage, you may want to camp farther down in the trees. Fishing at the lake is reported to be good.

From Lost Man Lake the Lost Man Trail climbs—strenuously in places—to the top of 12,800-foot Lost Man Pass, about 0.5 mile to the south. From here the route crosses to the head of the Roaring Fork River and reaches Independence Lake 0.3 mile south. After skirting around the south end of Independence Lake, the final 2 miles of the Lost Man Trail run alongside the Roaring Fork River, which, at this high elevation, is little more than a high mountain stream. While most of this last segment of the trail is easy to follow, some stretches may be faint. In these areas look for rock cairns that mark the way. From the upper trailhead another route climbs 500 feet in less than a mile to reach Linkins Lake, which is located in a small basin west of the Roaring Fork River. The beginning and the end of the Lost Man Trail are separated by only 4.5 miles.

Water is found all along this hike, but it must be treated before drinking. Watch for lightning during summer afternoons, especially above timberline.

# 50   SNOWMASS LAKE

**Distance: 17 miles one way**
**Difficulty: Strenuous**
**Hiking time: 2 days**
**Elevation: 9,550 to 12,462 feet**
**Management: White River NF**

**Wilderness status: Maroon Bells–**
   **Snowmass WA**
**Season: July to September**
**USGS maps: Maroon Bells, Snow-**
   **mass Mountain, Capitol Peak**

The Maroon Bells–Snowmass Wilderness is one of the most popular wilderness areas in Colorado, and for good reason. Highlighting this 181,138-acre wilderness are several Fourteeners, including what are likely the most photographed peaks in the state—the Maroon Bells. This nice overnight hike accesses the heart of this wilderness area, visiting Crater Lake before crossing west over Buckskin Gulch to Snowmass Lake. The route then drops north along Snowmass Creek to eventually end at Snowmass Fall Ranch near Snowmass Village.

To begin this hike, drive 0.5 mile west from Aspen on Colorado Highway 82 to the Maroon Creek Road. Turn south and drive 9.5 miles to the trailhead at the upper parking lot. Because of traffic congestion during the summer, visitors must park at the Aspen Highlands Ski Area and ride a free shuttle bus to the trailhead. The end of this hike is located a few miles past Snowmass Village, which is located west of Aspen.

From the trailhead this hike follows the Maroon Bells–Snowmass Trail southwest for 1.75 miles to scenic Crater Lake. In this first segment, the route passes Maroon Lake as it gains about 500 feet along a mostly moderate grade. Extensive stands of aspen in the area make

*The Maroon Bells mirrored in Maroon Lake*

this a nice autumn excursion. Additionally, views of the stunning Maroon Bells, which rise about a mile southwest of Crater Lake, can be enjoyed throughout. Sometimes referred to as the "Deadly Bells," these two 14,000-foot summits of crumbling sedimentary rock have served as the backdrop for fatal climbing accidents on numerous occasions. For hikers following established trails, however, these mountains are anything but a threat. Their distinctive layers of purplish rock, combined with their rugged outline, make them two of the most recognizable mountains in the nation.

Near Crater Lake two trails branch off, the West Maroon Pass Trail, which heads south, and the Maroon Bells–Snowmass Trail, which climbs west along Minnehaha Gulch toward the high point of the hike—Buckskin Pass. Following the latter trail, the route continues for 3 miles, climbing from an elevation of 9,580 feet to 12,462 feet. Grades along this ascent are mostly moderate, although the trail does become steeper as it draws closer to the pass. Less than a mile before reaching Buckskin Pass, the Maroon Bells–Snowmass Trail intersects with the turnoff for Willow Pass; after topping Willow Pass, this trail drops to Willow Lake before traversing another saddle and entering the East Snowmass Creek drainage. Known as the East Snowmass Trail, that route eventually ends at Snowmass Falls Ranch.

The views from Buckskin Pass are outstanding. To the west stands 14,092-foot Snowmass Mountain, with its obvious snow-filled basin. Named by the Hayden Survey in 1873, Snowmass is also one of the

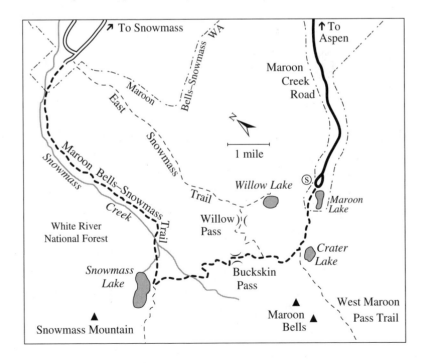

state's most remote Fourteeners, as climbers must follow an approach route of 8.5 miles just to reach the base of the mountain. Standing 2 miles to the north of Snowmass is 14,130-foot Capitol Peak. Like Snowmass, Capitol is easily recognizable from a distance. Characteristically light in color, this prism-shaped rock is unmistakable due to its steep slopes and pronounced summit. Also named by the Hayden Survey, the peak was thought to resemble the U.S. Capitol Building. One of the most difficult Fourteeners to climb, Capitol Peak was not conquered until 1909.

Beyond Buckskin Pass the Maroon Bells–Snowmass Trail drops 1,600 feet over the next 3 miles to reach Snowmass Creek. After crossing the creek the route climbs 200 feet over the next mile to reach Snowmass Lake, the largest of all lakes in the Maroon Bells–Snowmass Wilderness. Snowmass Lake is an incredibly popular destination for backpackers, and campfires are prohibited within 0.25 mile of its shores. Although stopping here for the night means sharing the area with dozens, if not hundreds, of other campers, the lake does mark the halfway point for this hike.

From Snowmass Lake, continue following the Snowmass Creek drainage north. About 2 miles north of Snowmass Lake the trail passes a couple of beaver ponds where it crosses the creek via a large log jam. From this point the trail follows closely along the east side of the creek for the remaining 6.5 miles to the Snowmass Falls Ranch trailhead. In this last segment the trail drops 2,600 feet along easy to moderate grades.

Watch for lightning in the vicinity of Buckskin Pass and along other high portions of this hike. Although water is found along much of the route, be sure to treat it first. Given the popularity of this hike (the Forest Service claims this is one of the most heavily backpacked trails in Colorado), you may want to plan your trip for after Labor Day.

# 51 ELECTRIC PASS

**Distance: 11 miles round trip**
**Difficulty: Strenuous**
**Hiking time: 7 hours**
**Elevation: 9,880 to 13,500 feet**
**Management: White River NF**

**Wilderness status: Maroon Bells–**
   **Snowmass WA**
**Season: July to September**
**USGS map: Hayden Peak**

Accessing the summits of the Maroon Bells, Snowmass Mountain, and other lofty peaks in the Elk Mountains would be the subject of another book entirely, but it is possible to hike established trails to a variety of vantage points that put you on virtually the same level as nearby 13,000- and 14,000-foot summits. One such vantage point is 13,500-foot Electric Pass, considered Colorado's highest trail-accessible pass.

To reach the beginning of this hike, drive 0.5 mile west from Aspen on Colorado Highway 82, turn south onto Maroon Creek Road, then

*Aspen line the lower portion of the trail to Electric Pass.*

make an immediate left onto Castle Creek Road (Forest Road 102). Follow this paved route 12 miles south to a gravel road that turns right. Follow this route for 0.6 mile to the trailhead at the road's end.

Setting out among beautiful aspen forests, this hike follows the Cathedral Lake Trail as it climbs along Pine Creek. Because this first stretch of the trail climbs 2,000 feet in 3.2 miles, you can expect a variety of grade changes, as well as some level areas. The first mile of the route climbs at a mostly moderate pace to reach a basin, where it levels off somewhat. After breaking out of the aspens, the trail begins traversing open meadows and rock-slide areas. After the 2-mile mark it reaches the head of the first basin, where a series of short but very steep switchbacks climb to the basin above. Although there is much more climbing to come, this is by far the most difficult part of the hike.

Shortly after topping the switchbacks, the trail reaches a signed fork. While the right-hand trail heads on to Electric Pass, the route to the left continues for another 0.4 mile to Cathedral Lake. Situated at an elevation of 11,866 feet, Cathedral Lake is a popular destination for day hikers and backpackers alike. Because it is situated above treeline and surrounded by rugged summits—the most imposing of which is 13,943-foot Cathedral Peak—Cathedral Lake is a terrific destination in itself. Because of its popularity, however, campfires are prohibited within 0.25 mile of the lake.

Shortly after turning right at the above-mentioned trail junction, the route to Electric Pass reaches timberline, then continues on through waist-high willows. Like the aspens below, the willow bushes

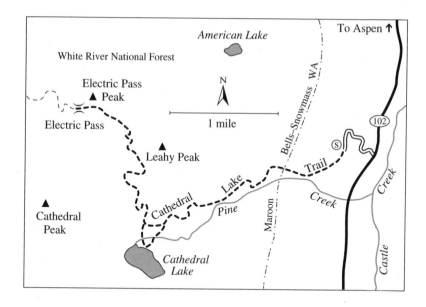

put on a showy display of colors in the fall. After reaching a second turnoff for Cathedral Lake, the trail bends northward to head into a basin above. While the route climbs another 1,600 feet in the next 1.5 miles, the going is surprisingly easy. As the trail makes its way toward Electric Pass, it passes beneath the crumbling summit of Cathedral Peak, below which is an extensive rock glacier. Eventually, the trail begins switchbacking up the east side of the basin, where it reaches a high ridge that extends southeast to 13,322-foot Leahy Peak. From the ridge top you can look into the American Lake area, which sits above the Castle Creek drainage to the east. From the north end of this ridge, the trail skirts along the rocky south face of 13,635-foot Electric Pass Peak to eventually reach Electric Pass.

From the pass you can look directly west into Cataract Creek, which is part of the Conundrum Creek drainage. An old, unmaintained, and difficult trail drops deftly from the pass in this drainage. Rising beyond this canyon is the unmistakable outline of the Maroon Bells. True to their name, these summits sport a purplish tint that characterizes the Maroon Formation. Beyond the Bells you can make out Snowmass Mountain with its extensive snowfield, as well as many other peaks. Dominating the skyline directly south of the pass is Cathedral Peak. It obscures the view of 14,265-foot Castle Peak, which sits directly behind it, but Castle Peak is visible along much of the trail leading up to the pass. Farther south, several slightly lesser peaks stand guard over passes that lead to the Crested Butte area. To the east you can make out the Sawatch Mountains, as well as numerous other ranges.

As the name suggests, lightning can pose an extreme danger on Electric Pass. All water must be treated before drinking. Expect some crowds on weekends and holidays.

# 52 LAMPHIER LAKE

**Distance: 6 miles round trip**
**Difficulty: Moderate**
**Hiking time: 4 hours**
**Elevation: 10,030 to 11,720 feet**

**Management: Gunnison NF**
**Wilderness status: Fossil Ridge WA**
**Season: July to September**
**USGS map: Fairview Peak**

Nestled just below timberline, Lamphier Lake is the destination of a nice hike into the newly established 33,060-acre Fossil Ridge Wilderness Area. Not only is the lake particularly scenic, but the fishing can be good as well.

To reach the beginning of this hike, follow US Highway 50 east from Gunnison to Parlin—a distance of about 12 miles. Turn left and drive northeast to Ohio City. Turn left again and drive 7 miles north on Forest Road 771 to the Gold Creek Campground. The trailhead is north of the road, a short distance beyond the campground.

Following the South Lottis Trail, the hike to Lamphier Lake begins by paralleling Lamphier Creek a short distance from the right bank. Climbing easily at first, the trail passes among aspen stands and timbered areas of Engelmann spruce and subalpine fir. After nearly a mile the route crosses Lamphier Creek and continues along the west bank of the stream. This segment of the hike soon climbs at a more moderate rate as it ascends the drainage bottom. Near the halfway mark the route pulls away from the creek a bit and follows closely along the foot of the drainage's steep west side. This rocky face is actually the eastern end of 12,749-foot Fossil Mountain and Fossil Ridge, which stretches to the west beyond. Consisting of limestone that was formed during the Paleozoic era, Fossil Ridge is true to its name in that it is chock-full of fossils.

Within the last mile to the lake, the South Lottis Trail crosses Lamphier Creek again, climbs a final pitch of moderately steep terrain, and turns west to reach the east shore of Lamphier Lake. Nestled in a glacial basin, the lake is engulfed by 12,985-foot Square Top Mountain to the west and rocky ridges to the north and south. Cut precisely into

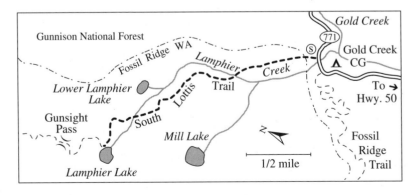

the horizon just north of the lake is 12,167-foot Gunsight Pass. From Lamphier Lake the South Lottis Trail climbs for another mile before topping Gunsight Pass. From there it drops into its namesake drainage before reaching the Lottis Creek Campground on Taylor River Road. From end to end, the South Lottis Trail covers 10 miles along the eastern end of the Fossil Ridge Wilderness.

Established with the passage of the Colorado Wilderness Act of 1993, the Fossil Ridge Wilderness encompasses part of a mountainous area long known to locals for its recreational opportunities. Because the area has been popular among trail-bike enthusiasts as well as hikers, other portions of the Fossil Ridge area have been set aside as a recreation management area. Existing trails in this 43,900-acre tract of land are open to off-road vehicles, but it has been withdrawn from all future mining and timber harvesting activities.

Although water is found along this hike, it must be treated before drinking. Lightning can pose a threat during summer thunderstorms, although this hike never traverses especially exposed terrain. Should you plan to hike on to Gunsight Pass, however, the danger increases greatly.

# 53   SILVER BASIN

**Distance: 13.5 miles round trip**
**Difficulty: Moderate**
**Hiking time: 8 hours**
**Elevation: 8,640 to 10,250 feet**
**Management: Gunnison NF**

**Wilderness status: Raggeds WA**
**Season: July to September**
**USGS maps: Marcellina Mountain,**
    **Anthracite Range**

Rising along the eastern end of the Raggeds Wilderness, the Ruby Mountain Range makes a colorful backdrop for this loop hike, which follows the Silver Basin and Dark Canyon trails.

To reach the beginning of the hike, drive 11.5 miles west from Crested Butte on Kebler Pass Road (County Road 12) to the signed turnoff for Horseranch Park. Drive north on this rough but passable dirt road for 0.3 mile to the trailhead at road's end.

This hike begins by following the south end of the Dark Canyon Trail for 2 miles to its signed intersection with the Silver Basin Trail. Originally a 4WD road, this portion of the Dark Canyon Trail is quite easy to follow as it is well marked and mostly level. Because this trail encounters many nice aspen stands along the way, it is especially scenic in the fall. Nice views of Marcellina Mountain to the west and the Beckwith Peaks to the southwest can be had year-round.

At the Dark Canyon–Silver Basin trail intersection, turn right to follow the Silver Basin Trail as it heads toward the foot of the Ruby Mountains. A short distance beyond this turn the route enters the Raggeds Wilderness Area, and less than 0.3 mile from the junction it reaches a second intersection. A right turn at this point leads south to

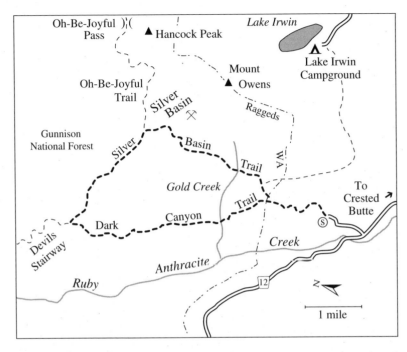

Lake Irwin, but the Silver Basin Trail continues straight ahead and soon begins climbing along a more moderate grade. As the trail gains in elevation, additional views of the West Elk Wilderness to the south open up, as do vistas of the Ruby Range directly east. From this proximity it is easy to see how these mountains got their name. Characterized by shades of deep red, the Ruby Range is composed of the same Maroon Formation that gives the Maroon Bells their distinctive color.

In the first 2 miles following the turnoff from the Dark Canyon Trail, the Silver Basin Trail climbs a total of 1,200 feet to reach this hike's high point of 10,250 feet. In this segment the route crosses two forks of Gold Creek that flow west from Gold Basin. It then reaches Silver Basin itself. Graced by numerous species of wildflowers, Silver Basin is made all the more scenic by the up-close views it affords of the Ruby Range directly east. The highest of these peaks is 13,058-foot Mount Owens, but several other summits in the range easily top the 12,000-foot mark. Of course, other portions of the Raggeds Wilderness are visible from Silver Basin as well. Of particular interest is the deep canyon to the west through which Anthracite Creek flows. Adding a historical footnote to the hike are the many tailings piles scattered about the surrounding mountain slopes. Silver Basin witnessed a fair amount of mining activity during the late 1800s.

Continuing north through the basin along a mostly level grade, the Silver Basin Trail eventually meets the west end of the Oh-Be-Joyful Trail about 5 miles from the start of the hike. Climbing moderate to strenuous grades, this side route continues for nearly 3 miles before reaching 11,740-foot Oh-Be-Joyful Pass. Continuing east from the pass, the Oh-Be-Joyful Trail then crosses into a 5,500-acre tract of land that was added to the Raggeds Wilderness with the passage of the 1993 Colorado Wilderness Act. Just beyond the Silver Basin–Oh-Be-Joyful trail junction, the Silver Basin Trail descends 1,750 feet in 2.3 miles before reconnecting with the Dark Canyon Trail. By turning right at this junction you can follow the Dark Canyon Trail north for 12.5 miles to reach a trailhead near the Erickson Springs Camp-

*Hikers take in a view of the Ruby Range along the Dark Canyon Trail.*

ground, just west of the wilderness. Along the way the Dark Canyon Trail descends the Devils Stairway—a drop of 1,200 feet in 0.75 mile. This hike turns left at the junction, however, and continues south for 6.5 miles to return to the Horseranch Park trailhead. Because this final section of the hike climbs from an elevation of 8,640 feet to 9,400 feet over a distance of about 6 miles, the grades are mostly easy.

Although water is found along much of this hike, you must treat it before drinking. Watch for lightning, especially during the afternoon thunderstorms that frequent this high country in the summer.

# 54 BECKWITH PASS

**Distance: 5 miles round trip**
**Difficulty: Easy**
**Hiking time: 3 hours**
**Elevation: 9,640 to 9,970 feet**

**Management: Gunnison NF**
**Wilderness status: West Elk WA**
**Season: June to October**
**USGS map: Anthracite Range**

While the West Elk Wilderness is the stuff that memorable multiday hikes are made of, this nice little day hike accesses a great view of this extensive wilderness as it climbs from the Lost Lake Campground to 9,970-foot Beckwith Pass.

To reach the start of this hike, drive 15 miles west from Crested Butte on Kebler Pass Road to the turnoff for Lost Lake (Forest Road 706), then drive 2 miles south to the trailhead, which is located at the northeast end of the Lost Lake Campground.

From the trailhead, the Beckwith Pass Trail heads east as it alternates between spruce and fir forests, aspen stands, and open meadows. While the route gains about 300 feet along its entire 2.5-mile length, the trail actually drops a couple of hundred feet in the first mile. After this low point the trail then climbs along mostly easy grades to gain 500 feet in the remaining 1.5 miles of the hike. As it draws closer to

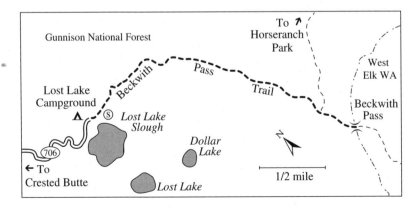

the pass, the trail encounters open parklands and meadows with incredible views of nearby 12,432-foot East Beckwith Mountain. To the north, the Ruby Range rises along the eastern end of the Raggeds Wilderness. Just shy of the pass, the Beckwith Pass Trail intersects a side route that drops to the vicinity of Horseranch Park on Kebler Pass Road.

Upon reaching Beckwith Pass, the trail crosses through a gate to enter the West Elk Wilderness beyond. It then descends into the head of Cliff Creek. While the pass serves as the turnaround point for this hike, it is possible to continue south along the Beckwith Pass Trail for another 8 miles to its junction with the Castle Pass Trail. About 1.5 miles south of Beckwith Pass, the Lowline Trail branches left to head southeast over Swampy Pass.

From Beckwith Pass itself you can look deep into the eastern side of the West Elk Range. Included in this panorama is a distant collection of pinnacles known as the Castles. Volcanic in origin, the West Elk Range formed as a broad dome that was covered with volcanic material during a fiery period some 35 million years ago. Known as West Elk Breccia, the dark rock of the West Elk Mountains has since been eroded into interesting formations that are widely scattered about the range. In addition to the unusual geologic features, this wilderness is also home to mule deer, elk, bighorn sheep, and the like.

Lightning is a very real threat along the upper portion of this hike and on Beckwith Pass. Some water is found along the route, but it must be treated before drinking

# SOAP CREEK

**Distance: 15 miles one way**
**Difficulty: Moderate**
**Hiking time: 2 days**
**Elevation: 7,500 to 10,050 feet**
**Management: Gunnison NF**

**Wilderness status: West Elk WA**
**Season: June to October**
**USGS maps: West Beckwith Peak,**
**  Big Soap Park**

At 176,000 acres, the West Elk Wilderness features many 12,000 and 13,000-foot peaks that rise abruptly above its timbered valleys and open grassy parks. Thanks to a 200-mile network of trails, a great variety of hikes are possible throughout most portions of the West Elk Mountains. One such hike traverses the heart of the wilderness, from north to south, by way of the Little Robinson and Soap Creek trails. Despite the fact that portions of this route are quite remote, this hike is surprisingly easy. Because the completion of this hike does require a lengthy shuttle, you may want combine a portion of the route described here with other trails to create a loop that will return you to your car. Two possibilities are mentioned below.

To reach the beginning of this hike, drive 17 miles east from Paonia on Colorado Highway 133 to the turnoff for Kebler Pass Road on the right. Drive 1.6 miles to a right turn marked by a pack outfitter's sign.

Follow this occasionally rough but passable road (known as Coal Creek Road and Forest Road 709) south for 9.9 miles to the Robinson Creek trailhead. Beyond the trailhead the road enters a large parcel of private land.

From the trailhead the Little Robinson Trail contours about 0.75 mile across a hillside covered with Gambel oak, skirting around the private land that encompasses the valley bottom below. Beyond the private holding the trail enters a nice aspen forest. Aspens are in plentiful supply for the next 5 miles of this hike. About 1 mile from the trailhead, the Little Robinson Trail reaches the first of several trail junctions. While the Kaufman Creek Trail turns right to eventually climb Kaufman Ridge to the south, the Little Robinson Trail heads left to continue along the Little Robinson Creek drainage in a southeasterly direction.

Beyond the intersection with the Kaufman Creek Trail, the Little Robinson Trail climbs a total of 2,500 feet in nearly 5 miles to reach the head of the Little Robinson Creek drainage above. About 3 miles from the trail junction the Little Robinson Trail meets the Castle Pass Trail, which heads east to Beckwith Pass (see the Beckwith Pass hike). Less than 0.5 mile farther it reaches the Little Robinson Cow Camp. Serving as backcountry headquarters for various ranches with grazing allotments in this area, the camp includes a fenced pasture for holding

*Aspen trees along the Little Robinson Trail in the West Elk Mountains*

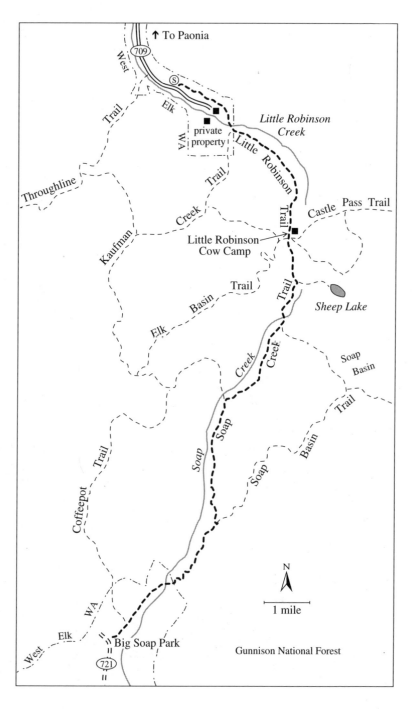

To Paonia

709

West

S

Elk

Trail

WA

private property

Little Robinson Creek

Little Robinson

Throughline

Kaufman

Creek

Trail

Trail

Castle Pass Trail

Little Robinson Cow Camp

Trail

Sheep Lake

Basin

Trail

Elk

Creek

Creek

Soap Basin

Soap

Soap

Basin Trail

Coffeepot

Trail

Soap

Soap

N

1 mile

WA

West

Elk

Big Soap Park

721

Gunnison National Forest

cattle and a small log cabin. A trail junction here accesses the Elk Basin Trail, which heads west to connect with the Kaufman Creek Trail.

Continuing south from the cow camp, the Little Robinson Trail covers another mile before reaching the top of a ridge that separates the Little Robinson Creek drainage from the Soap Creek drainage beyond. Although the Little Robinson Trail climbs some moderately steep stretches in this last mile, it is still not an overly difficult route to hike, even with a backpack. The highest portion of this trail affords some nice views of West Beckwith and East Beckwith mountains to the north and Kaufman Ridge to the west.

Shortly after crossing into the head of the Soap Creek drainage, the route passes through an old log fence, where it then takes up the Soap Creek Trail. Just past the fence a little-used trail heads left to continue 1 mile before reaching Sheep Lake. Along the first mile of the Soap Creek Trail, the route drops gently along a large park that follows the uppermost reaches of Soap Creek. Nice views from this section of the route face east, where 13,035-foot West Elk Peak rises on the skyline, and south, into the Soap Creek drainage. Some suitable camping areas may be found among the trees that line these meadows. While forests in this area consist solely of spruce and fir, more aspen glades are found downstream a bit. About 1 mile from the fence, the Soap Creek Trail crosses its namesake in the vicinity of several beaver dams, then continues downstream along the creek. Just beyond this stream crossing the Soap Creek Trail connects with the upper end of the 7-mile Soap Basin Trail, which heads east for a bit to reach Soap Basin, a large basin that opens up along the base of West Elk Peak. The Soap Basin Trail then heads south to eventually join back up with the Soap Creek Trail. In so doing it provides a nice loop hike possibility, should you be unable to arrange for a shuttle to pick you up at the south end the Soap Creek Trail.

Beyond the turnoff for the Soap Basin Trail, the Soap Creek Trail continues southward, staying close to the creek for the next 3 miles or so. About 2 miles south of the Soap Basin–Soap Creek trail junction is an additional junction from which the south end of the Kaufman Creek Trail takes off. If you choose, you could return to the Robinson Creek trailhead by following the 8-mile Kaufman Creek Trail north to its junction with the Little Robinson Trail. In so doing you would complete a nice 17-mile round-trip hike.

About 3 miles from the Soap Creek–Soap Basin trail junction, the Soap Creek Trail begins to contour along the east slope of the drainage to avoid a rough and narrow corridor along the creek below. After 2 miles, the trail reaches a level that is about 500 feet above the creek bottom. Encountering the south end of the Soap Basin Trail at this point, the Soap Creek Trail then descends sharply back into the drainage bottom by way of a series of switchbacks. Once it reaches the drainage bottom, the Soap Creek Trail continues downstream for another 3 miles to a trailhead at Big Soap Park. Within the last mile, the route also intersects the south end of the Coffeepot Trail. This trailhead is accessed by the 4WD Soap Creek Road (Forest Road 721), which begins north of the Blue Mesa Reservoir dam.

Water found along this hike must be treated before drinking. Watch for lightning in the higher elevations. While only a handful of hikers visit this portion of the West Elk Wilderness, the area does receive heavy use during the fall hunting season.

# 56 CRAG CREST

**Distance: 10 miles round trip**
**Difficulty: Moderate**
**Hiking time: 7 hours**
**Elevation: 10,152 to 11,189 feet**

**Management: Grand Mesa NF**
**Wilderness status: None**
**Season: July to September**
**USGS map: Grand Mesa**

One of the largest flat-topped mountains in the world, Grand Mesa offers a great opportunity to both learn about the complex geology of Colorado and enjoy some truly unique scenery. The premier hiking trail on Grand Mesa is the Crag Crest National Recreation Trail, which loops for 10 miles over one of the high points along the mesa top. From this memorable route, hikers can enjoy sweeping panoramas of surrounding mountain ranges and relish the quiet solitude of pristine forestlands as well.

To reach the beginning of this hike, drive 17 miles east from Grand Junction on Interstate 70 to the turnoff for Colorado Highway 65—a paved route that climbs up and over Grand Mesa. Continue south on Colorado Highway 65 for 34.5 miles to Forest Road 121. Turn left and follow this paved route for 2.5 miles to where it splits. Bear left and drive another 0.9 mile to the trailhead for the Crag Crest Trail. Parking is available on the right side of the road; the trail begins on the left.

From the trailhead the Crag Crest Trail climbs slightly before reaching a junction less than 0.25 mile north. At this intersection continue straight ahead on the middle trail. The route to the left is the trail you will be returning on, while the right-hand trail is a short side route that is unrelated to this hike. Beyond this junction the route continues to climb at an easy pace through some nice forests of Engelmann spruce and subalpine fir. This combination is found all along the hike, although a few aspen trees are scattered among the steeper slopes above. After 0.75 mile the route levels off as it passes Upper Eagleston Lake, and at about 1.25 miles out the route encounters Bullfinch Reservoir No. 1 and the signed turnoff for Butts Lake. Nearly a mile in length, Butts Lake is plainly visible from the crest above. After passing these two lakes, the Crag Crest Trail begins to climb again, but this time along a more moderate grade. As it ascends it draws closer to the rocky ridgeline of Crag Crest itself. The route climbs through several short switchbacks and crosses a few boulder fields before it finally reaches the top. In this first 2 miles of the hike, the Crag Crest Trail climbs about 900 feet.

Upon reaching the top, the Crag Crest Trail follows its namesake westward for 3 miles or so. As it does, the geology of Grand Mesa reveals itself quite plainly. Capped by a 200- to 600-foot-thick layer of dark basaltic rock that originated from volcanic fissures some 10 million years ago, the layers of sedimentary rock that underlay Grand Mesa were spared a more rapid rate of erosion than might normally have occurred. When these softer underlayers did erode away along the edge of the mesa, parts of the basalt top subsequently dropped, often along a curved slip face. These chunks of caprock, in turn, tilted inward toward the center of the mesa. Eventually filling with water, these basins today form a string of elongated lakes along the base of Crag Crest. Other forces have been at work in the shaping of Grand Mesa as well. The entire mesa was uplifted over the last 10 million years to its present height. And, over the last 100,000 years, intermittent glaciers have scoured the mesa's surface, leaving behind still more lakes, moraines, and such.

Geology lessons aside, Crag Crest is an interesting landform to hike along as the trail follows the summit of the crest the entire way. In some places the trail is barely 4 feet wide, with sheer drop-offs on either side. Of course, the views from this high route are spectacular. Included in the panorama are the Raggeds and West Elk wilderness areas to the east and southeast, the entire western half of the San Juan Mountains far to the south, Battlement Mesa and the Roan Cliffs to the north, the Uncompahgre Plateau to the west, and, visible on an especially clear day, Utah's La Sal Mountains even farther west. Add to these faraway landmarks the mesa's high point—11,234-foot Leon Peak, which rises to the east—and you have vistas worth writing home about.

After following the narrow spine of Crag Crest, the trail eventually reaches the gentler western end of the landform. Here the route passes among a quiet spruce and fir forest before dropping off to the south. Before doing so, however, it intersects with a trail that leads north to the Cottonwood Lakes. After turning left at this trail junction, continue for a mile to the next intersection, which is well signed. While a right turn at this point leads 0.5 mile to the west trailhead for the Crag Crest Trail, the route to the left returns you to your car at the east

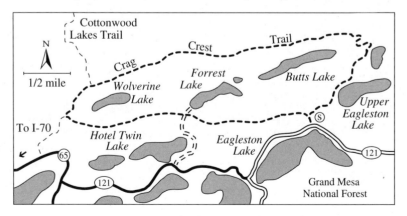

trailhead via the 3.5-mile return portion of the Crag Crest Trail. Along this last leg of the hike expect to find more spruce and fir forests, along with some open meadows. You also encounter some short climbs and drops along the way, but nothing too dramatic. Near the halfway mark of this last segment of the hike is an unsigned intersection that may cause some confusion. The trail running south to north accesses nearby Forrest Lake, but you must continue straight ahead (east) to complete this loop trip.

Bring a good supply of water as none is available along most of this hike. Be wary of lightning along the exposed upper portion of this trail, and use plenty of caution near dangerous drop-offs. This is an extremely popular hike, so you may want to plan accordingly.

*The Crag Crest Trail follows the summit of its namesake.*

# 57 WEST SPANISH PEAK

**Distance: 5 miles round trip**
**Difficulty: Strenuous**
**Hiking time: 4 hours**
**Elevation: 11,005 to 13,626 feet**
**Management: San Isabel NF**

**Wilderness status: Spanish**
   **Peaks WSA**
**Season: July to September**
**USGS maps: Cucharas Pass,**
   **Spanish Peaks, Herlick Canyon**

Standing as true sentinels along the southeast edge of Colorado's mountain province, the Spanish Peaks have long served as important landmarks for all who pass within sight of them. The Indians called them Huajatolla, or "Breasts of the World." Early Spanish explorers used them as easily identifiable landmarks on their conquest's northern frontier. And today they provide modern-day motorists along Interstate 25 with one of the most stunning vistas in the state. Anyone who has driven by these sharply rising mountains and envisioned standing on the summit may be shocked to know that the taller of the two peaks, 13,626-foot West Spanish Peak, is accessible via a short hike.

From Walsenburg, drive west on US Highway 160 for about 11 miles to the turnoff for Colorado Highway 12. Drive south 5 miles to La Veta and then another 17.5 miles to Cucharas Pass. Turn left onto Forest Road 415 and drive 6 miles on this passable gravel road to 11,005-foot Cordova Pass (formerly known as Apishapa Pass). The trail begins on the north side of the pass.

From the start, the West Peak Trail heads northeast along a broad and gentle ridge for about 2 miles. Along this first section of the hike grades are easy to nonexistent. Within this segment, the route encounters a variety of environments—forests of Engelmann spruce, corkbark fir, and limber pine; stands of aspen trees; and natural meadows. These open areas offer an exciting view of West Spanish Peak, which

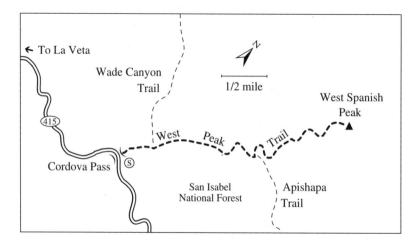

rises suddenly to the east. About 0.25 mile from the trailhead, the West Peak Trail intersects the Wade Canyon Trail, which descends to the north. Seldom used, this side route is easy to miss. At the 1.5-mile mark, the West Peak Trail intersects the upper end of the Apishapa Trail, which heads south for 4 miles before reaching Forest Road 416 south of Cordova Pass. Beyond this second junction the West Peak Trail climbs along a series of switchbacks through what remains of the forest. Among this final stand of trees you may note the bleached trunks of bristlecone pines. This close to timberline, these trees are especially picturesque.

After climbing easy to moderate grades for less than 0.5 mile from the junction with the Apishapa Trail, the West Peak Trail reaches timberline and the real start of the climb. Towering before you at this point is the bare summit of West Spanish Peak. Because this route ascends a total of 2,000 feet in about 0.5 mile, the task of climbing to the summit might seem rather daunting. Well, the climb is strenuous all the way to the top, but the going is actually not too bad. Although no official route leads to the summit, several bootleg trails do lace their way up the peak's southwestern ridgeline. And, while the steep sides of this mountain are rocky, these rocks do not easily give way when stepped upon. Add to these pluses the fact that the scenery is tremendous all along the hike and the possibility that you might see some bighorn sheep skirting about the slopes, and you will find yourself on top in no time.

Upon reaching the top, you are treated to an incredible 360-degree view. Rising just east is East Spanish Peak, which, at 12,683 feet, is nearly 1,000 feet lower than West Spanish Peak. Beyond it stretch the Great Plains. Although these prairie lands appear to be featureless, you may be able pick out canyons, washes, and mesas. To the north is the Cucharas River Valley, and beyond it 12,349-foot Greenhorn Mountain. To the northwest is La Veta Pass and then 14,345-foot Blanca Peak, which marks the southern end of the Sangre de Cristo Wilderness Area. Continuing southward into New Mexico, the Sangre de Cristo Mountains themselves can also be seen a few miles to the west, just beyond the Cucharas Pass area. Included in this portion of the range is 14,047-foot Culebra Peak, which can be seen to the southwest. And looking southward you can see the forested upper reaches of the Purgatoire River.

Scattered all across the lower lands that surround the Spanish Peaks are dozens of volcanic dikes, which appear as vertical curtains of rock protruding from the surrounding terrain. A geologic anomaly, these impressive formations were developed as lava-filled fissures in sedimentary rock during the Tertiary period. The source of this lava was the Spanish Peaks themselves, which formed as massive intrusions of molten rock, or stocks. While the Spanish Peaks are quite impressive even today, it is believed that they once stood much higher. Given the unusual quantity of these volcanic dikes, the geologic scenario that the Spanish Peaks portray is indeed one for the textbooks.

Bring water as none is found along this route. Because lightning is a very real threat on this exposed peak, you should plan your hike for the early-morning hours, especially during the summer. Use caution when descending from the summit.

# 58 BARTLETT TRAIL

**Distance: 11 miles round trip**
**Difficulty: Moderate**
**Hiking time: 7 hours**
**Elevation: 7,720 to 11,660 feet**
**Management: San Isabel NF**

**Wilderness status: Greenhorn**
**Mountain WA**
**Season: June to October**
**USGS maps: Rye, San Isabel**

Established with the passage of the Colorado Wilderness Act of 1993, the 22,040-acre Greenhorn Mountain Wilderness Area encompasses the high point of the Wet Mountains—12,347-foot Greenhorn Mountain. Within this wilderness are a number of trails that climb steeply from the base of the mountain to the summit. One of these is the 5.5-mile-long Bartlett Trail, which ascends some 4,000 feet up its eastern face.

To reach the beginning of this hike, drive south from Pueblo on Interstate 25 to the exit for Colorado Highway 165 and the town of Rye. Drive 8 miles west to Rye and turn left in the center of town. Continue south for about 2 miles to where Forest Road 427 turns right. Follow this road for nearly 3 miles to its end at the national forest boundary. The Bartlett Trail begins here.

From the trailhead, the Bartlett Trail heads west along a drainage bottom for a short distance before climbing southwest to cross into the North Apache Creek drainage, which is directly south. Within this first

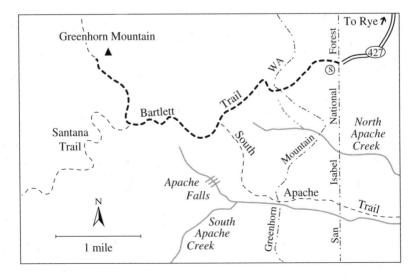

*A ponderosa pine frames a scene in the newly established Greenhorn Mountain Wilderness.*

2 miles the trail climbs mostly moderate grades over terrain that can be hot and dry during the summer months. Vegetation in this area includes Gambel oaks, along with scattered pinyon and ponderosa pines. After crossing two different forks of North Apache Creek (these streams are not always flowing), the Bartlett Trail eventually reaches a high ridge. Up to this point the route has provided some expansive views of the plains to the east. Upon crossing into the next drainage, however, vistas instead extend southward down the South Apache Creek drainage and beyond to the Spanish Peaks. At this elevation the dominant species of trees include ponderosa pine and Douglas fir. Shortly beyond the ridge top, the Bartlett Trail encounters the upper end of the 3-mile-long South Apache Trail. Unfortunately, the trailhead for this route is on private land and closed to the public. The trail does feature a 0.5-mile side route to beautiful Apache Falls, and South Apache Creek is home to a threatened species of fish known as the greenback cutthroat trout.

Beyond its intersection with the South Apache Trail, the Bartlett Trail continues climbing west across the upper reaches of the South Apache Creek drainage. Along this segment of the route you can expect to climb some strenuously steep grades, in addition to more moderate ones. As the route nears the 5-mile mark, it intersects the upper end of the Santana Trail, which branches left. Six miles long, this difficult route climbs a total of 3,400 feet along the west side of the wilderness. Within a mile of the Santana Trail junction, the Bartlett Trail reaches the end of an old road that follows the crest of the range. Now closed to vehicles, the last 0.5 mile of this road is included in the Greenhorn Mountain Wilderness. Reaching above timberline, the summit of Greenhorn Mountain is less than a mile north of this point.

Little or no water is found along this trail, so be sure to pack plenty before setting out. Watch for lightning along the higher reaches of this trail.

# 59 RAINBOW TRAIL

**Distance: 29.7 miles one way**
**Difficulty: Moderate**
**Hiking time: 4 days**
**Elevation: 8,546 to 9,700 feet**
**Management: San Isabel NF**

**Wilderness status: None**
**Season: June to October**
**USGS maps: Poncha Pass,**
**   Wellsville, Howard, Coaldale**

Forming a sweeping, 100-mile-long arc along the northern and eastern slopes of the Sangre de Cristo Mountains, the Rainbow Trail offers a truly great opportunity to enjoy an extended backpacking trip in beautiful mountain terrain. The description below covers a 30-mile segment of the route stretching from US Highway 285 to the Hayden Creek Campground.

To reach the beginning of this hike, drive 5.3 miles south of Poncha Springs on US Highway 285 to the trailhead. To reach the end of this hike, at Hayden Creek Campground, drive 20 miles southeast of Salida on US Highway 50 to Coaldale. Turn right onto County Road 6 and continue for about 5 miles to the campground. If you do not have time to complete the entire route, you may want to begin or end at the Bear Creek trailhead, which is near the halfway point between US Highway 285 and Hayden Creek. To reach the Bear Creek trailhead, drive 3 miles southeast from Salida on US Highway 50 to Forest Road 101 (also known as Bear Creek Road). Turn right and follow this route for 5 miles to its end. The last few miles of this road require a high-clearance vehicle.

Actually an old route that settlers used to access mountain lands as far back as 1912, today the Rainbow Trail is open to mountain bikes and trail motorcycles (ATVs and all other vehicles 40 inches or greater in width are prohibited). When the Sangre de Cristo Wilderness Area was established in 1993, its eastern boundary was drawn to exclude the Rainbow Trail so that the route would remain multiple-use. While motorcycles do temporarily impact one's chances of finding solitude along this hike, conflicts between cyclists and hikers are rare.

From US Highway 285, the Rainbow Trail heads due east up a small drainage for about a mile, after which it turns north to continue climbing. After 2 miles, the trail levels off to contour along at an elevation of 9,500 feet—about 1,000 feet higher than the trailhead. While ponderosa pines are common near the trailhead, Douglas firs, Engelmann

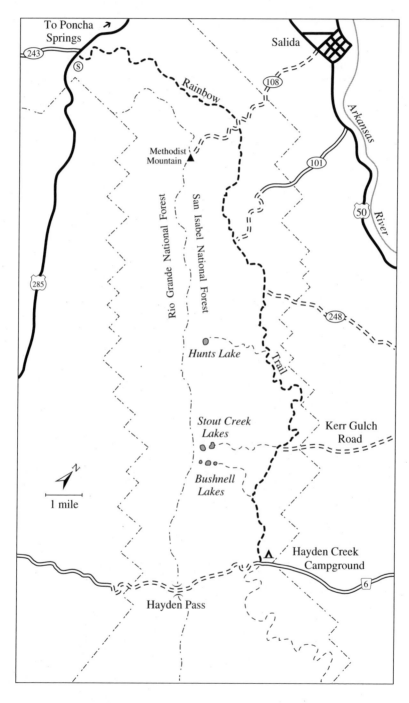

spruce, and aspens become more prevalent as the route gains altitude. For the next 2.5 miles the route dips in and out of the heads of some small drainages until it reaches the upper end of Sand Gulch. The trail then drops along the Sand Gulch drainage for the next mile before continuing east to King Gulch. After crossing King Gulch the Rainbow Trail covers another 2 miles before it intersects the 4WD Methodist Mountain Road (Forest Road 108), which accesses the 11,707-foot summit of nearby Methodist Mountain. Up to this point the Rainbow Trail is not too difficult to follow as the grade changes are easy to moderate and the trail itself is well maintained. Additionally, the scenery along this portion of the hike takes in both the Arkansas Valley to the north and the Collegiate Range, with its plethora of 14,000-foot peaks, to the northwest.

After meeting the Methodist Mountain Road, the Rainbow Trail follows the road uphill for a short distance before turning off to continue in a southwesterly direction. Maintaining a generally level elevation, the trail crosses Silverheel and Columbine gulches before reaching Rock Creek about 3 miles beyond Methodist Mountain Road. In another mile the route crosses Bear Creek—the first reliable source of water along the hike. A mile farther the Rainbow Trail reaches the Bear Creek trailhead, 12.5 miles from the start of this hike and 17.2 miles from the end.

South of the Bear Creek trailhead, the Rainbow Trail climbs from an elevation of about 8,900 feet to 9,700 feet in the next mile. It then drops back down to about the 9,000-foot level, where it crosses two secondary forks of Howard Creek. Keep in mind that the trail crosses private land in the vicinity of these crossings. From Howard Creek the route continues southeast for another 2 miles or so before reaching a 3-mile-long side trail that climbs to Hunts Lake. Because this route enters the Sangre de Cristo Wilderness, it is closed to all vehicles. Past this trail junction, the Rainbow Trail climbs for a short distance before dropping some 500 feet into the West Creek drainage. From this point the route continues along at an elevation between 8,500 and 8,600 feet for the next 4 miles before reaching Stout Creek, where the Kerr Gulch Road provides vehicle access to the trail. Branching right from the Rainbow Trail a short distance beyond this trailhead is a wilderness route that follows Stout Creek upstream for 4 miles to the Stout Creek Lakes. Nearly 3 miles from that junction is another intersection with the Bushnell Lakes Trail. Like Stout Creek Lakes and Hunts Lake, the Bushnell Lakes are nestled among scenic glacial basins situated near the crest of the mountains above.

Between Stout Creek and the turnoff for Bushnell Lakes, the Rainbow Trail climbs nearly 1,000 feet in 2 miles to reach an elevation of 9,400 feet. Beyond this point the route descends 1,600 feet—mostly along North Prong Creek—in 2.5 miles to reach the Hayden Creek Campground. While the Hayden Creek Campground marks the end of this hike, the Rainbow Trail continues southwest for another 53 miles before reaching its southern terminus near Music Pass.

Water is not always available along the first 12 miles of this hike. Where water is found, be sure to treat it before drinking. Lightning can occasionally pose a threat along portions of the Rainbow Trail. Because this is a multiple-use trail, hikers must share the route with horseback riders, mountain bikers, and trail motorcyclists.

# 60 NORTH CRESTONE LAKE

**Distance: 12 miles round trip**
**Difficulty: Moderate**
**Hiking time: 7 hours**
**Elevation: 8,800 to 11,840 feet**
**Management: Rio Grande NF**

**Wilderness status: Sangre de Cristo WA**
**Season: July to September**
**USGS maps: Rito Alto Peak, Horn Peak**

Forming a 70-mile-long crest of 13,000 and 14,000-foot peaks, the Sangre de Cristo Range encompasses some truly extraordinary mountain terrain. Nestled in glacial valleys on the steep western slopes of the range are numerous alpine lakes, most of which are accessible via established trails. North Crestone Lake, which is situated at the head of the Lake Fork of Crestone Creek, makes for a memorable day hike or overnight excursion.

Drive 18 miles southeast from Saguache to the small town of Moffat, and then another 12 miles east to Crestone, located on the eastern edge of the San Luis Valley, at the base of the Sangre de Cristo Range.

*The Sangre de Cristo Mountains near North Crestone Lake*

From Crestone, drive a little over 2 miles north on Forest Road 950 to the North Crestone Creek Campground.

From the North Crestone Creek Campground, the North Crestone Trail begins by following its namesake creek northeast for a little over 2 miles to where the Lake Fork branches right. Climbing along easy to moderate grades, this first segment of the hike gains about 1,000 feet. Within a mile of the North Crestone Creek–Lake Fork junction the trail switchbacks up the north slope of the drainage to reach a level that is 200 feet or so above the creek bottom. The route meets the lower ends of the North Fork Crestone and Loop trails, which branch to the left. These two routes climb toward the crest of the range, where two additional trails make a connection to form a loop over Venable Pass and Phantom Terrace.

After keeping right at this junction, the North Crestone Trail continues climbing for nearly 4 miles before reaching North Crestone Lake, one of the largest lakes in the Sangre de Cristo Range. Although it maintains a moderate grade for most of the way, the trail does make a strenuous 600-foot climb up a steep headwall just below the lake itself. Along the Lake Fork of North Crestone Creek are some nice fishing holes, along with beautiful little waterfalls. While the first half of this trail encounters expansive stands of aspen, its upper end climbs beyond the normal elevational range of the tree and instead passes through spruce and fir forests. North Crestone Lake is surrounded by several high peaks, including 13,931-foot Mount Adams directly south and 13,554-foot Fluted Peak to the northeast.

Used liberally in this part of the Sangre de Cristo Range, the name Crestone, which is Spanish for "Cock's Comb," alludes to the inherent ruggedness of these mountains and testifies to the early influence that Spanish explorers had on the area. The name Sangre de Cristo, which translates to "Blood of Christ," is thought to have been assigned to the mountain range in 1647 when a group of conquistadors camped near San Luis Lake looked up to see the peaks bathed in the brilliant

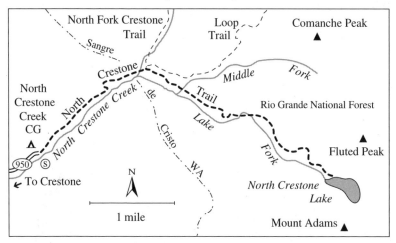

159

vermilion light of sunset. Interestingly, the remains of stone fortresses built by the early Spaniards have been found near 14,197-foot Crestone Needle, which is a few miles down-range from North Crestone Lake. And an American expedition during the 1850s found a skeleton dressed in Spanish armor stashed away in a cave.

Water is found along most of this hike, but it must be treated before drinking. Although not a persistent threat, lighting strikes are possible on the higher reaches of this hike. Forest Service regulations prohibit camping within 300 feet of North Crestone Lake.

# 61 GREAT SAND DUNES

**Distance: 3 miles round trip**
**Difficulty: Moderate**
**Hiking time: 2 hours**
**Elevation: 8,050 to 8,690 feet**
**Management: Great Sand Dunes NM**

**Wilderness status: Great Sand**
    **Dunes WA**
**Season: Year-round**
**USGS map: Zapata Ranch**

Great Sand Dunes National Monument encompasses a 39-square-mile area of sandy dunes on the eastern end of the San Luis Valley. Towering nearly 700 feet above the valley floor, these swells of sand are considered the tallest dunes in North America. For hikers of all ages, the Great Sand Dunes offer an enormous sandbox in which to explore. Because these sands are constantly shifting, no actual trails exist within the dunes. There is, however, a 1.5-mile route that climbs to what is probably the highest point in the dunes.

To reach Great Sand Dunes National Monument, drive 14 miles east from Alamosa on US Highway 160. Turn left onto Colorado Highway 150 and drive 19 miles north before reaching the visitor center. This hike begins at the Dunes parking area, which is about 1 mile north of the visitor center.

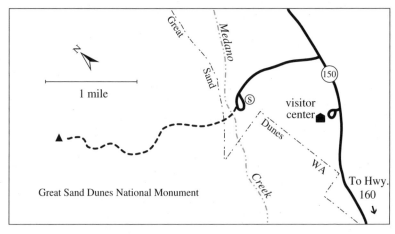

*Grass growing among the dunes of Great Sand Dunes National Monument*

From the parking area, cross Medano Creek to reach the foot of the dunes in about 0.5 mile. From here you can pick any of the dune crests, which ascend to the 8,690-foot summit of what appears to be the tallest dune in the monument. In the last mile to the top, the route climbs 690 feet along moderate to strenuous grades. Hikers should keep in mind that walking in soft sand is somewhat difficult and tiring. Of course, the return trip to the trailhead can be a matter of free-form bounding down the faces of the dunes. Some visitors have even taken to skiing the fall lines that the dunes provide.

Upon leaving the line of cottonwoods just north of the picnic area, this hike enters an environment that is unique in a number of respects. The first of the area's unusual features to be encountered is Medano Creek, which, in essence, dictates the dunes' eastern and southern boundaries by constantly eating away at the encroaching sands. Surfacing in the spring or after a summer rain, Medano Creek normally flows beneath the surface through the porous sand. Geologically speaking, the dunes were formed when sands being blown across the expansive San Luis Valley were deposited at the foot of a low saddle in the Sangre de Cristo Mountains. This saddle effectively funnels the prevailing winds up and over the range. While the sands continue to be blown by the wind, the main dunes are established enough to warrant representation on topographic maps. This is in part due to the sand's 7-percent moisture content.

Beyond Medano Creek the loose sands support scattered tufts of Indian ricegrass, blowout grass, a plant known as the scurfpea, and prairie

161

sunflowers. Reaching a surface temperature of 140 degrees and holding little moisture, these shifting sands constitute an extremely harsh environment—not just for plants, but for animals as well. Although an occasional deer, coyote, or other animal may wander a short way into the dunes, the only mammal that successfully inhabits them is the kangaroo rat. The dunes are also home to two species of insect that are found nowhere else on earth—the Great Sand Dunes tiger beetle and a species of circus beetle.

Water is not available along this hike, so bring plenty. While it is perfectly acceptable to walk barefoot, bring your shoes in case the sands become unbearably hot. Do not enter the dunes during electrical storms as lightning strikes the area with great frequency.

# 62 PENITENTE CANYON

| | |
|---|---|
| **Distance: 3 miles round trip** | **Management: BLM** |
| **Difficulty: Easy** | **Wilderness status: None** |
| **Hiking time: 2 hours** | **Season: Year-round** |
| **Elevation: 8,000 to 8,450 feet** | **USGS map: Twin Mountains SE** |

Since its discovery by rock climbers in 1985, Penitente Canyon has been visited by technical scramblers from as far away as Europe, Africa, and South America. Although relatively shallow, Penitente Canyon is enclosed by sheer cliff faces nearly 100 feet tall. Other places, such as the area above the canyon's rim to the west, feature unusual rock formations and outcrops. For hikers, a short and easy trail links both areas to create an interesting excursion.

To find Penitente Canyon, drive north from Del Norte on Colorado Highway 112 for 3.1 miles to the turnoff for County Road 33. Turn north and follow this good gravel road 9.5 miles to the signed left turn

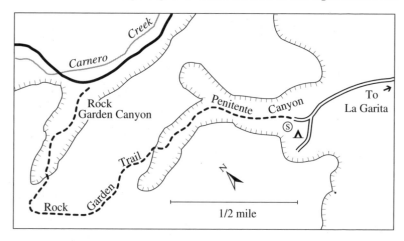

*A religious painting on the wall of Penitente Canyon*

for Penitente Canyon. Drive 1 mile west to where the road forks in the developed camping area. Bear right and drive a short distance farther to the trailhead. Penitente Canyon can also be reached from the small village of La Garita, which is a couple of miles east of the canyon.

From the trailhead the trail follows the canyon bottom northwest for 0.3 mile to where the canyon forks. While traveling along this first section of the hike you can see a beautiful image of the Virgin Mary painted about 40 feet above on a canyon wall. This religious image attests to the canyon's longtime use as a place of worship by a little-known sect of the Catholic religion known as the Brothers Penitente. Founded during the early nineteenth century, the Penitente movement began when Spanish settlers in the Southwest were isolated from the Catholic Church in Europe.

Upon reaching the fork in the canyon, turn left to follow the sign that points west to the Rock Garden Trail. A short distance up this side canyon the route begins climbing to the north, following rock cairns as it does. A bit of scrambling is required, but none of it is very difficult. Upon reaching the canyon's rim you get a nice look back into Penitente Canyon. Gazing out across the higher terrain to the west, you begin to see different species of trees growing in the area. Ponderosa pines and Douglas firs are most evident, but junipers and pinyon pines are plentiful as well. In addition, several aspens can be found growing in protected places.

Once the trail climbs out of the canyon it heads northwest across an area that features numerous outcrops of volcanic rock that have been eroded into well-rounded shapes. This volcanic material originated in the San Juan Mountains to the west. The trail is not well established here, so you follow the rock cairns, which are located at sporadic intervals. Less than 0.5 mile from where the route climbs out of Penitente Canyon, it turns east to drop into Rock Garden Canyon, the next canyon north. Descending about 75 feet in all, the trail follows this canyon a short distance east to the canyon's mouth and a rural road that follows Carnero Creek west. The mouth of Rock Garden Canyon marks the turnaround point for this hike.

There is no water in or near Penitente Canyon, so bring a quart or two. Lightning can occasionally pose a danger during afternoon thunderstorms.

# 63 WHEELER GEOLOGIC AREA

**Distance: 15 miles round trip**
**Difficulty: Moderate**
**Hiking time: 8 hours**
**Elevation: 10,800 to 11,800 feet**
**Management: Rio Grande NF**

**Wilderness status: La Garita WA**
**Season: July to September**
**USGS maps: Pool Table Mountain,**
 **Wagon Wheel Gap, Halfmoon**
 **Pass**

Certainly one of Colorado's more unusual geologic formations, the Wheeler Geologic Area is also one of its most remote natural features. Volcanic in origin, the white tuff of the area has eroded into a variety of hoodoos, pinnacles, and canyons. So unusual are these formations that they captured the interest of the then chief of the U.S. Forest Service, Gifford Pinchot, and his boss, Teddy Roosevelt, who made the Wheeler formations the centerpiece of a 300-acre national monument in 1908. Due to lack of access, however, the area was redesignated as a geologic area in 1969 and its size was increased to 640 acres. Today a rough and lengthy 4WD road reaches the Wheeler Geologic Area, as do a number of hiking trails. This hike follows the shortest of these trails, the East Bellows Trail. New signs along the route refer to it as the Wheeler Trail.

To reach the beginning of this hike, drive 7.3 miles southeast on Colorado Highway 149 from Creede to Pool Table Road (Forest Road 600). Turn north and continue 9.7 miles along this good gravel road to the signed trailhead at the Hanson's Mill site. All that is left of the old mill is a large pile of sawdust. From Hanson's Mill, Forest Road 600 continues for another 13.7 miles northeast and then west to reach the Wheeler Geologic Area. Meanwhile, the East Bellows Trail heads north and northwest to reach the Wheeler Geologic Area.

From the trailhead, the East Bellows Trail sets out due north in a forest of Engelmann spruce and subalpine fir. In the first 0.5 mile the trail maintains a relatively level grade, but it soon begins to descend easily after it reaches the head of the East Bellows Creek drainage. In the next 1.5 miles the route continues to descend easily until it reaches the creek itself. Portions of this first segment traverse open meadows, and in the last 0.3 mile before reaching the creek the trail parallels a deep canyon, that of East Bellows Creek, which runs a short distance to the west. In the last 100 yards or so the trail drops through a handful of short switchbacks before reaching the creek.

A sizable stream at this point, East Bellows Creek is favored by trout fishermen, and it is home to beavers as well. It may be difficult to cross in the early summer when high waters prevail. Beyond the crossing, the East Bellows Trail continues north into an interesting little canyon known as Cañon Nieve. About 0.5 mile from the crossing the trail turns left up a side canyon to head northwest. Following this drainage for the next 2 miles, the route climbs easily through open

*Unusual tuff formations typify the Wheeler Geologic Area.*

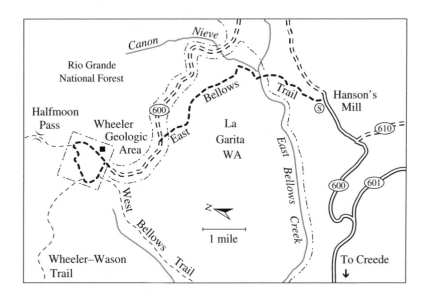

meadows before reaching another patch of spruce and fir. Beyond this forest area the trail enters expansive Silver Park, through which it continues for another mile. Here and in other open areas along the hike, you can gain some rather nice views of the surrounding alpine mesas, and you may spot a few deer or elk in the early-morning hours. Running along the north side of the park is the 4WD road, which accesses the Wheeler area as it snakes in and out of the trees. About 5.5 miles from the trailhead the East Bellows Trail reaches the road, which it then follows for about a mile to the boundary of the geologic area. In this last mile the route drops 350 feet into the head of West Bellows Creek. To the west you can see the rather deep canyon this drainage has carved for itself.

The 4WD road ends at a fence and signboard that mark the boundary of the Wheeler Geologic Area. While this road was "cherry-stemmed" out of the 25,640-acre Wheeler addition to the La Garita Wilderness mandated by the Colorado Wilderness Act of 1993, the geologic Area was added to the wilderness. From the road's end it is about a 0.5 mile walk to the formations. As you approach them, the trail splits at a signed intersection. The right-hand trail continues on to the base of the rocks and then to a small log structure known as the shelter house, beyond which it continues to climb north for another 2 miles or so to reach 12,700-foot Halfmoon Pass. The left-hand trail climbs along the western end of the formations, then circles around the north end to connect with the trail to Halfmoon Pass. This route also intersects the upper end of the 10.7-mile Wheeler–Wason Trail, which begins near Creede, and the slightly shorter West Bellows Trail, which travels north along its namesake creek. This latter route begins on private land below.

No matter which trail you take once you're inside the Wheeler Geologic Area, you will get a close-up view of these stunning rocks. Reminders of the San Juan Mountains' fiery past, these formations evolved after ash and debris blown from volcanic vents settled in the area to form a thick layer of tuff. In the millions of years since, this soft, light-colored rock has been eroded into a seemingly endless variety of shapes and designs. While climbing about the formations is alluring, these pinnacles are fragile and the rock itself is quite crumbly. The Forest Service discourages climbing about the rocks. Should you decide to spend the night at the Wheeler Geologic Area, you can find several suitable camping spots near the end of the road just south of the geologic area.

Water is available in places along this hike, but it must be treated before drinking. Watch for lightning in the higher areas, especially during afternoon thundershowers.

# 64  POWDERHORN LAKES

Distance: 9 miles round trip
Difficulty: Moderate
Hiking time: 4 hours
Elevation: 11,200 to 11,859 feet

Management: BLM
Wilderness status: Powderhorn WA
Season: July to September
USGS map: Powderhorn Lakes

Although the 60,100-acre Powderhorn Wilderness Area is best known for its extensive alpine plateaus, this out-of-the-way wilderness also features some beautiful lakes and prime timbered areas. This hike accesses the heart of this wilderness in relatively short order by following the Powderhorn Lakes Trail to the wilderness area's namesake lakes. Administered by both the BLM and the Gunnison National Forest, the Powderhorn Wilderness Area came into existence with the 1993 Colorado Wilderness Act. For years prior to that, the BLM's portion of the tract was included in the Powderhorn Primitive Area.

To reach the start of the Powderhorn Lakes Trail, drive 9 miles west from Gunnison on US Highway 50 to Colorado Highway 149—the road

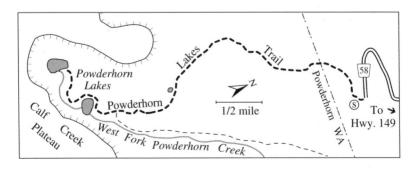

to Lake City. Turn south and drive another 20 miles to Indian Creek Road (County Road 58). Turn south here and drive a little more than 10 miles to the trailhead, which is at road's end. This gravel road is rough in places, but should be passable to most vehicles.

Upon entering a forest of Engelmann spruce and subalpine fir just beyond the trailhead, the Powderhorn Lakes Trail begins climbing easily to gain 600 feet in the next 1.5 miles. Well established, this route is easy to find throughout. At the 1.5-mile mark the trail enters the upper end of a large meadow that features nice views to the southeast. Included in this vista is the eastern portion of the Powderhorn Wilderness as well as several peaks that tower to around 14,000 feet in the La Garita Wilderness beyond. This meadow is a great place to spot deer and elk in the early morning and wildflowers during the midsummer months.

After crossing this meadow, the Powderhorn Lakes Trail follows the western edge of the opening for a short distance before continuing on toward the south through more spruce and fir forest. In the next 1.25 miles the route follows a mostly level grade before dropping into the West Fork of the Powderhorn Creek drainage. Although this descent is small, some short stretches of moderately steep grades must be climbed in both directions. The trail passes a small pond surrounded by timber; this makes a nice place to rest.

Upon reaching the West Fork of the Powderhorn Creek, the Powderhorn Lakes Trail intersects a trail that follows the creek downstream for a little way before crossing over to the Middle Fork of Powderhorn Creek. It eventually reaches Powderhorn Swamp and the Ten Mile Springs trailhead. The Powderhorn Lakes Trail turns right at this junction, however, and continues upstream for 0.5 mile before reaching Lower Powderhorn Lake.

Situated at an elevation of 11,650 feet, Lower Powderhorn Lake sits at the base of basalt-covered Calf Creek Plateau, which rises about 500 feet to the south. While the lake itself is surrounded by trees on three sides, the top of Calf Creek Plateau, like that of nearby Cannibal Plateau, is totally treeless for several miles. These are said to be the largest alpine mesas in the Lower Forty-eight states. From the smaller lower lake it is another 0.5 mile and a climb of 200 feet to Upper Powderhorn Lake, which is surrounded on three sides by cliffs. This cirque resulted in glacial action during the last ice age. Both lakes are quite scenic, and both are considered to have good fishing, especially for cutthroat trout.

Several old trails head out from the Powderhorn Lakes area to access different portions of the surrounding high country. One route provides a high route for returning to the trailhead, while another leads south to Devils Lake. A third route heads southeast to reach Skull Park. While all of these routes would be fun to explore, they are all hard to find due to lack of use. Only hikers who are skilled at orienteering should attempt to follow these routes.

Although water is available along this hike, it should be treated. Watch for lightning in higher areas along this trail. Backpackers should avoid camping on the lakes' shores.

# 65     FOURMILE FALLS

**Distance: 6 miles round trip**
**Difficulty: Easy**
**Hiking time: 4 hours**
**Elevation: 9,050 to 9,800 feet**

**Management: San Juan NF**
**Wilderness status: Weminuche WA**
**Season: June to October**
**USGS map: Pagosa Peak**

Spilling hundreds of feet over a precipice of dark volcanic rock, Fourmile Falls makes an interesting destination in the Weminuche Wilderness north of Pagosa Springs. Accessed by a short and easy hike, this spectacular feature of the rugged San Juan Mountains can be enjoyed by hikers of nearly all ages and abilities.

To reach the beginning of this hike from downtown Pagosa Springs, turn north onto County Road 400 at the Subway food franchise. In 8.4 miles bear right onto Fourmile Road (Forest Road 645), then drive another 4.6 miles to the trailhead, which is at road's end. Two trails head out from the Fourmile trailhead; follow Fourmile Trail, the right-hand route.

Within the first 0.25 mile the Fourmile Trail drops slightly within an old-growth forest of Engelmann spruce and fir before reaching a small creek. After crossing this stream the trail climbs a short distance before crossing into the Weminuche Wilderness. The trail then enters a large meadow through which it continues north for about 0.25 mile. This opening provides a nice view of 12,137-foot Eagle Peak to the northeast. You may also see a few aspens growing along the meadow's edge. After entering the forest again the Fourmile Trail continues for

*In winter Fourmile Falls is reduced to a thin veil of water.*

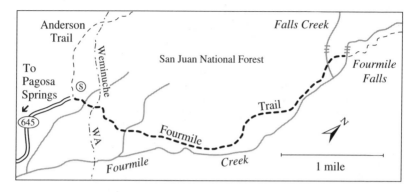

another 0.5 mile before climbing about 400 feet along a mostly easy grade. Upon crossing a second small creek the trail maintains a mostly level grade until it makes one final ascent to the base of Fourmile Falls. In this last climb the trail gains about 300 feet, again over a mostly easy grade.

The higher of the two Fourmile Falls is created by Falls Creek as it drops some 300 feet over a sheer face of dark breccia. Breccia is a conglomerate rock that consists of debris and ash blown from volcanoes many millions of years ago. Forming an imposing wall of cliffs, this rock has obviously proven to be resistant to erosion. A short distance beyond the first waterfall is a second fall, formed where Fourmile Creek drops into the lower portion of the canyon. Although smaller, this second cascade features a higher volume of water.

While this hike turns around at Fourmile Falls, the Fourmile Trail climbs above the falls and continues north for another 3 miles to reach Fourmile Lake. The other trail that begins at the Fourmile trailhead—the relatively new Anderson Trail—reaches Fourmile Lake in 8 miles. If you combine the Anderson Trail with the Fourmile Trail, you can enjoy a 14-mile loop hike along the eastern slopes of 12,640-foot Pagosa Peak.

Water is available along this hike, but it must be treated before drinking.

# 66   FISH LAKE

**Distance: 12 miles round trip**
**Difficulty: Strenuous**
**Hiking time: 8 hours**
**Elevation: 9,040 to 12,050 feet**
**Management: San Juan NF**

**Wilderness status: South San Juan WA**
**Season: July to September**
**USGS maps: Elephant Head Rock, Summit Peak**

On a September day in 1979, an event occurred that took wildlife experts and land managers by complete surprise. On that day a bow hunter killed an attacking grizzly bear with a pocket knife. What was so unusual about this incident was that it took place in the South San Juan Mountains of southwestern Colorado. Grizzlies were thought to have been extinct in the state for dozens of years, so this encounter rekindled hope for many that grizzly bears still lived in Colorado. While researchers have since scoured the South San Juans for signs that this unfortunate sow was not a loner, concrete evidence has yet to be discovered. Nevertheless, many experts do feel there is a good chance that a grizzly bear may eventually be spotted in some remote alpine basin or among the thick forests of the area. If visiting an area where such a legendary creature may still exist sounds intriguing, then the trail to Fish Lake on the western slope of the South San Juan Wilderness is a good place to start.

From Pagosa Springs drive 7 miles south on US Highway 84 to Blanco Basin Road (County Road 326). Turn left and drive 10 miles to Castle Creek Road (Forest Road 660). Turn right and drive 7 miles to the end of this occasionally rough but passable road. As of fall 1994, the last 3 miles of the drive were blocked by a washout.

Follow the Fish Lake Trail northwest from the trailhead for 1.25 miles as it continues downstream along the east side of Fish Creek. After dropping a couple of hundred feet in elevation in this first section, the Fish Lake Trail turns northeast to follow the North Fork of Fish Creek all the way to its headwaters. In the next 3 miles the route climbs easy to moderate grades along the drainage bottom. Although it crosses the stream on several occasions, the trail is easy to find throughout. Along this lower portion of the hike are several aspen

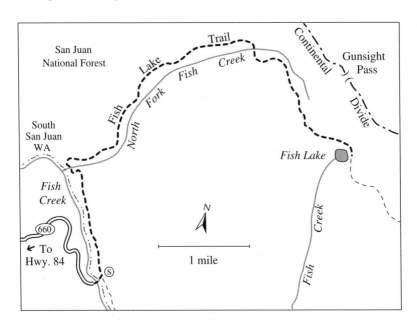

stands, along with small open meadows and evergreen forests. Mule deer and elk may be spotted in these openings during the early-morning hours.

Four miles from the trailhead the Fish Lake Trail begins to climb more steeply as it ascends the head of the North Fork drainage. This segment of the hike passes through nice old-growth forests of Engelmann spruce and subalpine fir. Shortly after reaching timberline, the trail levels off a bit to traverse some verdant alpine tundra. Views to the north take in some truly rugged terrain; the prominent notch to the northeast is 12,180-foot Gunsight Pass. After topping out on a small saddle, the Fish Lake Trail drops slightly to reach its namesake 6 miles from the trailhead. While Fish Lake is the turnaround point for this hike, the Fish Lake Trail continues for another 4 miles before reaching the Continental Divide Trail, about 1 mile north of Blue Lake. It was near Blue Lake that either the last grizzly bear in Colorado was killed or the first of many more encounters took place.

Water is available along the Fish Lake Trail, but it must be treated before drinking. Watch for lightning along the higher portions of this hike.

# 67 REDCLOUD AND SUNSHINE PEAKS

**Distance: 11.4 miles round trip**
**Difficulty: Strenuous**
**Hiking time: 7 hours**
**Elevation: 10,425 to 14,034 feet**
**Management: BLM**

**Wilderness status: Redcloud**
  **Peak WSA**
**Season: July to September**
**USGS map: Redcloud Peak**

Although they barely top the 14,000-foot level, the neighboring summits of Redcloud and Sunshine make for one incredibly fun hike. Not only will you enjoy memorable views from these peaks, but you can savor the fact that you have bagged two of Colorado's elite corps of mountains as well. Following the Silver Creek Trail, this hike falls within the 37,442-acre Redcloud Peak Wilderness Study Area, which is administered by the BLM.

To reach the start of this hike, drive 2.5 miles south from Lake City on Colorado Highway 149 to the turnoff for the Cinnamon Pass Road, which is also signed as the Alpine Loop Scenic Byway. Follow this road for 4 miles on pavement and then another 12.5 miles on gravel to the signed trailhead on the right side of the road.

Heading northeast from the trailhead, the Silver Creek Trail follows its namesake for the first 3 miles of this hike. Along the first 1.75-mile segment, the route continues up a rough road that was recently constructed to reach a mine above. While something of an intrusion in this proposed wilderness, the road is narrow enough to be easily converted into a foot trail when the mine work is completed. Beyond the point where this road turns northwest up a side gulch, the Silver Creek Trail

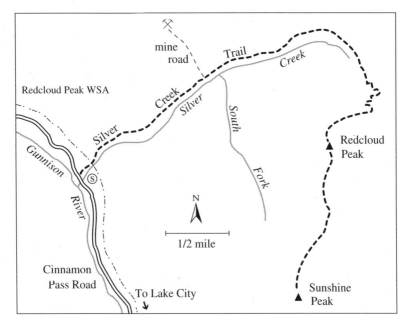

Redcloud Peak WSA

Gunnison River

Cinnamon Pass Road

To Lake City

N

1/2 mile

mine road

Trail

Silver Creek

Silver Creek

South Fork

Redcloud Peak

Sunshine Peak

continues straight ahead up the main drainage for another mile or so before reaching a scenic alpine basin at the head of Silver Creek. Up to this point the trail has climbed about 1,500 feet—mostly along easy to moderate grades. Because this basin is above timberline, it is an especially great place to enjoy the plethora of wildflowers that grow in the San Juan Mountains.

*Along the ridge that connects Redcloud and Sunshine peaks*

Upon reaching the head of the Silver Creek drainage, the trail (marked by cairns at this point) bends southward to begin the final 1,800-foot climb up the north face of 14,034-foot Redcloud Peak. In the next mile, the route climbs to the top of a saddle just east of the summit. It then continues on to the top by way of Redcloud Peak's northeast ridge. This final pitch ascends strenuously the entire way to the summit. Because the trail itself is rocky and loose in places, be sure to watch your footing, especially on the return trip down. Characterized by its deep orange hue, Redcloud Peak is heavily mineralized with iron oxides. It, along with Sunshine and other peaks in the area, are within the Lake City caldera—a huge volcano that eventually collapsed and filled with volcanic debris. There are several such calderas in the San Juan Range.

Once you have enjoyed the panorama from Redcloud—a 360-degree view that includes Uncompahgre and Matterhorn peaks to the north, the La Garitas to the east, the Needle Range to the south, and a jumble of peaks that stretch westward to Mount Sneffels—continue south for another 1.25 miles to 14,001-foot Sunshine Peak. In this easy traverse, the route drops a couple of hundred feet before climbing easily to this second summit. From the top of Sunshine you can look into the Lake Fork of the Gunnison River directly to the south and get an upclose view of 14,048-foot Handies Peak to the west. Return along the same route upon completing the climb.

As members of the Hayden Survey discovered in 1874 when they made the first recorded ascent of Redcloud, these summits are extremely dangerous places to be during electrical storms. Water is available along the lower half of the hike, but it must be treated. Although this route is not particularly exposed to dangerous drop-offs, the south face of Sunshine is ringed by high cliffs.

# 68 CONTINENTAL DIVIDE

**Distance: 31.5 miles one way**
**Difficulty: Moderate**
**Hiking time: 4 days**
**Elevation: 9,300 to 12,713 feet**
**Management: Rio Grande NF, San Juan NF**

**Wilderness status: Weminuche WA**
**Season: July to September**
**USGS maps: Howardsville, Storm King Peak, Rio Grande Pyramid, Weminuche Pass**

Within the more than 600 miles that it covers in the state of Colorado, the Continental Divide forms the headwaters of such famous rivers as the Yampa, Platte, Colorado, Arkansas, Rio Grande, and San Juan. Along the way the Divide tracks widely east to west as it snakes from mountain range to mountain range. One of these undulations occurs where the Divide crests along the San Juan Mountains—the largest mountain range in the U.S. Rockies. Within its final 200-mile stretch before reaching the New Mexico border, the Continental Divide nearly doubles back on itself as it traverses the state's largest

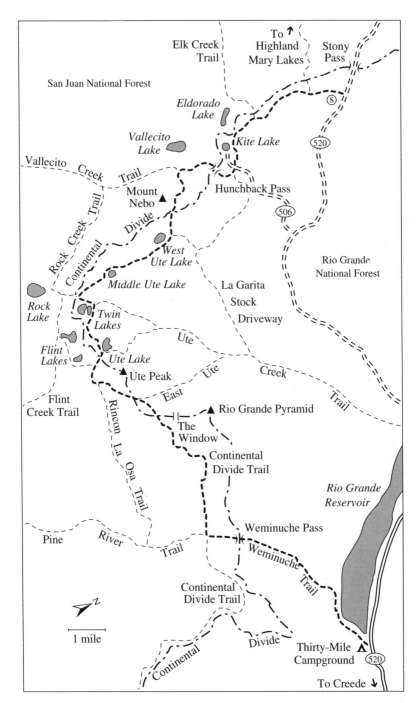

San Juan National Forest

Elk Creek Trail

To Highland Mary Lakes

Stony Pass

Eldorado Lake

Vallecito Lake

Kite Lake

Ⓢ

520

Vallecito Creek Trail

Rock Creek Trail

Continental Divide

Mount Nebo

Hunchback Pass

506

West Ute Lake

Middle Ute Lake

La Garita Stock Driveway

Rio Grande National Forest

Rock Lake

Twin Lakes

Ute

Flint Lakes

Ute Lake

Ute Peak

Ute

Creek

Trail

Flint Creek Trail

East

Rio Grande Pyramid

The Window

Continental Divide Trail

Rincon La Osa Trail

Rio Grande Reservoir

Pine River Trail

Weminuche Pass

Weminuche Trail

Continental Divide Trail

N

1 mile

Continental

Divide

Thirty-Mile Campground

520

To Creede ↓

wilderness area, the 488,544-acre Weminuche Wilderness. Encompassing more than 80 miles of the Continental Divide from end to end, the Weminuche Wilderness includes the longest undeveloped stretch of the Divide in the state. Thanks to the Continental Divide Trail, hikers can follow the Divide from Stony Pass to Wolf Creek Pass with very few intrusions. This hike description covers the 26-mile segment of the Continental Divide Trail between Stony Pass and Weminuche Pass.

This route begins at Stony Pass. To get there from Creede, drive 20.1 miles west on Colorado Highway 149 to the Upper Rio Grande River Road (Forest Road 520). Turn left and drive 33 miles west to within 0.5 mile of Stony Pass, which is on the Divide itself. The last 17 miles of this road require a 4WD vehicle. If you do not have a 4WD but you are willing to make the lengthy roundabout drive from Creede through South Fork, Pagosa Springs, Durango, and Silverton, you can access the Continental Divide Trail via the Highland Mary Lakes Trail (see Hike 73, Highland Mary Lakes). To reach the other end of this hike, drive just 10 miles west on the Upper Rio Grande River Road to Thirty-Mile Campground and the trailhead for the Weminuche Trail.

Beginning about 0.5 mile east of Stony Pass, this section of the Continental Divide Trail heads due south along a mostly level grade for the first 4 miles or so. The hiking is surprisingly easy, and because this stretch is well above timberline, the scenery is incredible in all directions. Looking east you can see the forested headwaters of the Rio Grande, while to the west is Cunningham Gulch (see Hike 73, Highland Mary Lakes). About 1.5 miles from the trailhead, the route

*One of the Flint Lakes, which lie along the Continental Divide in the Weminuche Wilderness*

intersects with a side trail that drops into Cunningham Gulch, where it meets the Highland Mary Trail to the west.

Beyond the Highland Mary area, the Continental Divide Trail continues south—still above timberline and still along level or easy grades—to reach the head of Elk Creek, which drops west to the Animas River. The Elk Creek Trail, in fact, is now part of the Colorado Trail, which runs from Denver to Durango. Just south of Elk Creek the mountains change abruptly as the Grenadier Range spikes the skyline with a number of sharply rising 13,000-foot peaks, and located at the head of Elk Creek is beautiful Eldorado Lake. The Continental Divide Trail, however, drops east from the Divide before reaching the lake itself. Leaving the Divide so as to avoid the rugged slopes of 13,136-foot Hunchback Mountain, the trail instead descends into the Kite Lake area, which lies outside of the Weminuche Wilderness. In this 2-mile diversion from the actual Divide, the route first descends about 1,000 feet, mostly along a rough 4WD road. It then intersects the 4WD route, which accesses Kite Lake to the right. After crossing this road the Continental Divide Trail then continues south to climb 700 feet in 0.75 mile before reaching 12,493-foot Hunchback Pass. Here the trail crosses the Divide again, then drops steeply into the head of Vallecito Creek. In the next mile the trail drops 1,000 feet to where Nebo Creek comes in from the east. The route then climbs east for a little over a mile to cross the Divide once more. In this ascent it gains nearly 1,200 feet to top a 12,500-foot saddle just north of 13,205-foot Mount Nebo. A quite impressive peak, Mount Nebo is especially beautiful this close.

Now east of the Continental Divide, the trail drops moderately for 2 miles to reach West Ute Lake, the first of five nice lakes that dot the headwaters of the Ute Creek drainage. From West Ute Lake the Continental Divide Trail heads south to climb up and over a 12,200-foot saddle before dropping to Middle Ute Lake. In this 2-mile stretch the trail climbs 400 feet and drops 200 feet before reaching the second lake, which is at an elevation of just under 12,000 feet. The trail then continues south for 1 mile to meet a trail that heads south to Rock Lake. From this intersection, which is located on the Continental Divide, the route bears left before dropping moderately to Twin Lakes. Beyond Twin Lakes the trail continues east to reach Ute Lake, the largest of the five lakes. Ute Lake, like most in this area, offers good fishing possibilities. Hiking in the vicinity of these lakes can be slow because of thick willows and soggy ground. Additionally, some portions of the trail may be indistinct and hard to find. Armed with topo maps, a compass, and the ability to use both correctly, many hikers pick their own route along the head of the Ute Creek drainage since it is treeless and wide open.

From Ute Lake the Continental Divide Trail ascends eastward to a ridge that extends south from 12,892-foot Ute Peak. At the top is an intersection with the Rincon La Osa Trail, which heads into its namesake drainage. Sometimes hikers mistakenly follow this better-defined trail. While the Rincon La Osa Trail drops east from the ridge, the Continental Divide Trail turns left on the ridge to follow it north toward Ute Peak. As it nears the top of this interesting little summit, the route cuts across its southern face to continue east along the Divide. In another mile it intersects the upper end of the East Ute Creek Trail, after which it reaches the head of the Rincon la Vaca drainage. In the next 2 miles the Continental Divide Trail drops a bit as it continues northeast into the Rincon la Vaca. Along this stretch of the trail you get a good look at an astounding landmark known as the Window. A 140-foot cut in the Divide above, the Window was often referred to as the Devil's Gateway by Spanish sheepherders. Just north of the Window is an impressive 13,821-foot mountain known as the Rio Grande Pyramid. After reaching a point that is a couple of miles east of the Pyramid, the Continental Divide Trail turns due east to begin its descent into the Rincon la Vaca drainage. Within a mile it drops below timberline to reach the drainage bottom, and in another mile it reaches a wide open park that runs north and south over low-slung Weminuche Pass. While the Continental Divide Trail continues east across this level meadow area, this hike turns north to reach 10,630-foot Weminuche Pass a mile north.

From Weminuche Pass follow the Weminuche Trail northeast for 5.5 miles to a trailhead at Thirty-Mile Campground. Dropping easily along Weminuche Creek, this trail descends a total of 1,200 feet over its entire length. Portions of this route cross open meadows, while other parts pass through forests of Engelmann spruce and subalpine fir.

Because most of this hike is above timberline, you must take extra precautions to avoid lightning, which is common during summer afternoons. Weather conditions in general can deteriorate rapidly at this elevation. Because the Continental Divide trail is indistinct in places, be sure you bring all necessary topographic maps. Water is found along most of this hike, but it must be treated before drinking.

# 69 VALLECITO CREEK– PINE RIVER LOOP

**Distance: 38.5 miles one way**
**Difficulty: Moderate**
**Hiking time: 5 days**
**Elevation: 7,916 to 12,000 feet**
**Management: San Juan NF**
**Wilderness status: Weminuche WA**

**Season: July to September**
**USGS maps: Vallecito Reservoir,**
   **Columbine Pass, Storm King**
   **Peak, Rio Grande Pyramid,**
   **Emerald Lake, Granite Peak**

With nearly 500 miles of trails, including the Continental Divide Trail (see Hike 68, Continental Divide), the 488,544-acre Weminuche Wilderness offers more long-distance hikes than any other area in Colorado. Many of the lengthy trails can be combined to create wonderful multiday hikes. Two such routes, the Vallecito Creek and Pine River trails, are easily connected by the Rock Creek and Flint Creek trails to offer a look at both high alpine terrain and forested valleys.

To begin this hike, drive north from Bayfield on County Road 501 to

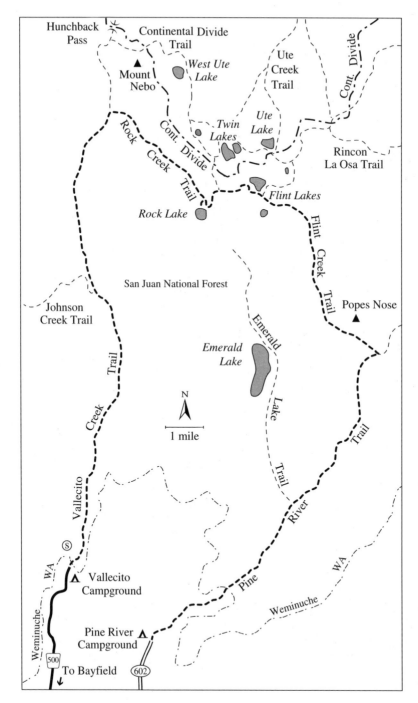

Vallecito Reservoir. Continue north on County Road 500, which follows the west shore of the reservoir, for 3 miles past the reservoir to the Vallecito Campground at the road's end. To reach the end of this hike, continue around to the east shore of Vallecito Reservoir on Forest Road 602 to the Pine River, then drive upstream along the river to the Pine River Campground. The shuttle distance between the two trailheads is about 11 miles.

From the Vallecito Campground, the Vallecito Creek Trail heads north along its namesake for 17 miles before reaching Hunchback Pass. With only minor exceptions, the portion of the Vallecito Creek Trail that this hike follows stays completely within the gently ascending drainage bottom. The Vallecito Creek Trail crosses the creek on a number of occasions, but all of these crossings are completed via well-constructed bridges. That these bridges were installed is indicative of the fact that the Vallecito Creek Trail is very popular, especially among horse packers. Stretches of the route can become a muddy mess after rain, thanks to the added traffic. About 8.5 miles from the trailhead the Vallecito Creek Trail intersects the east end of the Johnson Creek Trail. Climbing 3,500 feet in 6 miles, this side route reaches the top of 12,800-foot Columbine Pass before dropping into Chicago Basin at the head of Needle Creek (see Hike 71, Chicago Basin). About 14 miles from the trailhead and 3 miles short of Hunchback Pass, the Vallecito Creek Trail reaches the turnoff for the Rock Creek Trail. In this first segment, the hike gains 2,200 feet along mostly easy grades.

After turning right at the Vallecito Creek–Rock Creek Trail junction, this hike follows the Rock Creek Trail southeast for 5.5 miles. In its first 1.5 miles, the Rock Creek Trail climbs about 1,000 feet before leveling off some to continue along a large open meadow. After nearly 4 miles, the Rock Creek Trail intersects with a 0.25-mile side trail that leads south to Rock Lake. At 11,841 feet, Rock Lake is a popular destination for both backpackers and horse packers intent on fishing its cold waters. Beyond this turnoff the Rock Creek Trail climbs for another 0.5 mile before reaching both the high point of the hike and a second trail intersection. The left-hand trail leads up and over the Continental Divide to Twin Lakes (see Hike 68, Continental Divide), while the Rock Creek Trail stays right to continue east for another mile to the Flint Lakes and the upper end of the Flint Creek Trail. Situated at timberline, the Flint Lakes are quite scenic. Just before the largest of the Flint Lakes, this hike turns right onto the Flint Creek Trail, which heads down Flint Creek to the Pine River. The Rock Creek Trail turns left at this point to climb on to the Continental Divide Trail about 2 miles farther.

After turning onto the Flint Creek Trail continue downstream along the Flint Creek drainage for 7 miles to reach the junction with the Pine River Trail. In this segment of the hike the route drops 2,400 feet along easy to moderate grades. As you drop you may note the addition of aspen to the spruce and fir forest mix that predominates in the higher elevations. You can also enjoy a good view of the aptly named Popes Nose near the lower end of the Flint Creek Trail.

The lower end of the Flint Creek Trail intersects the 22-mile long Pine River Trail, which follows the Pine River (shown as Los Pinos River on most maps) northeast from the Vallecito Reservoir area to Weminuche Pass. After turning right onto the Pine River Trail, continue southwest for nearly 12 miles to the trailhead at the Pine River Campground. Although the trail stays close to its namesake for the entire way, there are some minor grade changes as the trail occasionally climbs and drops along the river's west side. Nearly 6 miles from the Flint Creek–Pine River Trail junction is the turnoff for the Emerald Lake Trail. This popular route climbs 1,700 feet in 4 miles to reach beautiful Emerald Lake, which was created by a landslide a long time ago. Measuring 1.5 miles long and 0.5 mile across, Emerald is Colorado's second largest natural lake. Because it is so popular among anglers, it is the destination for many of the hikers who venture up the Pine River Trail. In the final couple of miles, this hike crosses private land. Please respect all signs and fenced boundaries along the way.

Water is found all along this hike, but it must be treated before drinking. Watch for lightning in the higher terrain. While portions of this route are very popular, it is possible to camp in solitude by avoiding places like Rock Lake and the Flint Lakes and by choosing campsites far from the trails.

# 70   PIEDRA RIVER

**Distance: 8 miles round trip**
**Difficulty: Moderate**
**Hiking time: 5 hours**
**Elevation: 7,100 to 7,825 feet**
**Management: San Juan NF**

**Wilderness status: Piedra Area**
**Season: June to October**
**USGS maps: Devil Mountain,**
   **Bear Mountain**

With its headwaters on the Continental Divide in the San Juan Mountains, the Piedra River flows southwest through a maze of heavily timbered canyons before emptying into the San Juan River southeast of Durango. Virtually untouched, the middle portion of the Piedra River basin has been under consideration as a wilderness area for several years. Because of the potential for water development upstream, however, the proposed Piedra Wilderness was excluded from

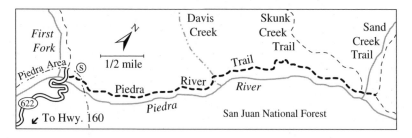

*The Piedra River framed by spruce and fir trees*

the Colorado Wilderness Act of 1993. It did, however, win designation as a special management area, which means it still has a chance for wilderness status pending settlement of water rights. This hike follows a 4-mile stretch of the Piedra River Trail.

To reach the beginning of this hike, drive 19 miles east from Bayfield on US Highway 160 to the signed turnoff for First Fork Road (Forest Road 622). Follow this narrow but maintained graveled road north for 12 miles to where it crosses the Piedra River. The trail begins just north of the river on the right side of the road. Parking is available on the left.

The Piedra River Trail starts by climbing easily among open stands of ponderosa pines. It then begins contouring about 100 feet above the north bank of the river. From this level it is possible to look down on many stretches of the waterway. Fishermen can access the river from most of this first portion of the hike. Although the trail for the most part stays well above the river bottom, it does drop briefly to within a short distance of the bank at one point. Farther upstream, the canyon closes in a bit and Douglas firs become more prominent. The canyon is also home to spruce trees, most notably the Colorado blue spruce, which grows close to the riverbank. Dangling from the trees are wisps of lichen known as old man's beard, which looks very much like Spanish moss, but is in fact a strictly high-altitude species. Trailside underbrush includes Gambel oak, wild roses, milkweed, and poison ivy.

As the trail nears the 2-mile mark it bends away from the river to contour around the normally dry Davis Creek drainage. The route also begins to climb at this point—gently at first, but more moderately after crossing Davis Creek. Over the next mile the route gains nearly 600 feet, bypassing Second Box Canyon in the process. Because it is walled in by tall cliffs, Second Box Canyon is too rugged for passage on foot. While it is possible to see the upper walls of the canyon in one or two places, the whole abyss never comes into full view.

Topping out as it skirts around a second side drainage, the trail then drops—steeply in places—for the next mile before reaching the Piedra River again. At this point the Piedra River Trail crosses through some nice meadows before reaching the mouth of perennial Sand Creek. Although Sand Creek marks the turnaround point for this hike, the Piedra River Trail continues for another 6 miles upstream before reaching Forest Service Road 631. The Skunk Creek Trail branches off a few feet west of the Sand Creek crossing and continues north for 5 miles before joining up with the First Fork Trail, which can then be followed back to the Piedra River trailhead. Shortly beyond the Sand Creek crossing, the Sand Creek Trail turns north to follow its namesake before reaching the upper portion of Forest Road 631. The turnoffs for the Skunk Creek and Sand Creek trails are not marked and both routes are very faint and difficult to follow. Good campsites are available in the vicinity of Sand Creek.

Upon turning around at Sand Creek, keep in mind that you have 500 vertical feet of moderate to strenuous climbing on the way back. Water is available in places, but it must be treated before drinking.

 # CHICAGO BASIN

Distance: 16.6 miles round trip
Difficulty: Strenuous
Hiking time: 2 days
Elevation: 8,000 to 12,680 feet
Management: San Juan NF

Wilderness status: Weminuche WA
Season: July to September
USGS maps: Mountain View Crest,
    Columbine Pass, Snowdon Peak

This is the most popular hike in the Weminuche Wilderness and for good reason. One of the most scenic areas in the San Juans, Chicago Basin is surrounded by the stunning 13,000- and 14,000-foot peaks of the Needle Range. Add to this the fact that the trailhead is accessible by way of a steam-powered narrow gauge train and you have an adventure that is steeped in both natural and historic lore. Be forewarned, however: some 6,000 people hike into Chicago Basin each summer, so this is no place to find solitude.

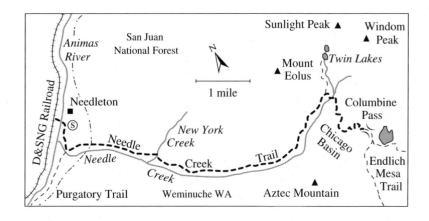

Most folks begin this excursion by riding the Durango & Silverton Narrow Gauge (D&SNG) Railroad north from Durango to the Needleton stopover. Not all trains make the stop to let off passengers, so be sure to specify that you will be hiking in from Needleton when you purchase your ticket. You will also want to find out what time to meet the train on your return trip. If you wish to bypass the train ride completely, you can hike an extra 11 miles down Purgatory Creek and upstream along the Animas River to reach the Needle Creek Trail.

From Needleton, the Needle Creek Trail heads south along the east side of the Animas River for less than a mile before reaching the Needle Creek drainage, which continues east. After intersecting the Purgatory Trail, the Needle Creek Trail begins climbing moderate to occasionally steep grades along the north side of Needle Creek. Staying on this side of the creek all the way to Chicago Basin, the trail follows what was once a stagecoach route. During the late 1800s, not only was Needleton a thriving little town but Chicago Basin itself was the site of several active mines. Today Needleton is but a few scattered cabins, and all of the mines in the basin above are nothing more than historical notations on the landscape. But, just as it was back then, access to the area is still provided by the narrow gauge railroad.

As the Needle Creek Trail climbs, it leaves behind the scented ponderosa pine forests in exchange for a forest mix of Engelmann spruce and subalpine fir. Scattered aspen stands are also encountered along much of the way. About 2 miles from Needleton the trail crosses New York Creek, which drains in from the northeast. Slide paths along this stretch of the hike testify to the fact that avalanches are a constant wintertime threat in the San Juan Mountains. After another mile or so, some nice views of the surrounding summits pop up in places where the trees thin out and in small openings. Additionally, nearby Needle Creek drops through some noisy but beautiful cascades that make for nice streamside lunch spots. About 7 miles from the start, the Needle Creek Trail reaches Chicago Basin.

Characterized by open meadows that spread across the valley floor,

*Old mine tailings in Chicago Basin*

Chicago Basin is completely engulfed by incredibly rugged mountains. To the south, along what is known as Mountain View Crest, rise 13,125-foot Mount Kennedy and 13,310-foot Aztec Mountain, and three 14,000-foot peaks—14,083-foot Mount Eolus, 14,053-foot Sunlight Peak, and 14,082-foot Windom Peak—tower to the north. Climbers intent on bagging these three summits head north from the Needle Creek Trail along a rugged route that follows Needle Creek up the basin's north wall to Twin Lakes. From the lakes, it is a relatively easy scramble east to Sunlight and Windom, and a somewhat more difficult ascent west to Eolus. A transplanted herd of mountain goats (these animals are not native to the San Juans) roams the Twin Lakes area, and they have become quite used to people. Having recently learned that human urine is high in salt, the goats have taken to digging up the ground wherever anyone has urinated. So acute is the dilemma that the Forest Service is asking hikers to relieve themselves only on solid rock, and not on fragile alpine soils.

While Chicago Basin is quite spectacular in its own right, it is well worth the trouble to climb beyond the basin to the top of 12,800-foot Columbine Pass—the turnaround point of this hike. In this last segment of the hike the trail climbs 1,600 feet in about 1.5 miles. From the pass the views extend north across the Needle Mountains—indeed, they are so sharp that the name is fitting—and east into the Vallecito Creek drainage. Beyond Vallecito Creek the San Juans continue to march eastward, stacking up against the skyline as they do. East of the pass, the Johnson Creek Trail (see Hike 69, Vallecito Creek–Pine

River Loop) drops to Columbine Lake before continuing on to meet the Vallecito Creek Trail below. A second route—the Endlich Mesa Trail—heads south from Columbine Pass over Trimble Pass and then on to City Reservoir. From Trimble Pass it is also possible to access Mountain View Crest.

Within Chicago Basin are many nice spots to camp. Because of severe overuse, however, campfires have been banned throughout the Needle Creek drainage. This has resulted in much cleaner campsites, but human impact on vegetation is still a problem. Undoubtedly, the popularity of the area will lead to new regulations in the future.

Water is found along this hike, but it must be treated before drinking. Lightning can pose a hazard in the higher reaches of the basin and on Columbine Pass. Because a considerable number of people hike into Chicago Basin, you may want to plan your trip for after Labor Day or, if the snows melt early, in June. Keep in mind the regulations concerning campfires.

# 72 CRATER LAKE

**Distance: 11 miles round trip**　　**Management: San Juan NF**
**Difficulty: Moderate**　　**Wilderness status: Weminuche WA**
**Hiking time: 7 hours**　　**Season: July to September**
**Elevation: 10,750 to 11,640 feet**　　**USGS map: Snowdon Peak**

The hike to Crater Lake is a popular one, and for good reason. Access to the trail's start is easy and, with only one real climb, the hike is relatively easy. Along the way the route crosses some impressive terrain before reaching a real gem of a lake. Whether you are looking for a nice day hike or an overnight destination, Crater Lake is an excellent possibility.

To reach the beginning of this hike, drive 44 miles north of Durango on US Highway 550 to the signed right turn for Andrews Lake. Turn and continue south for about 1 mile to Andrews Lake. Andrews Lake is 0.9 mile south of Molas Pass.

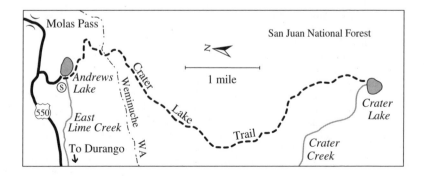

From the Andrews Lake parking area, the Crater Lake Trail circles south around the mouth of the lake. About 0.25 mile out the trail begins a 500-foot climb along a few long switchbacks. Recently reworked, this section of the route is easy to follow and the grade is easy to moderate. Because the terrain in this area is partially open, some nice views open up in various directions. Below you can occasionally see US Highway 550 winding its way over Molas Pass. Summits that come into view include Sultan and Kendall mountains to the north, the Twin Sisters and Jura Knob to the west, Engineer Mountain to the southwest, and Snowdon Peak directly east. The only drawback to this panorama is a powerline that was strung over Molas Pass in recent years.

After a mile, the trail levels off as it tops a ridge south of Andrews Lake. The route then begins to dip in and out of a number of shallow drainages as it heads south toward Crater Lake. Some of these grade changes may be moderate in difficulty, but they are short and never really a problem. As the trail makes its way to the lake, it crosses several open meadows where wildflowers grow in abundance. It also encounters a few small streams, some thickly timbered areas of Engelmann spruce and subalpine fir, and outcroppings of light-colored limestone.

Within the last 1.5 miles leading up to Crater Lake, the trail crosses marshy areas where the route may be a bit hard to find at first. A careful scan of the scene, though, quickly reveals the way. After 5.5 miles, the Crater Lake Trail reaches its destination, which is nestled just below timberline at the foot of 13,075-foot North Twilight Peak. A

*Crater Lake at dusk*

favorite among fly fishermen, Crater Lake is well stocked. Its shoreline harbors many nice camping spots and the scenery is unsurpassed, especially at dawn and dusk, when the rugged north face of Twilight is reflected in the still lake waters. It is possible to get a good look at the Needle Mountains to the east by climbing a small saddle that sits just above the lake. And, as many climbers already know, the summit of North Twilight can be accessed from Crater Lake. The route first tops the saddle and then follows the ridge south to the east flank of North Twilight Peak. From the summit it is possible to reach 13,158-foot Twilight Peak. The crossover to the higher summit involves a 400-foot drop and some scrambling over steep terrain.

All water along this hike must be treated before drinking. Watch for lightning during the frequent summer thunderstorms.

# 73 HIGHLAND MARY LAKES

**Distance: 8 miles round trip**       **Management: BLM, San Juan NF**
**Difficulty: Moderate**              **Wilderness status: Weminuche WA**
**Hiking time: 5 hours**              **Season: July to September**
**Elevation: 10,450 to 12,170 feet**  **USGS map: Howardsville**

Situated in a verdant alpine basin just west of the Continental Divide, the Highland Mary Lakes are a popular destination for day hikers and backpackers alike. Some come to try their luck at fishing, while others hike the steep trail simply to enjoy the surrounding scenery. Whatever your intent, these alpine lakes are worth the effort.

To reach the start of this hike, drive 4 miles east from Silverton on Colorado Highway 110 to the old town of Howardsville. Turn right onto Forest Road 589 and drive 4 miles up Cunningham Gulch to the trailhead at road's end. Although most of this road is passable to 2WD vehicles, the last 0.75 mile may require a 4WD.

From the trailhead the Highland Mary Trail begins to climb almost immediately. Alternating between moderate and strenuous grades,

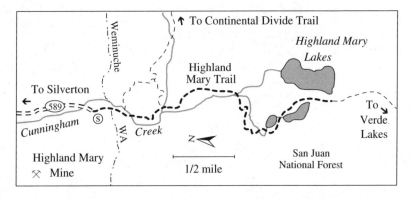

this route ascends some 400 feet in the first 0.25 mile. At this point the trail intersects a route that climbs 1,400 feet to reach the Continental Divide a few miles to the east. Continuing straight at this junction, the Highland Mary Trail levels off for a short distance before reaching a second turnoff for the Continental Divide (this route connects with the first a short distance east). It then begins climbing again and gains another 800 feet in the next 2 miles. Along this section the route occasionally crosses Cunningham Creek, which, at this elevation, is not difficult to negotiate. The trail also bends and twists a bit as it climbs along moderate to strenuous grades. As you climb up Cunningham Gulch, be sure to note the many old mines that dot the mountainsides. This drainage, along with most others in this part of the San Juans, was busy with mining activity during the last decades of the nineteenth century.

*Verdant alpine terrain typifies the Highland Mary Lakes region.*

After reaching timberline at the 11,600-foot level, the trail climbs for another 500 feet through open alpine tundra. Of the many wildflowers that grow here in July and August, blue columbine is the showiest. At the 12,000-foot level—about 3.5 miles from the start—the Highland Mary Trail reaches the first two lakes of the Highland Mary Lakes chain. Passing between the two, the trail continues south along the east shore of the second lake to access the third and largest of the lakes. Fishing is reported to be good to excellent in all three lakes, and vistas of the amazingly lush alpine tundra that covers the surrounding mountains are unforgettable. Domestic sheep can often be seen grazing across the slopes above the lake. While this hike turns around at the Highland Mary Lakes, it is possible to continue south for 0.5 mile to the Verde Lakes or west to the summit of 13,259-foot Whitehead Peak. In addition, because the Continental Divide Trail runs along the ridges a mile east of the Highland Mary Lakes, some people access it via this route (see Hike 68, Continental Divide).

Water is available along this hike, but it must be treated before drinking. Lightning is a frequent hazard in this high, open terrain during July and August, when afternoon thunderstorms are a common occurrence.

## 74    SILVER LAKE

**Distance: 3.5 miles round trip**
**Difficulty: Strenuous**
**Hiking time: 3 hours**
**Elevation: 10,600 to 12,186 feet**

**Management: BLM, private**
**Wilderness status: None**
**Season: July to September**
**USGS map: Howardsville**

In addition to encompassing some of the most scenic mountain terrain in the state, the San Juan Mountains also feature a wealth of historical treasures left over from one of the largest mining booms ever witnessed in the West. With the town of Silverton serving as the hub of the lode-laden San Juans' nineteenth-century mining activity, the surrounding valleys and mountainsides were thick with mining camps. One of these was located at Silver Lake, which is tucked away in an isolated basin well above timberline.

To reach the beginning of the hike from downtown Silverton, drive north on Greene Street (the town's only paved street) to Colorado Highway 110. Turn right and follow this paved route for 2 miles to County Road 2, which bears right where the pavement ends. Follow this road up Arrastra Creek for 0.8 mile to a fork in the road. Bear left and continue driving toward the upper end of Arrastra Gulch. The road becomes a 4WD route about 1.5 miles from Colorado Highway 110. The parking area for this hike is located 2.1 miles from Highway 110 at a switchback in the road. Although the road does continue another 0.5 mile, it has been blocked off to vehicles by a small rock slide. Because of the great number of mining claims in this area, portions of this hike (including the parking area and Silver Lake) are on private land. While hiking access is permitted by the land owners, disrespect for the property can result in closures. Be sure to stay on the trail and leave all structures and relics alone.

From where you park your vehicle, this hike follows the remaining 0.5 mile of the road to the Mayflower Mine. This section of the hike is moderately steep, and because it cuts acoss an open mountainside, the scenery is spectacular. Spreading out before you is the steep-sided Arrastra Gulch with its plethora of mines and tailings piles. Strung across the skyline in places are the cables of an old mining tram that hauled ore from the Mayflower Mine to a mill located far below on the Animas River. Visible from much of this hike, the Mayflower Mill now sits idle and its accompanying tailings have since been reclaimed.

Upon reaching the Mayflower Mine you can enjoy the remains of this once-productive hole. The top station of the ore tram is still in place, although it is no longer functional. Piles of planks are all that remain of some buildings, and heaps of rusting pipes and other scrap metal lie discarded to the side. The mine itself was sealed up with concrete in September 1993 to prevent people from entering it. Entering these abandoned mines is a risky adventure at best, and has proven deadly in some cases. From the mine the trail crosses a pile of scrap metal before climbing south along the foot of some cliffs to the left. In the next 0.75 mile the trail ascends steeply over slopes of loose rock and among boulder fields. Sturdy boots are a real plus here. After climbing up some steep switchbacks the trail encounters a vertical headwall, which it tops by following a narrow shelf of rock. At this point the trail enters Arrastra Basin, where it takes up an easy grade for the last 0.5 mile to the lake. Because this stretch of the trail crosses alpine tundra, it is spotty in places.

At the lake are seemingly endless piles of old boards, along with several buildings in varying stages of disrepair. Rusty machinery and discarded pipes are scattered about, lengths of cable are strewn here and there, and tailings piles reveal the locations of the many shafts that dot the surrounding mountainsides. Beginning in the late 1800s, mines in the Silver Lake area produced $11 million in precious metals before shutting down in 1901. In the vicinity of Silver Lake there were large

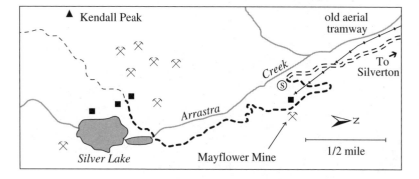

mills, boardinghouses, and even a post office. Rumors persist that dishonest miners used to hide high-grade silver ore in the lake and that these ill-gotten riches are still on the lake bottom today. History buffs enjoy Silver Lake for its wealth of historical memorabilia. Those who are looking for pristine alpine scenery, though, may find it a bit much.

When you return to your vehicle, exercise caution descending the steep slopes into Arrastra Gulch. Although water is readily found along this hike, it should not be consumed because mining activity in the area has left heavy metals and other toxic remnants in the lake

*Historic structures surround Silver Lake near Silverton.*

and streams. Lightning can pose a danger during afternoon thunderstorms. Do not disturb any structures or relics found along this hike. And do not enter old mines or buildings as they are not safe.

# 75  SPUD LAKE

**Distance: 2 miles round trip**
**Difficulty: Easy**
**Hiking time: 2 hours**
**Elevation: 9,360 to 9,800 feet**

**Management: San Juan NF**
**Wilderness status: None**
**Season: June to October**
**USGS map: Engineer Mountain**

Probably the easiest hike in this book, Spud Lake is a great excursion for family members of nearly all ages. From ages four to 84, all can reach this beautiful little lake for a picnic and some fine fishing. Of course, its easy access makes this beautiful lake a very popular destination, so don't count on solitude. The lake was named for nearby Spud Mountain; their official names are Potato Lake and Potato Hill.

To reach the beginning of this hike, take US Highway 550 about 27 miles north from Durango and turn right onto Old Lime Creek Road (Forest Service Road 591) just past Cascade Creek. From the turnoff it is 2.9 miles to the trailhead, which is on the left side of the road. Old Lime Creek Road is gravel but usually passable for most vehicles.

The Spud Lake Trail begins by winding its way through some old aspen groves. Recently rebuilt, the wide route is easy to follow and grades are very gentle throughout. As the route draws closer to the lake (after the 0.5-mile mark), it passes several beaver dams that may offer wildlife-watching opportunities for those who can wait patiently. Mule deer and elk also inhabit the forests along the way, along with a variety of smaller game. After passing a small pond on the left, the trail tops a small ridge, beyond which is the lake itself.

Shaded by 11,871-foot Potato Hill (known to locals as Spud Mountain) to the north and by the magnificent 13,000-foot peaks of the West

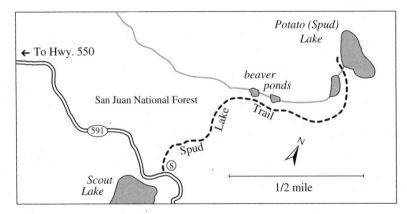

Needle Range to the east, Spud Lake is a scenic destination all summer long, but September is especially beautiful, as the area's many aspens are bathed with a brilliant golden glow. Anglers may have good luck at Spud Lake, although the fishing is not always consistent: it mostly depends on whether the trout are hungry or not. As for the geology of the area, consisting of older metamorphic rock, Spud Mountain and the West Needles are actually exposed portions of the Precambrian core of the San Juan Mountains. Unlike other reaches of this extensive mountain range, traces of volcanic activity here were long ago eroded away.

Be sure to treat all water before drinking, or, better yet, simply pack a quart before setting out. Although Spud Lake is not particularly exposed, you should watch for lightning during afternoon thunderstorms.

# 76    COLORADO TRAIL

Distance: 23 miles one way
Difficulty: Moderate
Hiking time: 3 days
Elevation: 10,880 to 12,490 feet
Management: San Juan NF

Wilderness status: None
Season: July to September
USGS maps: Snowdon Peak,
    Engineer Mountain, Ophir,
    Silverton

Covering 469 miles in its journey from Denver to Durango, the Colorado Trail accesses a variety of mountain terrain throughout the state. Built mostly by volunteers under the direction of Gudy Gaskill, this trans-state trail linked many existing trails to form one continuous route. On September 4, 1987, completion ceremonies were held at three locations along the trail. One of these sites was 10,880-foot Molas Pass, about 45 miles north of Durango. While portions of the Colorado Trail still need work, hikers can choose to complete either the entire route or countless different segments of it. One particularly interesting stretch of the trail heads 12 miles west from Molas Pass to the head of Cascade Creek, then turns south to follow three lesser routes to Coal Bank Pass. What makes this an especially nice excursion is the fact that most of the route is at or above timberline. This translates into unbelievable scenery throughout.

To begin this hike drive 45 miles north from Durango on US Highway 550 to Molas Pass. The Colorado Trail crosses the highway just north of the pass. While this hike description begins at the pass itself, it is best to drive 1 mile west of the pass to Little Molas Lake, where a trailhead provides plenty of parking. Because this hike is one way, you will need to arrange for a shuttle at Coal Bank Pass, located farther south on US Highway 550.

From Molas Pass the Colorado Trail heads due west to circle around the south end of Little Molas Lake, then switchbacks up a moderately sloping ridge to the west. Widely scattered spruce and fir trees grow along this open mountainside, along with some taller, standing dead snags left over from the old Lime Creek Burn of 1879. The fact that evidence of the fire is still noticeable more than 100 years later points out just how fragile life is in the subalpine environment. After climbing nearly 400 feet in 1 mile, the trail reaches an old road near the ridge top. Turn right and follow this road for a short distance to where the trail turns off sharply to the right. From this point the route heads north to begin traversing the head of the North Lime Creek drainage. Above timberline at this point, the Colorado Trail flirts with the last reaches of forest over the next 10 miles or so.

From the top of the ridge overlooking Little Molas Lake, the Colorado Trail climbs another 400 feet over 0.75 mile before reaching an elevation of about 11,600 feet. In the next 2 miles the route contours north and west at this elevation. Rising directly northeast is 13,368-foot Sultan Mountain. At mile 4 the route drops slightly to a 11,520-foot saddle that separates North Lime Creek from Bear Creek to the north. The trail then bends westward again to eventually cross into the head of West Lime Creek. A number of peaks are easily visible from the trail along this segment; besides Sultan Mountain, the panorama takes in 13,432-foot Twin Sisters, 12,614-foot Jura Knob, 12,968-foot Engineer

*Hikers pause near Engineer Mountain along the Pass Creek Trail.*

Mountain, 13,077-foot Snowdon Peak, and the more distant Needle Mountains.

Six miles out the Colorado Trail drops down a few switchbacks before crossing Lime Creek. The route then heads south for about 0.5 mile before turning west again. Continuing at an elevation of about 11,500 feet, the Colorado Trail travels above the head of West Lime Creek for the next 4 miles. Towering to the right is a line of dark volcanic cliffs and a pair of summits known as the Twin Sisters. Upon eaching the far end of the West Lime Creek drainage, the trail encounters an open terrace that lies on the divide between the Lime Creek and South Mineral Creek drainages. From here the Colorado Trail climbs an easy saddle to the west, where it reaches this hike's high point of 12,490 feet. From this saddle the route drops into the head of the Cascade Creek drainage. Here, a little over 12 miles from Molas Pass, the Colorado Trail intersects the upper end of the White Creek Trail.

At the junction between the Colorado and White Creek trails, this hike turns left onto the latter route to begin heading south toward Engineer Mountain and Coal Bank Pass. Maintaining an elevation of around 12,000 feet, the 3.5-mile White Creek Trail circles around the west side of a 12,703-foot unnamed mountain before continuing straight east toward the verdant slopes of Jura Knob. Upon reaching the south slope of this interesting little summit, the route turns south again and intersects with the Engine Creek Trail and the Engineer Mountain Trail. From this junction the hike continues south, following a 2-mile stretch of the Engineer Mountain route along a broad and mostly open ridge top. Not too far away is the unmistakable silhouette

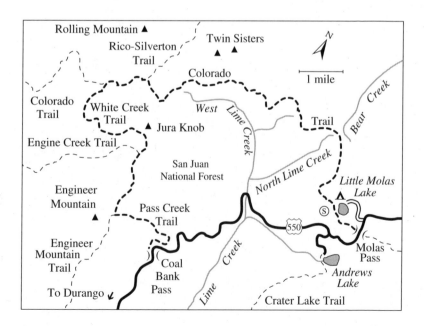

of Engineer Mountain. Along this segment of the hike, the Engineer Mountain Trail drops easily to an 11,650-foot saddle before climbing slightly to reach the foot of Engineer Mountain and the top end of the Pass Creek Trail. Climbers headed for Engineer Mountain's summit use this route to access the rugged north ridge of the mountain. While this ridge route to the top looks quite unsettling from here, it is actually relatively easy. The final leg of this hike turns left onto the Pass Creek Trail and follows it for 2.2 miles, dropping from 12,000 feet along mostly moderate grades to the trailhead at 10,600-foot Coal Bank Pass.

Water is found along much of this hike, but it must be treated before drinking. Watch for lightning all along this route as it is exposed throughout.

# 77 GOULDING CREEK

**Distance: 5.4 miles round trip**
**Difficulty: Strenuous**
**Hiking time: 4 hours**
**Elevation: 7,880 to 10,070 feet**

**Management: San Juan NF**
**Wilderness status: None**
**Season: June to October**
**USGS map: Electra Lake**

Short and steep, the Goulding Creek Trail reveals some splendid timbered areas, a string of beautiful meadows, and a dose of old-fashioned cowboy memorabilia.

*An idyllic aspen-ringed meadow in the upper reaches of the Goulding Creek drainage*

To reach the Goulding Creek trailhead, drive about 16 miles north of Durango along US Highway 550. About a mile past the Tamarron Resort, turn left at a small sign for the trail. The trailhead itself is located less than 0.25 mile down this dirt road.

Starting out along a fairly level grade among some nice aspen forests, the Goulding Creek Trail takes up a series of often steep switchbacks less than 0.5 mile from the start. As it climbs, the trail encounters some scattered ponderosa pines—some of them quite large—along with an occasional Douglas fir and thick undergrowth of Gambel oak. This stretch of the route can be somewhat hot on summer afternoons because of its exposure to the sun. As the route climbs you can catch an occasional view of the highway and Tamarron Resort below, and of imposing Missionary Ridge, which rises along the eastern horizon. You may also hear the whistle of the Durango & Silverton Narrow Gauge Railroad, which winds its way through the trees below.

After climbing some 1,500 feet in 2 miles, the Goulding Creek Trail levels off a bit where it passes through a cool aspen forest. In places you may spot a cliff face looming to the south. As part of the Hermosa Cliffs, which rise above US Highway 550 for several miles, this rock buttress is an example of the Hermosa Formation, which includes shales and sandstones deposited during the Pennsylvanian period in marine environments. Upon reaching a fence and gate, the trail begins to climb along a more moderate grade before encountering the upper end of Goulding Creek. While the creek may be dry below, it is usually flowing at this elevation. The trail then enters the first of a series of beautiful tree-ringed meadows. Wildflowers are numerous in these openings, as are cows. The first meadow contains the remains of an old

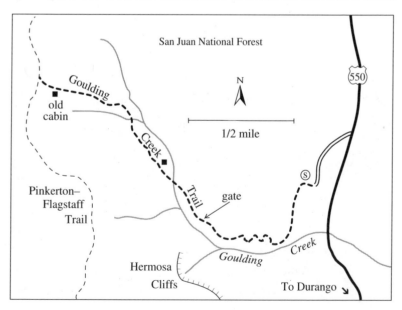

log cabin to the right, while the last meadow holds a small cabin that is still used by cowboys who run cattle in th area. Although not open to the general public, the small structure does make for an idyllic scene. About 0.25 mile above the cabin, the Goulding Creek Trail reaches the Pinkerton–Flagstaff Trail and the turnaround point for this hike. The Pinkerton–Flagstaff Trail runs for 8.5 miles along the crest of a lengthy ridge that separates the Animas River drainage from the Hermosa Creek drainage to the west. Glimpses of the heavily forested Hermosa area through the trees are quite impressive.

Be sure to bring a quart or two of water on this hike, as water may not be available during dry periods. Any water collected from Goulding Creek drainage must be treated before drinking.

# 78 ANIMAS CITY MOUNTAIN

**Distance: 6 miles round trip**
**Difficulty: Moderate**
**Hiking time: 4 hours**
**Elevation: 6,680 to 8,161 feet**

**Management: BLM**
**Wilderness status: None**
**Season: March to November**
**USGS map: Durango East**

Durango residents have long enjoyed both the beautiful pine forests and the spectacular scenery that a visit to the top of nearby Animas City Mountain provides. Managed by the Bureau of Land Management, the trail that loops across this mountain's sloping summit is currently designated as a combination hiking, biking, and equestrian route. The locally prominent mountain was named after Animas City, which actually preceded Durango by a few years. First settled in the 1870s, Animas City was a bit standoffish in 1880 when General Palmer brought his Denver & Rio Grande Railroad to southwestern Colorado. Miffed by the rebuff, Palmer established his own town 2 miles to the south and named it after the Mexican city of Durango. Over the years Durango outgrew its civic rival and eventually annexed it.

To reach the start of the Animas City Mountain Trail from downtown Durango, drive north on Main Avenue to 32nd Street. Turn left and drive uphill to West Fourth Avenue. Turn right and drive another block to the signed trailhead.

Two trails head out from the trailhead; follow the white arrows to take up the recently constructed foot trail that switchbacks up the south slope of the mountain before topping the mounain's south end. Climbing along mostly moderate grades, this new section of trail is a a huge improvement over the old route, which climbed strenuously along an old, rocky jeep road. Pinyon pine and juniper trees are encountered along this climb, with ponderosa pines growing here and there as the trail gains elevation. These taller evergreens are the dominant tree species on the mountain's flat but sloping topside. Gambel oak also grows in patches along much of this hike.

After climbing some 400 feet in the first 0.75 mile, the Animas City

Mountain Trail reaches the lower, south end of the mountain. It then begins following the east rim of the mountain, which is defined in places by high cliffs of Dakota Sandstone. Several points along this portion of the route offer some truly great scenery. Looking south you immediately get a nice view of Durango. As you continue around to the north, the vista begins to take in more of the expansive Animas River Valley. Walled in by the red cliffs of Missionary Ridge to the east, this flat-bottomed valley was carved by the Animas River as it flows south from the San Juan Mountains, meandering widely as it tracks through the valley. You can see how some bends in the river were eventually cut off from the river to become small oxbow lakes. You can also see that the verdant pasturelands within the valley are being swallowed up by housing developments. In the 2 miles that the trail runs adjacent to the east rim, it ascends a total of 1,000 feet.

Upon reaching the northeast corner of the mountaintop, the trail traverses the crest of the mountain's higher north end. Characterized by ponderosa pines, this area is frequented by mule deer and elk, especially in the winter. About 3 miles from the trailhead the route reaches the 8,161-foot summit of Animas City Mountain and a bird's-eye view of Falls Creek Valley to the north. From here follow an old road as it descends due south down the middle of the mountain's flat top. Although closed to motor vehicles, this route is very popular among mountain bicyclists. Here, as on all stretches of the Animas City Mountain Trail, you should walk with caution as some bicyclists carelessly

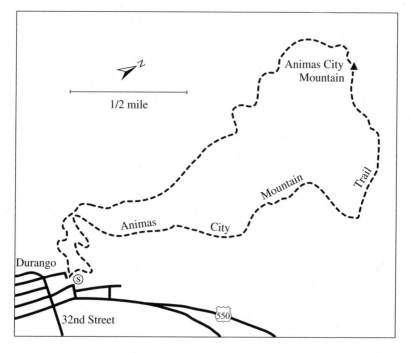

*The city of Durango as seen from Animas City Mountain*

careen down the trail with little regard for what is around the next bend. In 1.75 miles the trail returns to the south end of the mountain. From this point you can either continue down the old roadbed to the trailhead or return by way of the recently constructed trail.

Bring plenty of water as non is available along the trail. Lightning can pose a hazard during strong thunderstorms. Watch for out-of-control bikers along all sections of this hike.

# 79 WETTERHORN BASIN

**Distance: 9 miles round trip**
**Difficulty: Moderate**
**Hiking time: 6 hours**
**Elevation: 10,760 to 12,500 feet**

**Management: Uncompahgre NF**
**Wilderness status: Uncompahgre WA**
**Season: July to September**
**USGS map: Wetterhorn Peak**

Formerly known as the Big Blue, the Uncompahgre Wilderness encompasses a pair of Fourteeners, dozens of 13,000-foot summits, many miles of pristine streams, and some incredibly picturesque alpine basins. One of these scenic basins spans the head of Wetterhorn Creek in the western half of the wilderness. Accessed by a moderately easy trail, Wetterhorn Basin makes a memorable destination for hikers of many abilities.

To reach the start of this hike, drive 12 miles north from Ouray on

*The view along the hike into Wetterhorn Basin*

US Highway 550 to Owl Creek Pass Road (Forest Road 858). Turn right and drive about 14 miles to the turnoff for West Fork Road (Forest Road 860). Turn south and drive 5 miles to the trailhead, which is at road's end, north of the wilderness area. The last 1.5 miles of this road require a high-clearance vehicle.

Following the Wetterhorn Trail for the entire way, this hike sets out among scattered stands of Engelmann spruce and subalpine fir before reaching timberline after the first mile. Beyond treeline the remaining 3.5 miles of this hike traverse some beautiful alpine meadows that fill

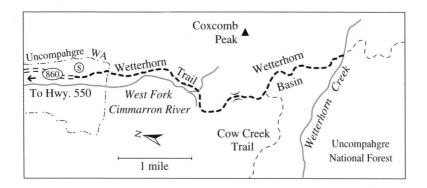

with blue columbine, Indian paintbrush, and a variety of other wild-flowers in the midsummer months. In places, the trail follows closely along the West Fork of the Cimarron River, a nice stream that features many cascades and a small waterfall. Well established and easy to follow, the first 2 miles of the Wetterhorn Trail climb along mostly easy grades. Only as it draws to within 0.5 mile of the pass that leads to Wetterhorn Basin does it take up a more moderate climb. A few switchbacks are encountered, but the grade is never overly difficult.

After 2.5 miles the Wetterhorn Trail has climbed some 1,800 feet to reach the high point of this hike—a 12,500-foot unnamed pass. Rising directly east of the pass is 13,656-foot Coxcomb Peak, and dominating the skyline to the southeast is the 14,015-foot summit of Wetterhorn Peak. Wetterhorn Peak is thought to be the conduit of an extinct volcano. Of course, the peak has since been sculpted by glaciers that gave it its rugged profile. From the pass you can look south across the Wetterhorn Basin and southwest into the deep Cow Creek drainage. Facing back to the north, you can look straight down the West Fork drainage toward the Owl Creek Pass area. Towering above the pass are several stunning rock pinnacles, the most visible of which is Chimney Rock.

South of the pass the Wetterhorn Trail drops moderately into Wetterhorn Basin, where it connects with the upper end of the 5.4-mile Cow Creek Trail. This route winds its way northwest into the Cow Creek drainage to reach a trailhead at the end of the Cow Creek Road (Forest Road 857). Beyond this intersection, the Wetterhorn Trail continues south into the Wetterhorn Basin, where it reaches Wetterhorn Creek and the turnaround point of this hike. From the creek crossing, which is at an elevation of 11,900 feet, the Wetterhorn Trail does continue on to climb another 600 feet before reaching a pass that separates Wetterhorn Basin from the head of Mary Alice Creek to the south. From this point the route drops to a trailhead south of the Uncompahgre Wilderness.

Water is available along this hike, but it must be treated before drinking. Lightning can pose a danger to hikers along most of this trail, especially on the pass and in the open basin beyond.

# 80  BEAR CREEK

**Distance: 8.4 miles round trip**
**Difficulty: Strenuous**
**Hiking time: 6 hours**
**Elevation: 8,440 to 11,200 feet**
**Management: Uncompahgre NF**

**Wilderness status: None**
**Season: June to October**
**USGS maps: Ouray, Ironton,**
    **Handies Peak**

Of the four different Bear Creeks found in the western half of the San Juan Mountains, the one that drains into the Uncompahgre Gorge a couple of miles south of Ouray could well be the most spectacular. Although the creek bottom itself is far too rugged to follow, miners during the late nineteenth century were not deterred, and constructed a trail into the upper reaches of the drainage. In so doing they built one of the most improbable mountain trails in the Colorado Rockies. This hike follows the first 4.2 miles of the route, which has been designated as a national recreation trail.

To reach the beginning of the Bear Creek Trail, drive 2 miles south of Ouray on US Highway 550, to where the road passes through a small tunnel. The trailhead is on the right side of the road immediately beyond the tunnel. Additional parking is available on the left.

From the trailhead the Bear Creek Trail crosses over the road by way of the top of the tunnel. It then begins climbing up a longthy series of moderate to strenuously steep switchbacks along the east wall

*A hiker along the rugged Bear Creek Trail*

of the Uncompahgre Gorge. In its first mile the trail passes through scattered white firs, some of which are quite old and impressive. After about a mile of climbing, the trail encounters some picturesque limber pines as well. Upon entering an open area you can look straight down to see the trailhead directly below. Signs on either end of the switchbacks warn against tossing rocks down the slope so as not to injure other hikers. The trail crosses a talus slope, then traverses the first of many precipitous ledges to come. It then climbs some more switchbacks before finally leveling off. In the first 1.5 miles the Bear Creek Trail climbs some 800 feet.

From the top of the switchbacks you can enjoy nice views of both the Uncompahgre Gorge below and the highly scenic Mount Sneffels massif to the west. You can also begin to see the town of Ouray tucked in the canyon to the north. In addition to the terrific scenery, this vantage point also provides a good perspective on the geology of the area. Exposed along the lower reaches of the rugged Uncompahgre Gorge are the quartzites and slates of the Uncompahgre Formation. This formation dates back to the Precambrian era and includes some of the oldest rocks in Colorado. Exhibited in these slates are ripple marks that hint at the rock's sedimentary origins. As the Bear Creek Trail climbs up the last switchback, it crosses from this Precambrian rock to a deposit of much younger volcanic tuff above. Common across the higher reaches of the San Juan Mountains, this rock was deposited during the Tertiary period, between 40 million and 5 million years ago. Occurring in three different phases, fiery eruptions repeatedly spewed ash and lava across a broad dome of older rock to slowly build up a layer of volcanic material thousands of feet thick. The end result was the large and rugged San Juan Mountain Range.

From the top of the switchbacks the Bear Creek Trail contours east along an elevation of about 9,200 feet for the next 0.75 mile or so. It is along this stretch that you can really appreciate the hard work that went into this incredible trail. In places the miners actually blasted ledges out of the sheer canyon wall. They also built support cribbing out of logs and rocks, some of which is still visible. Soon after the trail

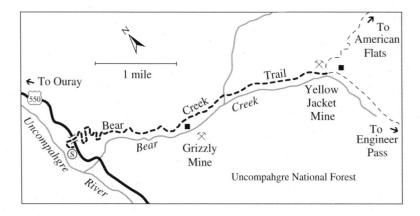

crosses a boulder slide area, it climbs along a moderate grade for 0.25 mile before reaching the old Grizzly Mine. Situated amid a stand of aspens on the left side of the creek are a few fallen-down buildings and some rusted machinery. The Grizzly Mine itself is located just across the creek and up the mountainside a bit.

Beyond the Grizzly Mine the Bear Creek Trail continues along the north wall of the canyon until it eventually reaches the creek bottom about 3 miles from the trailhead. The route then climbs sporadically for a little over a mile before reaching the Yellow Jacket Mine and the turnaround point of this hike. Along this last segment the trail crosses a side creek and continues on through forests of mostly Engelmann spruce and subalpine firs, and across open meadows. Like the Grizzly Mine, the Yellow Jacket Mine features old buildings and machinery, plus open mine shafts and tunnels. For safety reasons, it is best not to enter these deteriorating mines.

Although this hike turns around here, it is possible to continue on in one of two directions. From the Yellow Jacket Mine the Bear Creek Trail continues east to eventually reach the Horsethief Trail and American Flats in the southern tip of the Uncompahgre Wilderness. A second route turns south at the Yellow Jacket Mine to climb to 13,218-foot Engineer Pass. Portions of this second trail are indistinct, but the Forest Service plans to improve the route in the near future. While the Bear Creek Trail was built to access mines such as the Grizzly and Yellow Jacket, it also served as an alternate route to Engineer Mountain area for miners who did not want to pay the toll levied for passage on the Million Dollar Highway, which continued up the Uncompahgre Gorge. Built by Otto Mears, the Million Dollar Highway was a real engineering feat as it had to be etched out of sheer canyon walls. Today, US Highway 550 follows the same route.

Although water is available in the second half of this hike (it must be treated), the first 3 miles of the route are dry. Lightning can pose a hazard along the higher portions of this hike. Because of severe dropoffs, exercise extreme caution along much of this trail. Do not throw rocks over edges or cut switchbacks. Falling rocks may pose a hazard, especially after a rain.

#  BLUE LAKES

**Distance: 6 miles round trip**
**Difficulty: Moderate**
**Hiking time: 4 hours**
**Elevation: 8,350 to 11,730 feet**
**Management: Uncompahgre NF**

**Wilderness status: Mount Sneffels WA**
**Season: July to September**
**USGS maps: Mount Sneffels, Telluride**

Set in a scenic glacial basin, the Blue Lakes provide a nice destination within the 16,505-acre Mount Sneffels Wilderness. In addition to the access that this hike provides to higher terrain above, the fishing at all three lakes can be superb.

To reach the beginning of this hike, drive about 4 miles west from Ridgway on Colorado Highway 62 to Dallas Creek Road (Forest Road 851). Turn left and drive 14 miles south to the Blue Lakes trailhead, which is on a sharp bend near the road's end.

From the trailhead the Blue Lakes Trail follows the East Fork of Dallas Creek south for a short distance before beginning to climb up a ridge west of the creek. After following easy to moderate grades for the first 1.5 miles, the trail reaches a side creek that flows east into Dallas Creek below. By this point the route has gained a total of 2,000 feet in elevation. Beyond this stream crossing, the Blue Lakes Trail climbs a bit farther before reaching an elevation of 11,700 feet, along which it contours south for the next 0.5 mile. Within the next 0.75 mile, the trail gains another 300 feet before reaching the north shore of the lowest, and largest, Blue Lake. From here the Blue Lakes Trail ascends steeply eastward to gain 600 feet in less than 0.5 mile before reaching the middle lake. In the last 0.25 mile to the uppermost Blue Lake, the climb is negligible.

Situated above timberline, the middle and upper Blue Lakes provide the best views of the surrounding collection of particularly rugged summits. Included in the lineup are 13,809-foot Dallas Peak and 13,694-foot Gilpin Peak to the south, an unnamed 13,242-foot-high extension of Mears Peak to the west, and—the tallest of all—14,150-foot Mount Sneffels directly east. While the dark color of these summits belies the fact that this area resulted from an extensive period of volcanic activity, Mount Sneffels itself has been identified as an igneous intrusion that pushed its way up through existing layers of volcanic rock. For all its ruggedness, Mount Sneffels is a relatively simple climb from the Blue Lakes Pass area above the lakes. To reach the pass, continue east from the uppermost lake for another mile or so. Climbing strenuously much of the way, this ascent gains some 1,200 feet before reaching the 13,000-foot pass. Beyond the pass the route to the summit of Mount Sneffels takes off to the north to climb a couloir on the mountain's southeast face. While Mount Sneffels is accessible from the Blue Lakes, most climbers begin their ascent in Yankee Boy Basin on the east side of Blue Lakes Pass.

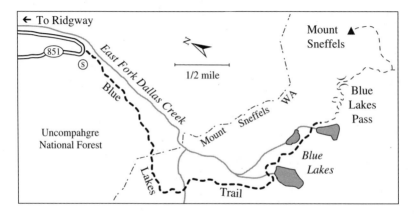

While water is available at the start of this hike and at the lakes, it must be treated before drinking. Watch for lightning in the vicinity of the lakes and above. Keep in mind that the rock in the Sneffels Range is quite rotten—use extreme caution when climbing around exposed areas. Because the area receives heavy use, you may want to plan your trip for a weekday. Campfires are banned within the East Dallas Creek drainage, so bring a stove.

# 82 SNEFFELS HIGH LINE

Distance: 14 miles round trip
Difficulty: Strenuous
Hiking time: 7 hours
Elevation: 8,900 to 12,250 feet
Management: Uncompahgre NF

Wilderness status: Mount Sneffels WA
Season: June to September
USGS map: Telluride

Although you would never know it by looking at the Uncompahgre National Forest map, a number of interesting trails explore the rugged mountain slopes north of Telluride. Perhaps the most intriguing route is the relatively new Sneffels High Line Trail. Completed in the summer of 1990, this loop trail connects several older routes with newly constructed sections to climb steeply above timberline. Traversing two alpine basins, this hike reveals some beguiling views along the way. The drawback is that, like most hikes in the Telluride area, the Sneffels High Line will put knots in your calf and thigh muscles. It is steep!

To begin this hike, drive to the north end of Aspen Street in downtown Telluride and park along the last block or two. Walk the remaining way to the trailhead, which features a signboard.

From the trailhead walk less than 50 yards north and turn left onto the Jud Wiebe Trail. As this route climbs west along the mountainside above Telluride, it offers nice views of the town and ski area in rather short order. Along the way it also encounters some big old Douglas firs. This portion of the Jud Wiebe Trail is very popular among mountain bicyclists, so watch out for them up ahead. Climbing moderate to steep grades, this hike gains about 600 feet in elevation in nearly a mile before reaching an intersection. The Jud Wiebe Trail turns right at the junction to reach a trailhead on the Tomboy Road just above town in a little more than 2 miles. This hike stays to the left at the junction and follows the Deep Creek Trail for about 100 yards before crossing Butcher Creek. The Deep Creek Trail intersects the Sneffels High Line Trail soon after; turn at this point to take up the less-used right-hand trail.

From its intersection with the Deep Creek Trail the Sneffels High Line Trail climbs along mostly moderate and strenuous grades to follow Butcher Creek uphill. Following the drainage bottom for the first mile or so, the trail passes through nice stands of aspen. Eventually, the trail climbs out of the drainage bottom to continue switchbacking up among some grassy meadows just to the west. From these open areas you gain some nice views looking south across the San Miguel River Canyon to the face of the Telluride Ski Area. Some very rugged 13,000-foot peaks just to the left of the ski slopes also come into view, as do the San Miguel Mountains off to the southwest. Included in this distant range are three Fourteeners and the lone spire of Lizard Head Peak. Continuing to climb along the mountain slopes just west of Butcher Creek, the Sneffels High Line Trail soon passes a small notch, through which you get a stunning view of the next drainage to the west—Mill Creek. This vista reveals just how steep these mountains actually are. Beyond this point the trail continues to climb until it reaches a stand of Engelmann spruce. This signifies that you have indeed been climbing, as you are now above the uppermost reaches ofthe aspen trees.

After switchbacking a bit farther the Sneffels High Line Trail crosses

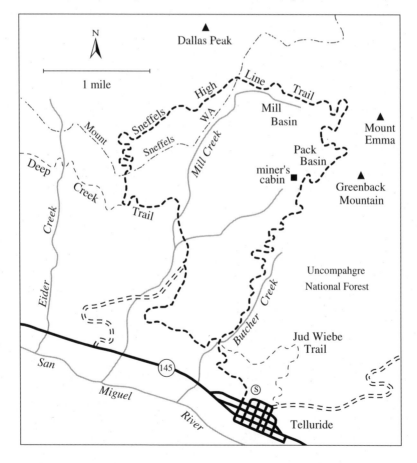

*A wintry scene along the Sneffels High Line Loop*

into the upper end of the next drainage west, where it continues along a short level stretch. Upon reaching the remains of an old miner's cabin at the edge of the forest, the trail climbs less than 0.5 mile amid some rather impressive old-growth spruce trees before reaching timberline at the lower end of Pack Basin. Sheltered by 12,997-foot Greenback Mountain to the south, 13,581-foot Mount Emma to the east, and an unnamed 12,490-foot ridge to the north, Pack Basin is a scenic little hideaway on the head of a side fork of the Mill Creek drainage. While the only distant view from this basin takes in the San Miguel Mountain Range to the southwest, the immediate peaks are incredibly rugged and scenic.

From Pack Basin the Sneffels High Line Trail climbs north to a small saddle from which it drops into Mill Basin at the head of Mill Creek itself. Marking the 12,250-foot high point of this hike, the saddle offers nice views of 13,809-foot Dallas Peak, among other rugged summits to the north. Composed of a dark volcanic rock, these jagged summits owe their existence to an intensive period of volcanic activity that occurred some 40 million years ago. The highest of these is 14,150-foot Mount Sneffels, which rises northeast from here.

After dropping into Mill Basin, the Sneffels High Line Trail briefly crosses a southern extension of the 16,505-acre Mount Sneffels Wilderness. Skirting its way around the head of Mill Creek, the route contours below Dallas Peak at about the 11,200-foot level before eventually dropping southward along a ridge that separates Mill Creek from Eider Creek to the west. Switchbacking down this steep descent, the trail loses some 800 feet in less than a mile before intersecting the Deep

Creek Trail west of Mill Creek. Turn left at this point, and continue to drop before reaching Mill Creek and the Mill Creek trailhead. This access point is located at the end of a 1-mile-long dirt road just west of town. From this point the hike covers a little over a mile along the Deep Creek Trail before reaching the start of the Sneffels High Line Trail, and about a mile more before ending at the Aspen Street trailhead.

Water is found along portions of this hike, but it must be treated. Watch for lightning in the higher terrain and mountain bicyclists along the lower Deep Creek Trail portion of the loop.

# *83* SHARKSTOOTH PASS

**Distance: 4 miles round trip**     **Management: San Juan NF**
**Difficulty: Moderate**     **Wilderness status: none**
**Hiking time: 2 hours**     **Season: July to September**
**Elevation: 10,900 to 11,936 feet**     **USGS map: La Plata**

Although Sharkstooth Peak is one of the smaller summits in the La Plata Mountains, it is one of the most spectacular. Protruding in splendid isolation a short distance north of the rest of the range, this sharply triangular summit is unmistakable, especially when viewed from the west. A short hike accesses Sharkstooth Pass, which, in turn, offers an upclose view of the rugged mountain.

To begin this hike, drive less than 0.5 mile north from Mancos on Colorado 184 to County Road 42. Turn right and follow this road (it becomes Forest Road 561 after it enters the national forest) for 12 miles

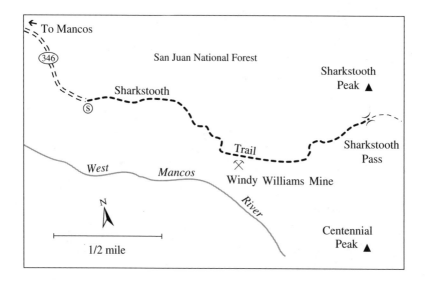

to Spruce Mill Road (Forest Road 350). Turn right and continue east for another 6.5 miles to Forest Road 346. Turn right and drive 1.5 miles to the Sharkstooth trailhead. The last few miles of this drive are rough but passable to most carefully driven vehicles.

Heading east from the trailhead, the Sharkstooth Trail begins by climbing moderately through a forest of Engelmann spruce and subalpine fir. After the first 0.75 mile, the route begins a more moderately difficult ascent. Near the 1-mile mark it encounters the old Windy Williams Mine. Besides tailings, little of the operation is left today. Beyond the mine the trail soon reaches timberline, then continues to climb among some nice alpine meadows. Following a few switchbacks, the route finally reaches 11,936-foot Sharkstooth Pass, which separates Sharkstooth Peak from Centennial Peak to the south. Along this last portion of the hike, nice views looking west across the forested foothills of the range and south to banded 13,232-foot Hesperus Mountain (the La Plata Range's highest summit) are afforded. From the pass itself, you can look east into the upper reaches of the Bear Creek drainage.

Although Sharkstooth Pass marks the turnaround point for this hike, it is possible to add to your excursion in one of two ways. The first option is to continue east along the Sharkstooth Trail, and drop into the Bear Creek drainage. After descending 1,400 feet from the pass in about 1.5 miles, the Sharkstooth Trail reaches Bear Creek and the Highline Loop Trail. A national recreation trail, the Highline Loop Trail follows Indian Ridge and upper Bear Creek to complete a 16-mile

*Looking down at Sharkstooth Pass and Sharkstooth Peak from nearby Centennial Peak*

loop hike. The second option is to scramble up 13,062-foot Centennial Peak, which rises just south of Sharkstooth Pass. The moderately difficult climb reaches the top in less than a mile, and the summit offers some interesting views. Looking across at Hesperus Mountain to the southwest and other peaks to the south, you gain an appreciation for the true uggedness of the La Plata Mountains. And looking north back at Sharkstooth Peak, you realize that, while the 12,462-foot summit is somewhat small in comparison to its neighbors, its profile is memorable.

Because water is not available along most of this hike, be sure to pack a quart or two. Watch for lightning in the exposed higher terrain.

## 84 GEYSER SPRING

**Distance: 2.5 miles round trip**
**Difficulty: Easy**
**Hiking time: 2 hours**
**Elevation: 8,600 to 9,120 feet**
**Management: San Juan NF**

**Wilderness status: None**
**Season: June to October**
**USGS maps: Dolores Peak,**
  **Groundhog Mountain**

Short and easy, the hike to Geyser Springs reveals one of Colorado's most surprising geological features: the state's only true geyser.

This hike begins at an obscure trailhead on the West Fork Road. To find it, drive 13 miles northeast from Dolores on Colorado Highway

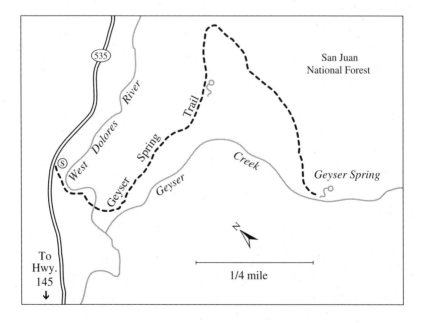

145 to the West Fork Road (Forest Road 535). Turn left and follow this road for 20.3 miles to the trail's start on the right side of the road. Although the Forest Service has installed a sign at the trailhead, it is sometimes removed by vandals. The trail begins at a point along the road just to the right of a private drive. It then follows a fenced access lane for a short way to the West Dolores River.

From the trailhead the Geyser Spring Trail follows the West Dolores River upstream for a short distance before crossing to the east bank. As there is no bridge here you will definitely get your feet wet, and you may not be able to cross at all during periods of high water. Beyond the crossing, the trail winds easily among some nice stands of aspen. After crossing a sall creek, the route continues to climb up an easy grade on an old road. Old thermal springs that have since dried up are evidenced by barren patches of brine-encrusted ground along the way. Depending on the direction of the wind, you may get a whiff of sulfur—an aroma similar to that experienced in the geyser basins of Yellowstone National Park. You may even see a wisp of steam floating up from small springs that are hidden in the woods.

After climbing for a bit, the trail drops for a short distance farther into the Geyser Creek drainage, where it reaches this hike's destination. Situated alongside the streambed, Geyser Spring is enclosed in a stone-lined pool. Although the thermal spring does not produce the fury and spectacle that Old Faithful and other Yellowstone geysers do, it does gurgle and bubble for about 12 to 15 minutes at 30- to 40-minute intervals. Unlike the thermal springs of Yellowstone, this one is not particularly hot. Rather, it is a constant 82.4 degrees Fahrenheit—a bit cool for soaking in. Upon erupting, Geyser Spring does emit sulfurous gases.

Although water is available in the West Dolores River and Geyser Creek, it must be treated before drinking. Use caution when crossing the West Dolores River in late spring, early summer, and after rainy periods.

# NAVAJO LAKE

| | |
|---|---|
| **Distance: 9.6 miles round trip** | **Management: San Juan NF** |
| **Difficulty: Strenuous** | **Wilderness status: Lizard Head WA** |
| **Hiking time: 7 hours** | **Season: July to September** |
| **Elevation: 9,393 to 11,154 feet** | **USGS map: Dolores Peak** |

It is easy to understand why Navajo Lake is the perhaps the most popular destination in the Lizard Head Wilderness. Not only is the lake situated in a beautiful alpine basin, but it also offers a handy base camp for climbers intent on climbing the nearby Fourteeners of El Diente, Mount Wilson, and Wilson Peak. Because of heavy use, a fire ban has been put into effect in the Navajo Lake Basin.

To reach the Navajo Lake trailhead, drive 13 miles northeast from

Dolores on Colorado Highway 145 to the turnoff for the West Fork Road (Forest Service Road 535). Drive 26 miles north, past the end of the pavement and past the Burro Bridge Campground, to a signed left turn for the trailhead.

Shortly beyond the trailhead, the Navajo Lake Trail intersects the Groundhog Trail, which climbs west. Afterstaying right at this junction, the route begins an easy climb along the east bank of the West Dolores River. Within 0.75 mile the route crosses the river to climb up the west bank. Because there is no bridge at this crossing, you can count on getting wet feet at the very least and having your hike blocked off cmpletely during high runoff. Beyond the crossing the trail climbs along easy to moderate grades through beautiful meadows and sporadic forests of Engelmann spruce and subalpine fir. A great variety of wildflowers grows in these meadows in July and early August. At the 1.5-mile mark the Kilpacker Trail comes in from the Meadows area to the southeast. Views along this portion of the hike include Dolores Peak to the northwest and El Diente to the east.

After 2.5 miles the trail begins to climb a much more strenuous grade along a series of steep switchbacks. In all this ascent climbs about 1,000 feet in less than a mile. At the top of the switchbacks the Navajo Lake Trail intersects the Elk Creek Trail. A left turn at this point leads 4.5 miles to Woods Lake, which lies north of the wilderness. This hike turns right, however, and continues on for another 0.5 mile to Navajo Lake. In this last stretch the route drops about 250 feet.

Situated at 11,154 feet in elevation, scenic Navajo Lake lies right at timberline. Fishing in Navajo Lake is reported to be poor, although the West Dolores River is considerably better. In both the lake and the river, artificial flies and lures are required. Beyond its namesake, the Navajo Lake Trail continues to climb astward through Navajo Basin before topping out on a 13,000-foot saddle just below 14,017-foot Wilson Peak. Climbers often use this route to access the peak. Because the Forest Service has recently replantedsome heavily trampled campsites near the lake's outlet, they ask that overnight visitors not camp in these areas.

While water is available along much of the hike, it must be treated

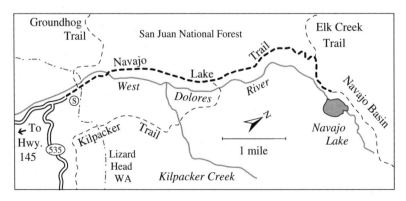

*Navajo Lake is nestled among the rugged San Miguel Mountains.*

before drinking. Also, watch out for lightning in the higher terrain. There is a fire ban throughout the Navajo Basin, so backpackers will need to bring a stove. Because Navajo Lake receives heavy use in midsummer, you may want to plan your visit for a weekday or after Labor Day.

# 86     LIZARD HEAD

**Distance: 12 miles round trip**
**Difficulty: Moderate**
**Hiking time: 8 hours**
**Elevation: 10,040 to 12,147 feet**
**Management: Uncompahgre NF,**
   **San Juan NF**

**Wilderness status: Lizard Head WA**
**Season: July to September**
**USGS map: Mount Wilson**

For at least the last 100 years, the sight of Lizard Head Peak has enthralled all who traveled across Lizard Head Pass between the towns of Dolores and Telluride. Protruding abruptly above the eastern end of the San Miguel Mountains, this 13,113-foot pinnacle of rock was featured in the logo of Otto Mears's Rio Grande Northwestern Railroad. In 1912 an erroneous newspaper story claimed that the landmark had actually collapsed, much to the shock of its readers. Today, the stunning spire still captures the imaginations of motorists heading north on Colorado Highway 145. Those who wish to get a much closer look at Lizard Head can follow a roundabout route to its base for a worm's-eye view.

To reach the beginning of this hike, drive 14.5 miles south from Telluride on Colorado Highway 145 to Lizard Head Pass. The well-marked trailhead is located just west of the highway.

From the trailhead the Lizard Head Trail contours north along the east slope of Blackface Mountain for about 1 mile before turning west to climb up a number of switchbacks. This first section of the route passes through patches of aspen and open meadows as it roughly parallels Highway 145 above Trout Lake and the Lake Fork Valley. After crossing a talus slope the trail begins ascending the switchbacks along moderate to strenuous grades; the surrounding forest incldes stands of Engelmann spruce and subalpine fir. The route encounters a junction at a small meadow. A right turn here leads 2 miles to Wilson Meadows, a beautiful open park located north of Blackface Mountain. The Lizard Head Trail heads left to continue climbing up Blackface Mountain.

Beyond the turnoff for Wilson Meadows, the Lizard Head Trail ascends more steeply among tall stands of spruce and fir. Around the 11,600-foot level the trail reaches timberline, where it levels off somewhat to follow the crest of Blackface Mountain west. While this open mountaintop is no place to be during inclement weather, it does provide exceptional views. To the south it is possible to pick out Highway 15 as it winds north toward Lizard Head Pass. To the east are the rugged summits of Pilot Knob, Golden Horn, and Vermilion Peak, among

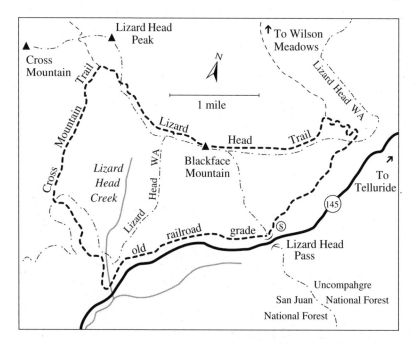

others. To the north you can look down upon Wilson Meadows, where you might spy mule deer or elk. And westward stand the spectacular San Miguel Mountains. Among these impressive wonders are three Fourteeners, a number of slightly lower mountains, and Lizard Head itself.

After topping the 12,147-foot summit of Blackface Mountain, the trail begins to drop down the relatively gently sloping west flank of the mountain. Eventually, the route reaches a saddle situated between the headwaters of Lizard Head and Wilson creeks. From here it climbs up a moderately steep ridge that extends south from Lizard Head. All along this section of the trail, views of the monolith are unobstructed and spectacular. About 6 miles from the trailhead, the route passes just beneath Lizard Head itself to reach a junction with the Cross Mountain Trail. Composed of old volcanic ash and cinder, Lizard Head is nearly unclimbable due to the crumbling condition of the rock. Climbers do, however, scale nearby 14,246-foot Mount Wilson, 14,017-foot Wilson Peak, and 14,159-foot El Diente with considerable frequency. Of these three Fourteeners, El Diente and Mount Wilson are considered difficult, and some climbers have died trying to scale them.

Although this hike turns left at the Lizard Head–Cross Mountain Trail intersection, it is possible to continue following the Lizard Head Trail north into Bilk Basin. Heading south on the Cross Mountain Trail, however, this hike drops some 1,800 feet in 3 miles to reach Colorado Highway 145 a couple of miles south of Lizard Head Pass. The Cross Mountain Trail segment of the hike descends easily among open meadows that afford wonderful views in various directions. Upon reaching the highway you can return to your car via a trail that parallels the highway to the north. Although not signed, this last 2-mile stretch of the hike actually follows an old railroad grade. You will be within plain view of the road, but there is still plenty of fine mountain scenery.

Water is available along this hike, although it must be treated before drinking. Watch for lightning during summer thunderstorms, especially along the exposed summit of Blackface Mountain. Although there are no exposed drop-offs along the Lizard Head Trail, those who attempt ascents of nearby peaks should be very careful.

*Lizard Head Peak from the summit of Blackface Mountain*

# 87  DILLON PINNACLES

**Distance: 4 miles round trip**          **Management: Curecanti NRA**
**Difficulty: Easy**                      **Wilderness status: None**
**Hiking time: 3 hours**                  **Season: Year-round**
**Elevation: 7,400 to 7,847 feet**        **USGS map: Sapinero**

This short and easy hike along the north shore of Blue Mesa Lake culminates with an up-close vista of the impressive Dillon Pinnacles. Rising at the south end of the West Elk Mountains, these unusual formations offer picturesque evidence that this region resulted from an extended period of volcanic activity.

Drive 21 miles west from Gunnison on US Highway 50 to where the road crosses to the south shore of Blue Mesa Lake. The Dillon Pinnacles trailhead is at the picnic area just before the bridge.

Setting out along the shore of the Blue Mesa Lake, the Dillon Pinnacles Trail follows a mostly level grade for about 0.75 mile until it reaches Dillon Gulch. The route then turns north to follow the gulch's bottom for another 0.25 mile. Along this stretch the trail climbs about 300 feet along a mostly easy grade. Upon reaching the 7,800-foot level, the trail turns left to contour west to a knoll that sits directly in front of the Dillon Pinnacles. An old jeep route continues up Dillon Gulch from where the Dillon Pinnacles Trail turns off. All along this hike, the plant community is predominantly sagebrush and grasses. Views of the lake to the south are nice throughout.

While the Dillon Pinnacles are visible along most of this hike, the best view is at the trail's end, which is marked by a small loop. Composed of West Elk Breccia, the pinnacles consist of ash and rock that was spewed from fiery volcanoes some 30 million years ago. Deposited in a layer thousands of feet thick, this volcanic material was eventually cemented together to make a conglomerate rock that has subsequently eroded into the cliff of spires before you. While palisades of

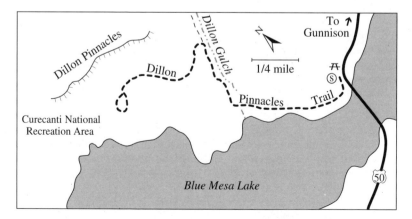

*The Dillon Pinnacles rise near Blue Mesa Lake.*

West Elk Breccia tower over portions of Blue Mesa Lake, the lower reaches of the Curecanti National Recreation Area feature the much older Precambrian rock that typifies the Black Canyon of the Gunnison.

Eagles—golden eagles in the summer and bald eagles during the winter—may be seen soaring in the vicinity of Blue Mesa Lake, and a variety of migratory birds frequent the shores of the lake below. Mule deer and elk are common to the Curecanti area, while coyotes, mountain lions, and black bears reside here as well. Given the fact that a lot of activity occurs on and about the lake, however, you will likely not see these shyer creatures along the Dillon Pinnacles Trail.

Bring water on this hike, especially on warm summer afternoons. Watch for lightning as thunderstorms can move quickly through the area.

# 88 OAK FLAT LOOP

**Distance: 2 miles round trip**
**Difficulty: Moderate**
**Hiking time: 2 hours**
**Elevation: 8,160 to 7,800 feet**
**Management: Black Canyon of the**
  **Gunnison NM**

**Wilderness status: Black Canyon**
  **of the Gunnison WA**
**Season: Year-round**
**USGS map: Grizzly Ridge**

Reaching a depth of 1,800 feet and spanning as little as 1,100 feet from rim to rim in places, the Black Canyon of the Gunnison is unmatched for its combination of narrowness and depth. Although most visitors view the Black Canyon from either the south or north rim, a handful of hardy souls actually descend into the canyon's depths by way of a few rough routes that access the bottom. While such an endeavor is beyond the realm of this guidebook, one established trail—the 2-mile-long Oak Flat Loop—does drop beneath the south rim for a short distance to offer a more in-depth look at the canyon and its ecosystems.

The Oak Flat Loop begins at the visitor center for the Black Canyon

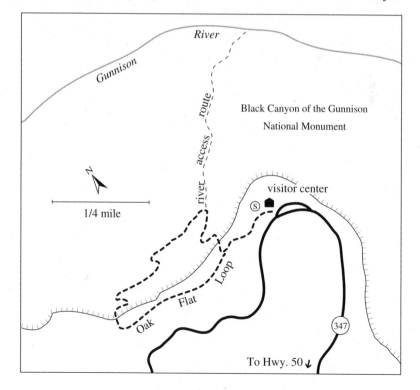

*Looking into the Black Canyon of the Gunnison from Oak Flat*

of the Gunnison National Monument. To reach the visitor center, drive
8 miles west from Montrose on US Highway 50 to Colorado Highway
347 and the turnoff for the monument. The visitor center is 7 miles
north.

Heading west from the visitor center, the signed Oak Flat Loop descends easily through a thick forest of Gambel oak for about 0.25 mile
before reaching the first trail junction. After turning right here the
route descends steeply through a few switchbacks before reaching Oak
Flat itself. Along this descent the trail passes among some Douglas firs
and a small stand of aspens. Both of these tree species find suitable
moisture and protection from direct sun in this below-the-rim location.
After dropping about 300 feet from its start, the Oak Flat Loop reaches
the signed turnoff for a river-access route. Quite rugged and un-
marked, this route to the bottom drops some 1,500 feet in less than a
mile. A permit is required from the Park Service to continue down this
route; it can be obtained from the visitor center.

Beyond the river-access turnoff, the Oak Flat Loop begins heading
west along a ledge of sorts. Shortly, the trail passes a rock outcrop with
an incredible view of a mile-long stretch of the canyon below. Of particular note is a narrow section a short distance downstream. Consisting of Precambrian schist and gneiss that dates back 1.7 billion years,

the dark walls of the canyon feature several light streaks that were formed when molten rock was injected into fissures and cracks. Thought to have been formed within the last 2 million years, the Black Canyon was cut into the dome-shaped Gunnison Uplift by the Gunnison River. Geologists theorize that the river first established its present course in a layer of softer volcanic rock before it reached the underlying Gunnison Uplift.

From the overlook, the Oak Flat Loop heads west for a short distance before beginning the climb back up to the canyon's rim. The trail passes another stand of aspens nestled at the base of a cliff, as well as more Douglas firs. The climb out of the canyon on this end of the loop is not nearly so steep as where the trail drops in below the visitor center. After reaching the rim the Oak Flat Loop heads east to return to the trailhead.

Bring water on this hike as none is found along the way. Watch for lightning during thunderstorms and use caution when hiking near dangerous drop-offs.

# 89  GUNNISON GORGE

Distance: 9 miles round trip
Difficulty: Moderate
Hiking time: 6 hours
Elevation: 6,500 to 5,300 feet
Management: BLM

Wilderness status: Gunnison
   Gorge WSA
Season: Year-round
USGS map: Black Ridge

Up for consideration as wilderness, the BLM-administered Gunnison Gorge Wilderness Study Area encompasses some truly beautiful canyon country that extends north from the Black Canyon of the Gunnison National Monument. Included in this area is one of Colorado's more alluring river corridors. So coveted is the run through this gorge that rafters go to the trouble of packing their gear into the canyon just so they can then float down the next several miles of river. Four hiking trails drop into this highly scenic canyon from the west rim. The longest of these routes, the 4.5-mile Ute Trail, offers as fine an introduction to the Gunnison Gorge as any. Currently, the Gunnison Gorge Wilderness Study Area encompasses 21,038 acres of prime canyon country.

To reach the beginning of this hike, drive north from Montrose on US Highway 550 to Falcon Road. Turn right and continue 3.6 miles to the end of the pavement. Here the route becomes the Peach Valley Road. About 7 miles beyond the pavement's end, turn right onto Ute Road and follow it 2.5 miles to the trailhead. This road is rough in places and may require a 4WD vehicle.

From the trailhead the Ute Trail drops easily down arid hillsides studded with pinyon pine, juniper trees, and sagebrush. After descending through an open basin, the Ute Trail reaches a bench that follows the top of the inner gorge's harder Precambrian rock. After following

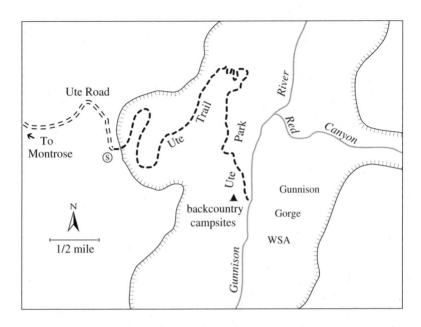

this bench north for less than a mile, the route turns east to drop down a series of steeper switchbacks. Up to this point the route has descended along mostly easy grades. Upon reaching the bottom of these switchbacks the Ute Trail heads due south across a bench area known as Ute Park before actually reaching the river. Stretching along a straight, comparatively open stretch of the Gunnison River, Ute Park historically served as a crossing point for the Ute Indians who once inhabited much of Colorado.

Upon reaching the river you can travel some distance both up- and downstream before being turned back by impassable canyon walls. The scenery is incredible, as the canyon's walls tower hundreds of feet above. Exposed within the inner portion of the Gunnison Gorge are the same dark Precambrian schists and gneisses that are found upstream within the Black Canyon of the Gunnison National Monument. Because this stretch of the Gunnison River is considered gold-medal water for trout fishing, you may want to bring a rod and reel. You may also encounter a rafting party camped at one of three backcountry campsites. Anyone who is interested in floating through the Gunnison Gorge should keep in mind that some Class III and IV rapids are found downstream. However, in an effort to minimize impact on the fragile canyon environment, the BLM has regulations for boaters. Parties cannot exceed twelve persons, open fires are prohibited, and portable potties are required.

Bring water on this hike as none is available until the river. This hike can be a hot one, especially in the summer. Watch for rattlesnakes in rocky areas.

# 90     MOUNT GARFIELD

**Distance: 4 miles round trip**
**Difficulty: Strenuous**
**Hiking time: 3 hours**
**Elevation: 4,800 to 6,765 feet**
**Management: BLM**

**Wilderness status: None**
**Season: Year-round**
**USGS maps: Clifton, Round**
   **Mountain**

One of the main geographical features of the Grand Valley, the Bookcliffs rise sharply to form a strikingly scenic wall that stretches deep into Utah. In the Grand Junction area, the Bookcliffs top out at a height of 6,765 feet in Mount Garfield. The short but challenging Mount Garfield Trail climbs to the top of Mount Garfield from a trailhead just west of the town of Palisade.

To reach the beginning of this hike, drive east from Grand Junction

*Looking through a crack in the rim from the summit of Mount Garfield*

on Interstate 70 to the Palisade exit—a distance of about 10 miles. From the exit drive south a short distance to the first paved road that turns west. Follow this road (signed as the G7 Road) for 1.5 miles through a residential area to where it turns. Turn right onto this gravel road and drive 0.2 mile under the interstate to the trailhead just north of the highway.

From the trailhead the Mount Garfield Trail heads north across a level area before reaching a steep-sided ridge of Mancos Shale. Following the spine of this ridge, the route climbs along a very strenuous grade for the next 0.5 mile. Deposited in a shallow sea over 75 million years ago during the Cretaceous period, Mancos Shale is a soft claylike material that swells greatly when wet and shrinks upon drying. Because of this, few if any plants can grow in the soil, thereby allowing rapid erosion. Along the Bookcliffs, and in many other places, Mancos Shale features exaggerated ripple patterns. Mancos Shale is very slick and gooey when wet, so it is a good idea to avoid this hike after a rain or snowfall.

After gaining approximately 600 feet along this ridge of Mancos Shale, the route continues to climb up a slope strewn with boulders of Mesa Verde Group sandstones. The Mesa Verde Group is composed of sands deposited in a shoreline environment along Cretaceous seas. Sandwiched in among these buff-colored layers are seams of coal, which resulted from plant-rich lagoons. While this section of the trail winds its way through rocky areas, it is not difficult to follow. Eventually, the trail reaches a shelf of relatively level ground that is not visible from below. After crossing this grassy area the route climbs again to a hidden valley that was burned over within the last few years. The result is thick grasses studded by a few charred skeletons of juniper trees. From here the Mount Garfield Trail climbs to traverse an open slope to a saddle just below the rim above. From this saddle climb a

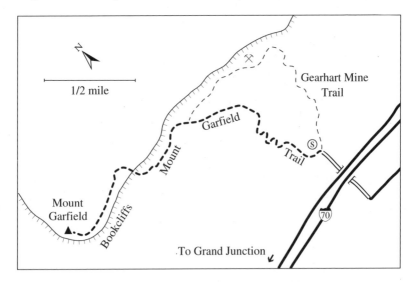

short distance farther to reach the top of the Bookcliffs. Although the scenery up to this point is spectacular, it is especially so from the very top. From the crest of the Bookcliffs it is less than 0.5 mile west to the summit of Mount Garfield. The climb along this last section of the trail is minimal.

Marked by a flagpole and a memorial to two brothers who died some years back, the Mount Garfield summit provides a 360-degree vista that is indeed tremendous. Spreading out directly below and to the west are highly eroded Mancos Shale slopes. Virtually barren, these exposures of shale contrast starkly with the pinyon pine and juniper forests that top Mount Garfield. Beyond these Mancos Shale badlands is the Grand Valley with its irrigated orchards and farm fields. Coursing across the valley and through the city of Grand Junction is the Colorado River. The Uncompahgre Plateau is draped across the horizon beyond. Grand Mesa rises to the east, as does Battlement Mesa. To the north in the distance are the light-colored Roan Cliffs, and opening up between the Roan Cliffs and Mount Garfield is Coal Canyon. As part of the 30,261-acre Little Bookcliffs Wild Horse Area, managed by the BLM, Coal Canyon is home to a herd of about eighty wild horses. Some of the horses are occasionally rounded up and put up for adoption so as to maintain a healthy balance between the feral animals and the delicate desert lands. It may be possible to spot some of these horses both from and on Mount Garfield, especially during the winter and early spring months.

While the Mount Garfield Trail provides the most direct route back to the trailhead, a second route—the 2.5-mile Gearhart Mine Trail, which branches east from the Mount Garfield Trail in the shelf area—offers a longer alternative. Indistinct and hard to find, it continues farther east to pass by the remains of an old uranium mine and an accompanying tramway. Because this route is not well used, it is difficult to follow in places.

Bring plenty of water on this hike as none is available along the way. During the summer you may want to head out early so that you can avoid the heat of the day. Lightning may pose a threat, especially on the summit. In addition, you must use careful footing along portions of this hike as a fall could prove disastrous.

# 91 MONUMENT CANYON

**Distance: 6 miles round trip**
**Difficulty: Moderate**
**Hiking time: 4 hours**
**Elevation: 6,200 to 5,300 feet**
**Management: Colorado NM**

**Wilderness status: None**
**Season: Year-round**
**USGS map: Colorado National Monument**

Embracing a ruggedly beautiful cross-section of canyons, cliffs, and mesa tops, Colorado National Monument offers some wonderful hiking opportunities within a short drive from Grand Junction. The hike described here follows the Monument Canyon Trail to the base of Indepedence Monument, the monument's flagship landform.

To reach the beginning of this hike, drive west from Grand Junction on Interstate 70 to the Fruita exit and follow the signs for Colorado National Monument. Continue south on Colorado Highway 340 for 2.4 miles to the entrance to the Colorado National Monument. Follow the monument's only road, Rim Rock Drive, south for 8.2 miles to the signed trailhead. There is limited parking for hikers on the left side of the road.

From the trailhead the Monument Canyon Trail begins dropping immediately into the head of a side drainage that eventually feeds into Monument Canyon. Within 200 yards is the turnoff for the 0.5-mile trail to the Coke Ovens—a cluster of beehive-shaped formations of Wingate Sandstone. Created by the erosion of the softer sandstone beneath caps of more resistant Kayenta Sandstone, these monoliths are clearly visible from the Monument Canyon Trail, which turns left at the trail junction.

Beyond the turnoff for the Coke Ovens, the Monument Canyon Trail begins to really drop in elevation as it negotiates steep switchbacks, areas of loose rock, and exposed drop-offs. In about 0.5 mile the route descends some 600 feet before reaching the relatively level canyon bottom. Originally built by John Otto shortly after the turn of the century, this route was part of his one-man campaign to bring attention to this

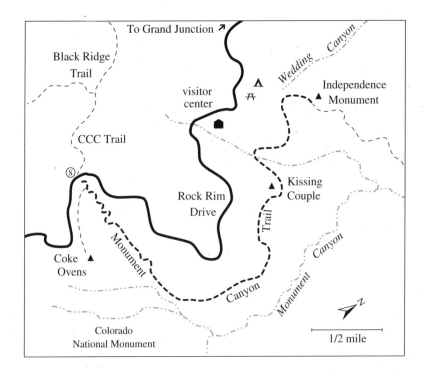

*The Kissing Couple (right) is a visual treat for hikers who venture into Monument Canyon.*

scenic area. His efforts paid off, and Colorado National Monument was established in 1911 by a stroke of President Taft's pen.

Along this descent you may want to stop and take in the geology of the canyon. Like the Coke Ovens, the canyon walls consist of Wingate Sandstone, a rock that tends to form sheer cliffs several hundred feet high. Wingate Sandstone was deposited as sand dunes during the Triassic period more than 200 million years ago. Atop the Wingate Formation is a layer of Kayenta Sandstone, and above that a layer of pinkish rock known as Entrada Sandstone. Like the Wingate Formation, Entrada Sandstone was formed from wind-blown sands. Although Entrada Sandstone forms the rimrock in most of the national monument, younger layers of substrata are identifiable in the higher terrain west of the trailhead. Included among them is the Morrison Formation, which has produced most of the dinosaur bones found in the Colorado Plateau region thus far.

Upon reaching the canyon bottom the Monument Canyon Trail heads east through forests of pinyon pine and Utah juniper. Such an ecosystem is standard for this elevation as semidesert conditions predominate here. Other plants include mountain mahogany, Mormon tea, yucca, and a renegade cottonwood tree or two stashed away along the dry streambeds. Among the resident fauna of the monument are mule deer, desert bighorn sheep, antelope ground squirrels, coyotes, and mountain lions.

After continuing 0.5 mile east from the bottom of its descent into the canyon, the Monument Canyon Trail begins to bend north as it follows the canyon wall. A little more than 2 miles from the trailhead the trail passes almost directly beneath an interesting formation called the Kissing Couple. From this upclose vantage point, the landmark is quite impressive. By this point you may have also noticed some dark metamorphic rock along the lower reaches of the canyon. Dating back 1.5 billion years, these Precambrian schists and gneisses form the core of the Uncompahgre Plateau, which reaches its northern terminus at Colorado National Monument.

After passing beneath an additional tower of Wingate Sandstone, the Monument Canyon Trail reaches the base of Independence Monument. While a spectacular view of this 450-foot-high monolith can be enjoyed from Rim Rock Drive above, the rock's base provides an equally impressive but very different vantage point. Once part of a large dividing wall, Independence Monument was worn away by erosin on both sides, leaving the freestanding flatiron behind. This whole scenario can best be envisioned from a low saddle just west of the formation. From this point you can see how Independence Monument separates Monument Canyon from Wedding Canyon to the nrth. From here you can also see the Pipe Organ, Window Rock, and Sentinel Rock on the far side of Wedding Canyon. And, framed in the mouth of Wedding Canyon just as it is framed in the mouth of Monument Canyon, is the verdant patchwork of farmlands that spread across the Grand Valley beyond.

Although the 6-mile Monument Canyon Trail continues for another 3miles from the base of Independence Monument to reach a trailhead just east of the national monument boundary, this hike turns around here to return to the upper trailhead. Don't forget that you have a 600-foot climb back to your car before finishing this hike.

Water is not available along this hike, so bring plenty, especially in the hot summer months. Although rattlesnakes tend to shy away from people, watch out for them anyway.

# 92 RATTLESNAKE CANYON

**Distance: 2.8 miles round trip**
**Difficulty: Easy**
**Hiking time: 2 hours**
**Elevation: 5,860 to 5,400 feet**
**Management: BLM**

**Wilderness status: Black Ridge**
**Canyons WSA**
**Season: Year-round**
**USGS map: Mack**

Containing the second-largest collection of natural arches in the country—behind only Arches National Park—Rattlesnake Canyon is as nice a slickrock paradise as any to be found on the Colorado Plateau. Besides the arches, the overall scenery is tremendous and the hike itself offers a real adventure.

You will need a 4WD vehicle to get to the start of the Rattlesnake

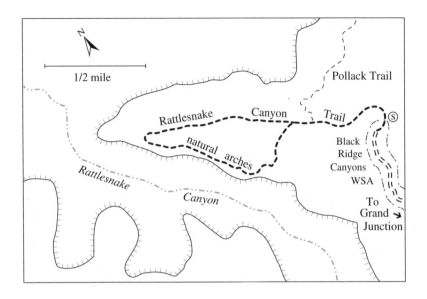

Canyon Trail (if you have a 2WD vehicle, see the next paragraph for
information on an alternate access). From Grand Junction, drive west
on Interstate 70 to Fruita and the turnoff for Colorado National Monument. Turn south onto Rim Rock Drive and drive 11 miles to the turnoff for Glade Park. Turn right and drive 0.2 mile to Black Ridge Road.
Turn right again and drive 13 miles to the trailhead. The first several
miles of this route require a high-clearance 2WD vehicle, while the last
3 miles definitely call for a 4WD. The route is marked with small
brown public-access signs.

From the trailhead the Rattlesnake Canyon Trail drops steeply for a
hort distance to the east before circling around to the west beneath the
trailhead area. After leveling off the trail intersects the Pollack Trail,
which begins at a trailhead at the east end of the WSA. Nearly 7
miles in length, the Pollack Trail offers access to Rattlesnake Canyon
to those who do not have a 4WD vehicle. It also traverses some truly
interesting canyon topography. Included in the rugged collection of
canyons and mesas that make up the Black Ridge Canyons WSA are
exposures of the Morrison and Summerville formations, and faces of
Entrada, Wingate, and Chinle sandstones. The lower sections of some
canyons feature dark Precambrian rock, The great folds and bends in a
few canyon walls resulted from faulting action. Flora within this semidesert terrain includes pinyon pines, junipers, Mormon tea, sagebrush,
saltbush, and a variety of grasses. Wildlife residents include mule
deer, coyotes, mountain lions, and a herd of about 150 desert bighorn
sheep.

After keeping left at the Pollack Trail junction, continue west for
nealy another 0.5 mile to reach the rimrock above Rattlesnake Canyon.

You should soon see the first arch in the red rock below. To reach the other arches, descend through this arch to the bench area, then continue northwest along the base of the cliffs to the right. The arches are tucked away in these folds of rock. Formed only partly by water and wind erosion, these arches also owe their existence to the cleaving action of ice in the wintertime. As water seeps into cracks it freezes and expands, thereby flaking off chunks of rock. The rock, Entrada Sandstone, is the same stuff of which the arches in Arches National Park are made. After enjoying the nearly one dozen arches in Rattlesnake Canyon, you can circle around to the north side of the pointed mesa top that forms a portion of Rattlesnake Canyon's north side. The route doubles back to rejoin the trail just west of the Pollack Trail intersection.

Bring plenty of water, as none is available along this hike and it can get quite hot in the summer. Watch for rattlesnakes when hiking in rocky areas, and exercise caution when climbing around the arches and near all precipices. Take care not to trample across cryptogamic soil, which forms a stabilizing crust over loose soil that might otherwise blow away. This combination of lichens and mosses is very fragile and it takes many years to heal after it is stepped on.

# 93 RUBY CANYON OVERLOOK

**Distance: 5 miles round trip**
**Difficulty: Easy**
**Hiking time: 3 hours**
**Elevation: 4,950 to 5,723 feet**

**Management: BLM**
**Wilderness status: None**
**Season: Year-round**
**USGS map: Ruby Canyon**

If you show up at the Rabbit Valley Recreation Management Area on a busy weekend, you might think that this is the last place in Colorado to find an interesting and peaceful hike. As a BLM-administered recreation management area, Rabbit Valley is often rife with noisy ATVs, motorcycles, and 4WD vehicles. While many trails and dirt roads in Rabbit Valley do accommodate the off-road vehicle enthusiasts who frequent the area, the 2.5-mile Rabbit's Ear Trail leaves the mechanized hum behind in favor of a lonesome, windswept mesa top with one of the best vista points in the entire Grand Valley area.

To reach the trailhead, drive 30 miles west from Grand Junction on Interstate 70 to Exit 2, which is less than 2 miles from the Utah border. From this exit turn south and drive 0.4 mile to where the road splits. Turn left (east) and drive another 4.4 miles on a good dirt road. The signed trailhead is on the right.

Named for the shape of the mesa's edge that it follows, the Rabbit's Ear Trail climbs a few hundred feet along an easy grade for the first 0.5 mile to reach a ridgeline, which it follows a short distance farther. From this section of the hike it is possible to look out toward the Bookcliffs to the north. All along this trail the dominant plant species is Utah juniper, but scattered rabbitbrush, saltbush, and Mormon tea are found here as well. Around the 1-mile mark is a nice view of a large meander in the Colorado River to the east. The trail then passes through an interesting cut in the sandstone before contouring up to the northern point of an unnamed mesa. Within the next 0.25 mile the trail makes its steepest climb—about 300 feet—to reach the mesa top directly south. Upon reaching the top, the trail follows the east rim of the mesa for slightly less than a mile to reach the Ruby Canyon Overlook, which is located on the southern edge of the mesa.

*An interesting formation near the Colorado River as seen from the Ruby Canyon Overlook*

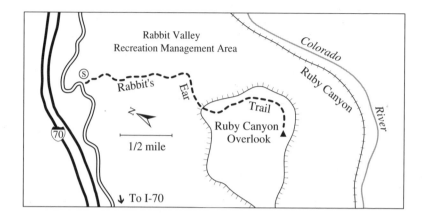

From the overlook the views are indeed wonderful. Front and center is Ruby Canyon, through which flows the Colorado River. Although railroad tracks follow its north bank, this stretch of the river is popular among rafters and kayakers. This is in large part due to the colorful sandstone walls that follow the river as it snakes its way toward Utah. Rising farther south is the 75,168-acre Black Ridge Canyons Wilderness Study Area. A real highlight among BLM wildlands, the Black Ridge Canyons WSA includes tangled slickrock canyons, isolated mesas, and the largest collection of natural arches outside of Arches National Park in Utah (see Hike 92, Rattlesnake Canyon). Beyond the Black Ridge Canyons area is the Uncompahgre Plateau, and in the distance to the southwest rise the La Sal Mountains near Moab, Utah. The Grand Valley and the city of Grand Junction are visible to the east, as are Grand Mesa and the Roan Cliffs beyond. And, as previously mentioned, the lengthy Bookcliffs line the skyline to the north as they stretch far into Utah's Green River Desert.

Bring plenty of drinking water on this hike as none is available along the way. Hiking in the summer can be especially hot in this arid desert terrain. Watch for rattlesnakes in rocky areas.

# 94 ROUBIDEAU CANYON

Distance: 8 miles round trip      Management: Uncompahgre NF
Difficulty: Moderate      Wilderness status: Roubideau Area
Hiking time: 5 hours      Season: June to October
Elevation: 9,120 to 8,400 feet      USGS map: Antone Springs

Slicing deeply through the eastern flank of the Uncompahgre Plateau, Roubideau Canyon offers a 20-mile corridor of pristine canyon country. In all, three modest trail systems access the canyon: one near its mouth, one in the middle, and one at the head of the drainage. This hike into Roubideau Canyon accesses the upper portion, where peren-

nial streams and beautiful forestlands predominate. Although the
Colorado Wilderness Act of 1993 did not designate the Roubideau as a
wilderness area, it did establish the 19,650-acre Roubideau Area. This
designation safeguards the canyon from further development, but it
does not settle the issue of water rights within the area.

To reach the start of this hike, you must first negotiate a maze of
rural roads that lead through the farmlands northeast of Montrose.
From Montrose drive north on US Highway 50 for 5 miles to the turnoff for Jay Jay Road. Turn left and follow Jay Jay Road for about 1.5
miles to a fork in the road. Bear left onto Jig Road, continue another
2 miles to Road 5850, and turn right. Follow this road for less than a
mile to Jasmine Road, which turns left. In 1.2 miles keep right on Hillside Road and follow it for 2 miles to where it bends right and graveled
Holly Road continues straight. Follow Holly Road for less than 0.5 mile
to its intersection with Transfer Road (also known as Forest Road 508).
Turn left onto graveled Transfer Road and follow it for 16.8 miles to
the signed turnoff for the Roubideau trailhead. Follow this road for 0.4
mile to its end, and the start of the Roubideau Trail. Although passable to most vehicles, Transfer Road is rough in places.

If you have a shuttle it is possible to hike this route one way, to the
Pool Creek trailhead. To reach it from the Roubideau trailhead, drive
3.2 miles farther south on Transfer Road to Divide Road (Forest Road
402). Turn right and drive about 4 miles to the signed turnoff for the
Pool Creek trailhead.

From the trailhead the Roubideau Trail begins dropping into the
canyon in very short order. The route actually follows an old road as it
descends along a mostly moderate grade to reach the canyon bottom.
This portion of the hike affords some nice views of the upper reaches of
Roubideau Canyon. It also passes a small stock pond, and encounters a

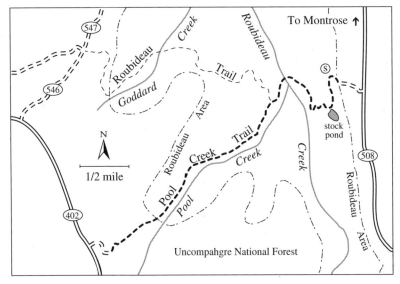

few impressive ponderosa pines near the canyon rim. The bulk of the forest type along this segment of the hike, however, is aspen, which grows in prodigious numbers. Open meadows occasionally break up the timbered areas. It should not take long for you to realize that this is a well-used grazing area for cattle.

After 0.75 mile and a drop of about 500 feet, the Roubideau Trail reaches Roubideau Creek, which drains north along the canyon bottom. Following the creek downstream from this point, the trail continues north to where it crosses over a relatively recent landslide. A little over 1 mile from the trailhead, the route crosses Roubideau Creek just downstream from where Pool Creek drains in. The Roubideau Trail then continues west, following Pool Creek upstream. In less than 0.5 mile the Roubideau Trail begins a steep climb up the canyon's west side. Just before the start of this steep ascent, however, this hike turns left onto the Pool Creek Trail, which continues to follow its namesake upstream. A sign marks this intersection.

Ascending an easy to moderate grade for much of the way, the 3.2-mile Pool Creek Trail reaches the Pool Creek trailhead after a climb of about 700 feet. This section of the hike features a considerable number of aspens. On the more shaded south side of the drainage, however, are surprisingly mature stands of Engelmann spruce and Douglas firs. The contrast between the drier aspen forests and the lush, north-facing evergreen slopes testifies to a difference in the amount of moisture available to plants in each of these environments.

Water is found along the way, but it must not be consumed as cattle frequently wade in the creeks of the area. This area receives heavy use during the hunting season in late fall, but is seldom visited during the rest of the year.

# 95 DOLORES RIVER CANYON

**Distance: 6 miles round trip**
**Difficulty: Easy**
**Hiking time: 4 hours**
**Elevation: 5,000 to 5,100 feet**
**Management: BLM**

**Wilderness status: Dolores River WSA**
**Season: Year-round**
**USGS map: Paradox**

After gathering strength in the San Juan Mountains, the Dolores River flows west and north before emptying into the Colorado River just inside Utah. While still in Colorado, the Dolores River twists and turns through a series of deep wilderness canyons that thrill thousands of rafters, canoeists, and kayakers each spring. One of these canyons, the 30-mile-long Dolores River Canyon, is the centerpiece of a 28,668-acre BLM wilderness study area of the same name. Hikers interested in exploring this corridor can follow an old jeep road, now closed to vehicles, that accesses the first few miles of the canyon's mouth. Along the way you can enjoy not just spectacular red-rock scenery, but some prehistoric and paleontological treats as well.

To reach the start of this hike drive 2 miles west from Naturita on Colorado Highway 141 to where Colorado Highway 90 turns off. Turn left and drive about 22 miles to Bedrock. Just beyond where the highway crosses the Dolores River, and just before the Bedrock Store, turn left and drive 2 miles south to where the road is closed.

From the road closure follow this old road south along the river's west bank for about 1 mile, to where it turns west to continue upstream. Rounding a prominent point in the canyon wall, this turn in the route is almost directly above the river itself, and offers a good view

*The Dolores River winds its way among soaring sandstone walls.*

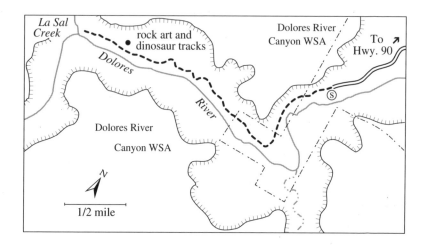

of the Dolores River as it meanders downstream toward Bedrock, and of a straight upstream stretch to the west. Already towering nearly 1,000 feet high at this point, the walls of the Dolores River Canyon include several layers of rock that represent different episodes of geologic history. Most impressive are the sheer faces of Wingate Sandstone, which provide the canyon walls with much of their vertical rise. Wingate Sandstone was formed as giant sand dunes during the Triassic period. Below these cliffs is the Chinle Formation, which includes sandstones and shales that were deposited in large flood plains and shallow lakes. Above the Wingate cliffs is Kayenta Sandstone, which originated in flood plains in the Triassic period. And above it is the Entrada Formation, which also began as large sand dunes. Younger deposits of the less distinct Summerville, Morrison, and Dakota formations constitute the highest reaches of the canyon corridor.

After turning west, the route continues upstream for another 2 miles before reaching the mouth of La Sal Creek, which drains from Utah to the west. Maintaining a level grade as it follows a bench above the river bottom, the route encounters pinyon pine and juniper forests along with open areas of sagebrush. About 2 miles from the trailhead, the route encounters two interesting features that are a short distance north of the road. If you turn right onto a small trail that river runners have worn down, you will soon reach several large boulders. Some of these boulders have petroglyphs etched into protected faces. Created by the Anasazi Indians several centuries ago, these images still mystify archaeologists and laypersons alike. And across the flat side of a particularly large boulder that stands upright are faint but unmistakable dinosaur tracks. After visiting these two relics of the past, you can continue following the road for less than a mile before reaching the mouth of La Sal Creek and the turn-around point for this hike. It is possible to continue exploring both the Dolores River Canyon and La Sal Creek upstream but you should expect to get your feet wet before too long. Although once a wild and free-flowing waterway, the Dolores

River has since been tamed by the McPhee Dam upstream. This means that the river usually flows at a fraction of its normal strength. While this drop in volume may allow hikers to wade across in the low-water season, it also means that rafters can enjoy the river for only a few weeks each year.

Bring water on this hike as any found along the way is not potable. Watch for flash floods, especially in the narrow side canyons. Rattle-snakes are found in the area, although they typically shy away from people.

# 96 PRATER RIDGE

**Distance: 7.8 miles round trip**
**Difficulty: Moderate**
**Hiking time: 5 hours**
**Elevation: 7,800 to 8,400 feet**

**Management: Mesa Verde NP**
**Wilderness status: None**
**Season: March to November**
**USGS map: Point Lookout**

Although much of Mesa Verde National Park's backcountry is off-limits to hiking, a few designated trails do pass through some appealing terrain. The longest of these routes is the Prater Ridge Trail. While it does not access any of the archaeological resources that the park is known for, the trail does offer spectacular scenery and an interesting array of plant species.

To reach the start of this hike, drive to Mesa Verde National Park, which is 8 miles west from Mancos on US Highway 160, or 10 miles east from Cortez. Drive 3.8 miles south from the park entrance to the Morefield Campground, turn right, and drive 0.5 mile to a parking

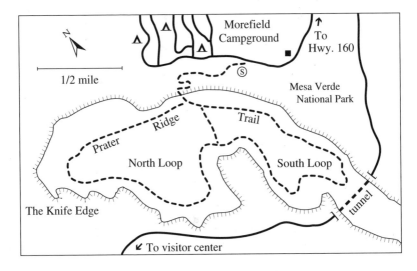

*Looking north from Prater Ridge toward the San Miguel Mountains*

area on the left side of the road. The trailhead is located just beyond the entrance booth for the camping area.

Although the Prater Ridge Trail starts out by crossing a grassy area, it soon enters a thick stand of Gambel oak, where it begins climbing the east face of Prater Ridge. As the dominant deciduous species of tree in Mesa Verde National Park, Gambel oak is plentiful all along this hike. For the next 0.5 mile or so the trail climbs an easy to moderate grade before reaching a couple of switchbacks just below the rim of the ridge. Growing nearby are some scattered Douglas firs. These taller evergreens grow throughout the park in protected areas such as this. Shortly after cresting the rim the route reaches the first of three trail junctions. While the Prater Ridge Trail follows the rim area of its namesake for most of the way, a short crossover trail divides the route into north and south loops. This hike turns right at the first trail junction to continue counterclockwise around the North Loop.

From this intersection the Prater Ridge Trail continues to climb in short but easy spurts as it heads for the ridge's high point at its north end. While Gambel oak continues to dominate the area, scattered pinyon pines and junipers also grow across the relatively flat top of the ridge. Shrub species include Utah serviceberry and mountain mahogany. As the trail nears the north end of Prater Ridge, some spectacular views open up. Close by is Point Lookout, an impressive face of sandstone and shale that towers over the park entrance. Along the horizon farther to the north are the silhouettes of Lone Cone Peak and the San Miguel Range. To the east rise the La Plata Mountains; to the west is elongated Sleeping Ute Mountain. Its resemblance to a reclining giant figures prominently in Ute Indian mythology.

After rounding the north end of Prater Ridge, the trail continues down the western rim of the ridge. This portion of the hike is especially interesting as open shelves of light-colored sandstone are traversed. Approximately 2.5 miles into the hike the Prater Ridge Trail reaches the second trail junction. As the sign indicates, a left turn here takes you back to the campground, thereby completing the North Loop portion of the trail. Instead, keep right at this point and continue along the western rim of Prater Ridge to complete the trail's South Loop. Shortly beyond the junction the route reaches some impressive pinyon pines, while a number of standing dead Douglas firs can be seen in the canyon just below. In addition to the varying plant life found along the Prater Ridge Trail, there is also a great variety of wildlife. Mule deer are plentiful and not particularly shy in Mesa Verde, and wild turkeys are a common sight. You might find black bear and mountain lion scat along the trail itself. With luck, you may even see such birds of prey as peregrine falcons and golden eagles soaring above the cliff faces of the ridge.

Eventually, the Prater Ridge Trail reaches the southern end of the ridge, where it begins heading north to follow the eastern rim back to the campground. Soon after the campground comes into view below, the final trail junction is reached. This is where the crossover trail returns from the west side of the ridge. It is a short distance from here to where the trail descends back down to the campground.

Water is not available along the Prater Ridge Trail, so bring plenty. Watch for lightning, especially during summer thunderstorms. Keep in mind that all artifacts found within the park are strictly protected by law.

# 97  PETROGLYPH POINT

**Distance: 2.8 miles round trip**
**Difficulty: Easy**
**Hiking time: 2 hours**
**Elevation: 6,970 to 6,640 feet**

**Management: Mesa Verde NP**
**Wilderness status: None**
**Season: April to November**
**USGS map: Moccasin Mesa**

Among Mesa Verde National Park's chief attractions are its impressive cliff dwellings, which were constructed during the thirteenth century. Counted among the largest such ancient structures in the

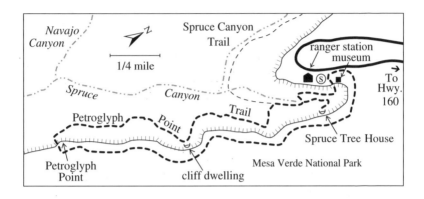

Southwest, these classic sites are enjoyed by hundreds and even thousands of visitors each summer day. Offering a considerably less crowded look at some of the park's other archaeological resources is the hike to Petroglyph Point. Awaiting hikers at the far end of this loop trail is a panel of exquisite rock art that dates back several hundred years.

To reach Mesa Verde National Park, drive 8 miles west from Mancos on US Highway 160, or 10 miles east from Cortez. Turn into the park and drive 20 miles south to the park headquarters. From the museum at the headquarters, follow the paved trail that leads down to the Spruce Tree House ruins. After making a sharp bend, turn right at the signed start of the Petroglyph Point Trail. Before setting out, however, be sure register at the ranger station, which is located just south of the museum. You can pick up a trail guide here as well.

Following the canyon wall just below the rim all the way to Petroglyph Point, this trail encounters several rocky areas and small stone stairways. It also cuts through some narrow passageways that may prevent heavier people from completing the hike. A few places could pose unsure footing for some, and a steep climb at the far end of the loop might be a bit precipitous for others. While such trail conditions may deter some people from hiking this route, it is an otherwise easy trail to follow. Along the way the route also intersects the Spruce Canyon Trail, which branches right.

This route accesses a number of archaeological and ecological points of interest. A short distance after turning off the paved way to Spruce Tree House, the Petroglyph Point Trail passes by a 300-year-old Douglas fir. Early ranchers incorrectly identified a Douglas fir growing next to nearby Spruce Tree House as a spruce, but the name has managed to stick to this day. Additional stands of this evergreen species are encountered later on, as well as Utah serviceberry bushes, Utah junipers, pinyon pines, and a patch of shrub live oak that is growing well north of the species' normal range.

About 1 mile out the Petroglyph Point Trail reaches a shaded grott with a small multiroom cliff dwelling located on a shelf just above. Nearby boulders have characteristic scrape marks, which resulted

*Prehistoric petroglyphs enthrall hikers in Mesa Verde National Park.*

from the sharpening of stone axes. This site dates back to around A.D. 1200, when the ancestral Puebloan Indians (commonly called the Anasazi, although this word is being discouraged as it is inaccurate) began building their homes among the canyon walls of the Four Corners region. Shortly after, however, they abandoned the canyons of Mesa Verde and moved south to the Rio Grande and Little Colorado River drainages. While a lengthy drought occurred at this time, other factors such as the depletion of topsoil may have also served to force their migration. Of course, all sites and artifacts within the park (and on all federal lands, for that matter) are strictly protected. Do not climb on any of the masonry walls or harm them in any way.

From this cliff dwelling the Petroglyph Point Trail continues south for another 0.4 mile before reaching the rock art panel for which Petroglyph Point is named. Spreading across a few square feet of the cliff face are a number of animals, human figures, designs, and handprints that have been etched into the smooth sandstone. While archaeologists have remained somewhat perplexed by the meaning of this prehistoric rock art, some Hopi elders did provide a translation during a visit in 1942. As the direct descendants of the ancestral Puebloans, these elders identified a number of clan symbols that indicate each clan's presence in Mesa Verde during previous times. They pointed out spiral designs that represent the Sipapu, or the place of emergence for the Pueblo and Hopi Indians, and they indicated some kachina figures as well. It is important not to touch these images as the oils on your hand can deteriorate the rock.

Just beyond the petroglyph panel, the trail climbs steeply to gain the canyon rim above. Offering a somewhat different view of both the scenery and the ecology of Mesa Verde National Park, the remaining half of this hike follows the canyon rim back to park headquarters. Various points along the mesa's edge offer nice views of both Spruce and Navajo canyons. Because the mesa tops are considerably drier than those areas just below the rim, the only trees that grow in appreciable numbers here are pinyon pines and junipers. After rounding the head of Spruce Canyon, the trail returns to the park headquarters.

Water is not available along this hike, so pack a quart or two before heading out. Lightning may pose a threat during periodic thunderstorms. Although the trail is open year-round, some icy spots may be present after heavy snowfall. Use extreme caution when hiking near drop-offs. Be sure to register at the ranger station before beginning the hike. Be aware that removing or disturbing artifacts in any way is strictly prohibited by federal law.

# 98   SAND CANYON

**Distance: 6 miles round trip**
**Difficulty: Easy**
**Hiking time: 4 hours**
**Elevation: 5,470 to 5,900 feet**
**Management: BLM**

**Wilderness status: None**
**Season: Year-round**
**USGS maps: Battle Rock, Woods Canyon**

Characterized by deep canyons and broad mesas, the far southwestern corner of Colorado features a variety of Anasazi cliff dwellings and ruins that date back to ancient times. While the best known of these archaeological sites are those found at Mesa Verde National Park and

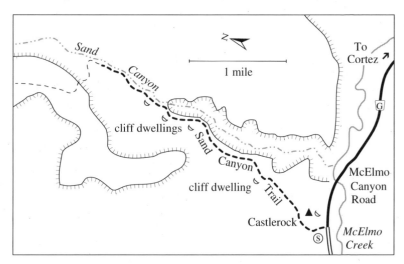

Hovenweep National Monument, other smaller ruins abound in these canyons as well. One location that features both archaeological wonders and a nice trail for hiking is picturesque Sand Canyon.

To reach Sand Canyon, drive 3 miles south of Cortez on US Highway 666 to McElmo Canyon Road (County Road G). Turn right and follow this paved road west for 12.5 miles to the trailhead, which is on the right, just past where the road crosses McElmo Creek.

From the trailhead the Sand Canyon Trail heads north for 100 yards o so across mostly bare sandstone before reaching a trail register and signboard. From this point it continues to the left of the nearby rock formation known as Castlerock. Castlerock is the site of an archaeological dig that is being conducted by the Crow Canyon Archaeological Center out of Cortez. Under the tutelage of professional archaeologists, students at the center have been working for the last few years to unearth artifacts and reconstruct the structures that once stood at the base of the pinnacles. From Castlerock the Sand Canyon Trail continues north, mostly across bare sandstone. The route along this section is marked by both rock cairns and small signs.

About 0.25 mile beyond Castlerock, the Sand Canyon Trail bears right at a sign to continue in a more northeasterly direction, heading up the Sand Canyon drainage along a broad shelf above the canyon bottom. Traversing an open forest of pinyon pines and junipers beyond this point, the trail here is well worn and easy to follow. For the next 1.5 miles the route is mostly level as it continues north along benches within the canyon. This section of the hike passes some nice cliffs and formations of Entrada Sandstone.

About 1 mile from the trailhead the Sand Canyon Trail reaches the first of severa prehistoric cliff dwellings along this hike. Tucked into a small but protective alcove, this well-preserved structure dates back to around A.D. 1200. Built by the Anasazi or, more correctly, the ancestral Pueblo Indians, cliff dwellings such as these represent the culmination of ancient civilization in the Four Corners area. Prior to A.D. 1200, the Anasazi lived in scattered settlements along valley bottoms and on mesa tops. It was not until the thirteenth century that they began constructing these cliff dwellings. Shortly after—just prior to A.D. 1300—an extensive drought, along with other factors, forced these cliff dwellers to abandon the region in favor of the Rio Grande and Little Colorado River drainages to the south. While these cliff dwellings have survived many hundreds of years, they are still quite fragile. Do not climb on the walls or camp within the ruins. And keep in mind that all artifacts—pottery shards, arrowheads, corn cobs, and so on—are protected by law and must be left alone.

Beyond this first cliff dwelling the Sand Canyon Trail rounds the next bend in the canyon wall to continue north. About 0.25 mile beyond the trail encounters the head of a small but deep side drainage of Sand Canyon's inner gorge. Soon the trail drops about 100 feet into the next side canyon north to reach the next lower bench within the canyon. Along the north wall of this side canyon you may note some additional cliff dwellings. After visiting the first two cliff dwelling sites, it is easy to recognize a pattern in these ancient structures. Nearly all of these cliff dwellings were built along south-facing canyon walls. This was undoubtedly to take advantage of the warm rays of the low winter sun. Still more dwellings are found around the next turn in the canyon to the north. Within this site, piles of rocks lying at the base of the ruins indicate that there were once many more rooms to this dwelling. You may also note the remains of a round underground room on the west side of the ruin. This was probably a kiva, which served as a center of religious activities.

Within the next mile the Sand Canyon Trail encounters more cliff dwellings before finally reaching the bottom of the canyon. At this point the route follows the normally dry wash bottom for another 0.5 mile before turning left to climb out of the canyon bottom to the west. This final section of the hike is quite interesting as it passes through a narrow corridor of sandstone rock. A few cottonwood trees, plus some tamarisks, grow within this riparian community.

Although this hike turns around where the Sand Canyon Trail begins climbing from the canyon bottom, it is possible to continue for another 3 miles up the canyon to reach its head to the north. The trail becomes steep and less distinct beyond this point, but it does reach the expansive Sand Canyon Pueblo at its far end. The Crow Canyon Archaeological Center has spent the last few years excavating the Sand Canyon Pueblo; archaeologists believe that the large complex may have served as a major religious center.

Bring plenty of water on this hike, especially in the hot summer months. Watch for flash flooding when in the canyon bottom. Keep in mind that ancient cliff dwellings are very fragile and should be treated with utmost care. All artifacts found on public lands are protected by federal law; you can enjoy these relics but leave them as they were.

# *99* HARPERS CORNER

**Distance: 2 miles round trip**
**Difficulty: Easy**
**Hiking time: 2 hours**
**Elevation: 7,600 to 7,510 feet**
**Management: Dinosaur NM**

**Wilderness status: Dinosaur**
**National Monument WA**
**Season: Year-round**
**USGS map: Jones Hole**

Despite the fact that Dinosaur National Monument is best known for its paleontological resources, there is only one place in the entire 211,141-acre monument where you can see dinosaur bones: at the Dinosaur Quarry in the far west end of the monument. What this unit of the National Park system does have in prodigious supply, however, are slickrock canyons, lonesome mesas, and miles of pristine river corridor. The short but highly scenic Harpers Corner Trail offers a memorable look at these treasures.

The Harpers Corner Trail begins at the end of the Harpers Corner Scenic Drive in the central portion of the monument. To reach the

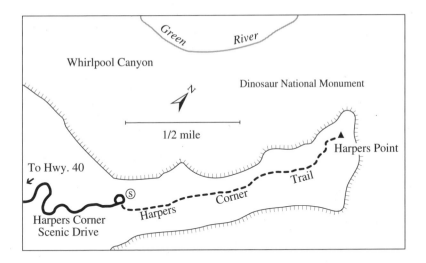

Green River

Whirlpool Canyon

Dinosaur National Monument

N

1/2 mile

Harpers Point

To Hwy. 40

Harpers Corner Trail

Harpers Corner
Scenic Drive

trailhead, drive 90 miles west from Craig on US Highway 40 to the Dinosaur National Monument headquarters. Turn right onto the Harpers Corner Scenic Drive and continue 31 miles north to the trailhead, which is at road's end.

From the trailhead the 1-mile-long Harpers Corner Trail heads northeast along a narrow and precipitous ridge before reaching Harpers Point at the end. While this trail dips and climbs a bit throughout, it is nevertheless an easy route to follow. Several numbered features

*Enjoying the view from Harpers Corner overlook*

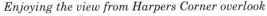

correspond to a printed trail guide, available at the visitor center. This pamphlet also mentions various species of flora that grow along the way, including pinyon pines and junipers, Douglas firs, such desert bloomers as phlox and Indian paintbrush, sagebrush, and even some grasses. The pamphlet points out some fossils that are embedded in a limestone shelf near the end of the trail and describes in some detail the folding and faulting action that led to the peculiar geology of this area. This geologic history is made evident by the fact that the walls of Whirlpool Canyon to the west consist of dark limestones and shales, while the Echo Park area to the east has been cut into a lighter-colored sandstone. Although the two canyons are at the same level, the rocks they have been cut into have been greatly displaced due to the bending and fracturing that took place as the area was being uplifted.

Geological discourse aside, these two canyons offer what may be the most dramatic view in Colorado's plateau region. Some 2,500 feet deep, Whirlpool Canyon, which is on the left side of Harpers Point as you are hiking out, engulfs the Green River within a spectacular corridor of rock. To the right, Echo Park is quite reminiscent of southern Utah's canyon country as it features entrenched meanders set in sheer walls of sandstone. Flowing in from the east, the Yampa River joins forces with the Green River in Echo Park. Their combined waters then flow around the north end of Harpers Corner, where they enter Whirlpool Canyon. In addition to naming Whirlpool Canyon during his epic 1869 float down the Green and Colorado rivers, John Wesley Powell also assigned titles to a number of other features in Dinosaur National Monument, among them the Gates of Lodore, Disaster Falls, Hells Half Mile, and Steamboat Rock. In more recent times—the 1950s, to be exact—these canyons were threatened by a proposed dam. Fortunately, conservationists won out.

While the views are spectacular all along the Harpers Corner Trail, the panorama is best from the observation point at trail's end. With a little luck you may even be the only person at the point during your visit. If so, be sure to take the time to really soak in the ambience of this special place. Return to your car along the same route.

Bring water as none is available along the way. Watch for lightning along this exposed route, and use extreme caution around the many precipices found along this route.

# 100 CHOKECHERRY DRAW

**Distance: 7 miles round trip**
**Difficulty: Easy**
**Hiking time: 4 hours**
**Elevation: 5,650 to 6,300 feet**
**Management: BLM**

**Wilderness status:**
 **Diamond Breaks WSA**
**Season: Year-round**
**USGS maps: Lodore School,**
 **Swallow Canyon**

Situated in the remote northwest corner of the state, the 35,380-acre Diamond Breaks Wilderness Study Area encompasses a rugged ex-

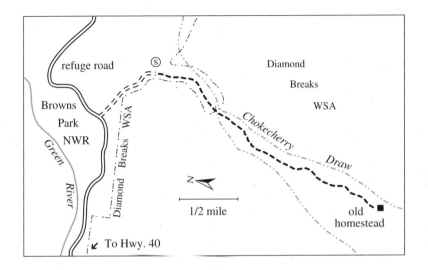

refuge road ⓢ Diamond

Breaks

Browns WSA

Park

NWR Chokecherry

Green River Draw

Diamond Breaks WSA

N

1/2 mile old
homestead

To Hwy. 40

tension of Utah's Uinta Range known as Diamond Mountain. Although few maintained trails enter this proposed wilderness, one well-established route does follow an old road, now closed to vehicles, up a drainage known as Chokecherry Draw. In addition to some nice views of this little-known corner of Colorado, the hike up Chokecherry Draw reveals the remains of an old homestead.

To reach the Diamond Breaks WSA and Chokecherry Draw, drive 31 miles west from Craig on US Highway 40 to the turnoff for Colorado Highway 318. Drive 60 miles northwest on this route to graveled County Road 83 in Browns Park. Turn south and drive 2 miles to the narrow bridge that spans the Green River. Immediately after crossing the bridge, turn left and drive east on a Browns Park National Wildlife Refuge road. Continue for 1.7 miles to a 4WD road that branches right. Follow this road for less than a mile to where it is closed.

Following an old road the entire way, this route is quite easy to follow. The grades are mostly easy as the road climbs a mere 650 feet over a length of 3.5 miles. About 0.75 mile beyond the trail's start the road reaches a fork in the drainage. After crossing the normally dry wash the road begins climbing along a gentle ridge that separates the two forks. A variety of different plants are common to this upland desert area. The two primary tree species that grow across these dry hillsides are pinyon pine and Utah juniper. These stunted forests are occasionally interspersed with sagebrush flats. Deciduous trees of the area include Gambel oaks and, of course, chokecherry trees.

Beyond the 2.5-mile mark the trail reaches a grassy meadow that stretches for nearly a mile to the homestead site and the turnaround point of this hike. A good place to spot mule deer at dawn and dusk, this meadow also allows unobstructed views north into Browns Park below. A sparsely populated valley that is well off the beaten path—even by Colorado's standards—Browns Park constitutes quite a find for anyone searching for the back of beyond. Encompassing much of the valley's floor, along with a lazy stretch of the Green River, is the Browns Park National Wildlife Refuge. The refuge harbors some important waterfowl habitat, while the Diamond Breaks WSA is home to a variety of wildlife, including mule deer, elk, coyotes, mountain lions, and black bears.

At the upper end of the meadow are the remains of an old homestead that dates back to the first decades of this century. All that is left today, however, are some scattered fence posts, a house foundation, and a few gnarled fruit trees. As early as 1826, Browns Park served as a rendezvous site for the famed mountain men of the era. Later, because of its isolation, the Browns Park area served as a hideout for such notorious outlaws as Annie Bassett, Butch Cassidy and the Sundance Kid, and Tom Horn. A short distance beyond the homestead is a small spring and beyond that is a nice outcrop of rock, the top of which makes an ideal place to take in the views.

Because water is scarce in Chokecherry Draw, and because any that is found must be treated first, it is best to bring your own.

*The trail into Chokecherry Draw*

# Index

# Index

Index

# About the Author

Scott S. Warren has been exploring Colorado for over 20 years, both on his own and in his earlier work for the U.S. Forest Service. An avid photographer, he holds a bachelor of fine arts degree in photography from Utah State University. His images have appeared in *Audubon, Outside, Sierra, Travel & Leisure,* and various *National Geographic* publications.